CORPUS JURIS HUMOROUS

—IN BRIEF—

A Compilation of

Outrageous, Unusual, Infamous, and Witty Judicial Opinions from 1256 A.D. to the Present

Compiled and Edited by

JOHN B. MCCLAY
ATTORNEY-AT-LAW

&

WENDY L. MATTHEWS
ATTORNEY-AT-LAW

BARNES
&NOBLE
B O O K S
NEW YORK

This edition published by Barnes & Noble, Inc.
by arrangement with the authors.

1994 Barnes & Noble Books

ISBN 0-56619-521-7

Printed and bound in the United States of America

M 9 8 7

THIS BOOK IS DEDICATED TO THE JUDGES AND COMMISSIONERS SERVING IN JUDICIAL SYSTEMS THROUGHOUT THE WORLD

... A judge's life, like every other, has in it much of drudgery, senseless bickerings, stupid obstinacies, captious pettifogging, all disguising and obstructing the only sane purpose which can justify the whole endeavor. These take an inordinate part of his time; they harass and befog the unhappy wretch, and at times almost drive him from that bench where like any other workman he must do his work. If that were all, his life would be mere misery, and he a distracted arbiter between irreconcilable extremes. But there is something else that makes it—anyway to those curious creatures who persist in it—a delectable calling. For when the case is all in, and the turmoil stops, and after he is left alone, things begin to take form. From his pen or in his head, slowly or swiftly as his capacities admit, out of the murk the pattern emerges, his pattern, the expression of what he has seen and what he has therefor made, the impress of his self upon the not-self, upon the hitherto formless material of which he was once but a part and over which he has now become the master. That is a pleasure which nobody who has felt it will be likely to underrate. ...

—LEARNED HAND[1]

---

[1]"The Preservation of Personality," presented as a commencement address at Bryn Mawr College, Bryn Mawr, Pennsylvania, June 2, 1927. [From Dilliard, Irving, *The Spirit of Liberty: Papers and Addresses of Learned Hand,* The University of Chicago Press, p. 43 (1952).]

ACKNOWLEDGMENTS

The editors wish to express their profound gratitude and appreciation to the many persons who have assisted in the preparation of this work, including but not limited to the following:

JON A. DIERINGER, ESQ.
Western State University College of Law, J.D. 1992
Member, State Bar of California
(Research)

J. MARK SUGARS, B.S. (Bio. Sci.), B.A. (Classics)
Candidate for Ph.D. (Classics)
University of California, Irvine
(Latin and Norman-French Translations)

THOMAS W. BOSSE, ESQ.
University of Notre Dame School of Law, J.D. 1991
Member, State Bar of California
Member, State Bar of Kentucky
(Research and Citations)

CHRISTOPHER D. LEWIS, B.A. (English)
Candidate for M.A. (English), 1995
California State University, Fullerton
(Research)

Janet S. Fohrman, Laura E. Stephens, Ardelis Malone, Jeanine Briggs, Eleanor Wahl, Denise P. McCall, Geri R. Grissom, Lynda M. Durham, Andrew Y. Nahm, Victoria A. Halliday, Ross Steiber, Kathleen Traeger, Brandee D. Turner, Maren E. Agnew, Kwang (Paul) Lee, Brian Kim, Eldridge Suggs IV, Sonya A. Webster, Barbara Martin, Kathy Derby, Linda Huth, Melanie Brown, Alessandra Capella, Joanne J. El Kareh, Susan H. Pruner, Julie L. Carrell, Anne Monaghan, Pamela C. Kurp, Laurin L. Jackson, Marty Longé, Jeanne Langford-Pirooz.

A special acknowledgment and thanks is extended to Douglas D. Alani, Esq., cofounder and co-lead counsel of McClay & Alani, a Professional Law Corporation, for his patience, tolerance and support throughout the duration of this project.

A further special acknowledgment and thanks is extended to the Honorable George Rose Smith (Associate Justice, Arkansas Supreme Court, 1949–1987) for his excellent sense of humor and valuable assistance in the preparation of this work.

This work is also specially dedicated by John B. McClay to his parents, Robert H. McClay and Virginia C. McClay, and by Wendy L. Matthews to her parents, Eugene C. Matthews and Shirley E. Matthews.

CONTENTS

FOREWORD

CORPUS: /kor' pəs/ *noun* [Lat.] Body; an aggregate.
JURIS: /jur' is/ *noun* [Lat.] Of law.
HUMOROUS: /hyoom̓ ə rəs/ *adj.* [< Lat.] Funny; amusing.
Corpus Juris Humorous: a collective body of humorous law.

———————————

Since we first published *Corpus Juris Humorous* in December 1991, the book has enjoyed a popular circulation within the legal community. It was anticipated that judges, lawyers, paralegals, law clerks and legal support staff would constitute our primary audience, since the subject matter of the book, although fascinating and humorous, is rather specialized and often technical. As such, we didn't consider marketing it to a wider readership.

To our immense delight, we underestimated the scope of mainstream interest in humorous law. Non-legal readers, humorists and commercial publishers alike were intrigued by it. If only, they urged, we could reduce the size of the book and cut down on the legal jargon (or at least explain it more adroitly) everyone could enjoy the gems of legal wit contained in *Corpus Juris Humorous*.

Inspired, we ruthlessly thumbed through the 288 cases in our original tome, harvested our favorites, eliminated the more obtuse legal recitations, wrote brief introductions and finally added a glossary explaining some of the frequently used legal terminology. The result, we hope, is an abridgment which retains all the wonderful humor of the original work, in a format which non-legal readers will find appealing and understandable.

Whatever you think about our legal system, we hope you will read the following cases with pleasure. After all, they are about real people, about you and me and the judges who had to make serious and often difficult decisions. We are confident that you won't be able to resist a chuckle at the wit, humor and wisdom created by our brethren in the long black robes, whom, incidentally, you may no longer find quite so remote and intimidating.

W.L.M. & J.B.M.   Santa Ana, California
                                                                    1994

INTRODUCTION

... The law has always been a hard task-master and requires of its advocates a serious approach and stern visaged application. When it comes face to face with life, as it unfolds in the drama of the courtroom, the law sometimes reaches its serious, stern results from facts which have been compiled with humor. So—while the end results of the law are deadly serious—there is about the lawyer (and even judges, occasionally) a spark of the humor of life—and a need for it. So let it be . . . for, while the end result is most serious to both plaintiff and defendant, what has brought about the necessity for the end result, is most humorous. . . .

—Randolph H. Weber[1]

U.S. District Judge

The cases and materials presented in this compilation represent the culmination of more than a decade and a half of ardent, resolute and purposeful research and collection. The process was both tedious and inherently gratifying. The real work, of course, was performed by the judges who wrote the opinions. Their wit, humor and literary acumen is self-evident. The cases and materials are reproduced in as complete a form as possible to enable the reader to appreciate the fabric of the judicial humor within a meaningful factual and legal context. They are presented verbatim et literatim, exactly as reported. The original language, grammar and spelling have all been retained, notwithstanding any obvious or technical improprieties. In many cases, the grammatical errors and arcane usages constitute an integral part of the humor of the writing. The judicial opinions are genuine and all

---

[1]From Aetna Insurance Company v. Sachs, 186 F. Supp. 105, 106 (1960).

have been reported, published and/or otherwise preserved in written form, generally in one or more of the officially recognized reporters. The opinions are drawn from a variety of judicial systems, each having its origin in the English common law tradition, including the United States, England, Canada and South Africa. Citations, and parallel citations where available, are provided.

For the most part, the cases and materials are self-explanatory. Where deemed helpful or appropriate, summaries of the court record and/or prior proceedings, as well as explanatory references, translations of Latin and Norman-French phrases and editorial comments are offset in braces { }. Internal abbreviations and deletions from the original text are denoted by triple-dot (...) ellipses. In certain cases, paragraphing was added to enhance readability. Such editing as was required reflects the subjective judgment of the compilers. Our objective was to retain as much of the structural cohesiveness and logical sense of the opinions as possible and not merely to provide a compilation of humorous excerpts. The materials are not presented in chronological order, but rather are loosely organized within the broad categories outlined by the chapter titles. Where ascertainable, we have set forth the full name of the judge authoring each of the judicial opinions included within the compilation, rather than simply noting his or her surname, as is the usual custom. In cases where it was impossible to identify the judge involved, particularly in the ancient opinions, the author is simply designated as "Anonymous."

Perhaps the most difficult editorial task we encountered was deciding which of the many cases and materials assembled should be included within this volume. The process was entirely subjective, involving the admittedly personal judgment and discretion of the editors. We did our utmost to include the best and most representative works within each of the broad subject matter categories outlined by the chapter titles. Many excellent cases and materials could not be included in this collection due to the inherent spatial constraints, and must await our follow-up volume, *Corpus Juris Humorous II*, which is currently being compiled and edited.

J.B.M.

Santa Ana, California
1991

CHAPTER I

Canine, *Equine*, *Feline*, *Bovine*, *Murine*, *Porcine*, *Anserine*, *Avian*, *Muline*, *Vespine*, *Piscine*, *Cervine*, *Cimicine*, *Lepidopterine* and *Grylline Law*[1]

Judicial Humor ... Again the advice must be a flat Never.
Judicial humor is neither judicial nor humorous. ...
—Hon. George Rose Smith[2]

In judicial language, that part of the Primer disapproving
judicial humor is hereby overruled, set aside, held for naught,
and stomped on!
—Hon. George Rose Smith[3]

---

[1]Dog, horse, cat, cow, rodent, pig, goose, bird, mule, wasp, fish, deer, bedbug, butterfly and cricket law.

[2]Hon. George Rose Smith, "A Primer of Opinion Writing for Four New Judges," 21 *Ark. Law Rev.* 197, 210 (1967).

[3]Hon. George Rose Smith, (Footnote 60) "A Critique of Judicial Humor," 43 *Ark. Law Rev.* 1, 25 (1990).

Concern for animal rights has always been a priority on the agenda of progressive judicial thinkers. The following ruling was written by Richard C. Barry, an eccentric, notorious and semi-literate Justice of the Peace for Tuolumne County, California, during the gold rush era of 1849–1851.

IN RE SIRUS JOD
Justice Court of California, Tuolumne County
Case No. 515 (1851)

R. C. BARRY, JUSTICE PEACE

This were a crimminel caze or suite in which one Sirus Yod or Jod butcher were indited by me fur cruelity to animules. The only testimmony projuced were that of Bill Foarde and Arkansaw who planely prooved that Cirus Jod had tied up a oxe in the sunshine all day without water or feade which were a shame and a outrage on the public morrels and desency. Jod defended hisself by sayeing the oxe was not his property nor did he owne him that he only tied him up so his owner could git him. I found Jod gilty and fined him the costs of Court 2½ ounses and ½ ounce for feading and wattearing the said oxe and the trubble the Constable has been att.

Sonora, Aug. 20, 1851
John Luney, Constable.

In the following case, the plaintiff, Aetna Insurance Company, filed a lawsuit requesting that the Court decide whether or not coverage applied to a loss under a homeowner's insurance policy. The insured homeowners, the Sachs, had submitted a claim to Aetna for carpet damage caused by their pet dog, André.

AETNA INSURANCE COMPANY v. SACHS
U.S. District Court, E.D. Missouri
186 F. Supp. 105 (1960)

RANDOLPH H. WEBER, DISTRICT JUDGE

... The law has always been a hard task-master and requires of its advocates a serious approach and stern visaged application. When it comes face to face with life, as it unfolds in the drama of the court-

2

room, the law sometimes reaches its serious, stern results from facts which have been compiled with humor. So—while the end results of the law are deadly serious—there is about the lawyer (and even judges, occasionally) a spark of the humor of life—and a need for it. So let it be with this opinion; for, while the end result is most serious to both plaintiff and defendant, what has brought about the necessity for the end result, is most humorous.

Our factual situation obviously had its inception when defendant obtained the insurance policy from plaintiff. If all had proceeded in the normal course of human events from that point on, this suit would never have been brought, for plaintiff insured against and was prepared for the usual expectancies of fire, wind and rain. But defendant purchased, and plaintiff issued, the rider, known commonly in the trade as a "floater." Now, "floater" provisions are covered by (and in this instance, rightly so) the rules of "maritime" law, for the risks are sometimes unusual.

In any event, the policy in question provided generally for damages and loss to the furnishings and personal property of the defendant for reasons other than fire, wind and rain, to-wit, theft and other fortuitous circumstances. What subsequently transpired after issuance brings into play the "floater" provisions of this policy.

Defendant and wife purchased in October 1957 a "French Poodle," which they appropriately and fascinatingly named "André." According to defendant, André was properly trained and "broke" and life was pleasant for the defendant and his wife until defendant and wife went on vacation and left André at a kennel for the duration. When they returned their first thoughts were of André and they promptly brought him back to their chateau, blissful in the reunion. But the home-like serenity was soon shattered, for madam soon spied André with his leg hoisted in masculine canine fashion and his purpose has been, and was being, accomplished. Madam did not testify, but defendant said she told him of the occurrence and he promptly surveyed the living room, dining room and hall and found signs of André's misfeasance. His next step was to notify his insurance agent and make claim under the "floater" provisions of this policy.

There was some dispute between the parties as to whether proper notice was given and claim made, but the Court is convinced that defendant gave notice within the terms and provisions of the policy, and plaintiff cannot escape liability on that point. Plaintiff did send an adjuster to the premises to survey the effects of where André, the French Poodle, had popped in, piddled and popped out. In fact, he testified that André gave a "command performance" while he was there.

Also, a rug specialist was sent to the premises and he too made a survey. He found spots ranging in diameter from the size of a "dime" to nine inches, and in number from 75 to 80. He testified that one or two could have been repaired, but not that many, for it would have been impossible to match the yarn in the rug, and the patches and repairs would have been as obvious as André's tell-tale marks. He also said that the spots would have been readily noticeable from the time they dried and that they extended throughout the living room, dining room, hall, stairway and were on the rug, furniture and drapes; which gives rise to the conclusion that André had the run of the house.

The owner of the kennel, where André spent just two weeks, gave as his opinion that a dog with good habits would not lose them in two weeks; that he properly cared for the dog and had provisions for outside relief facilities for the dogs in his kennels; and that four to five times a day would be a maximum amount of calls to nature for any dog, including André.

Plaintiff brought this declaratory judgment suit to determine its liability for threatened prosecution by the defendant and contended that this was just too many incidents to be liable for. Defendant answered and denied, claiming surprise in André's change of habits, and further contended that there were but four or five incidents and the rest of the spots were pure dribbles, and he counterclaimed for total loss of carpeting and for damages in the amount of $7,500 therefor.

At the rate of four or five calls per day, at best it would have taken André about sixteen days to make all the spots. But, on the theory that each incident is entitled to a dribble or two, it could probably be said, without fear of contradiction, that the spotting represents ten to twelve incidents and probably over a period of a week. In that length of time if the spots had not been seen, they at least should have been recognized by other sensory perception.

A review of the search books to the law reveals no cases in point. Either there never was a poodle as prolific as André, or, before such insurance, people caught them, put their nose in it and threw them

4

outside. Thus, we have a case of first impression. The testimony is that André met his demise, by truck, some few weeks after his prolific, piddlin' propensities were discovered and he, therefore, can never be made aware of his place in history unless he rests in some Valhalla from whence he can eat, sleep and answer his calls to nature, while still permitted to glance back occasionally to review the results, devastation, chaos and the indecision caused by his handiwork.

The unprecedented problem requires some decision, for the law, right or wrong, must conclude litigation. I would conclude this episode in the following manner:

For one or two occasions of André's imprudence we might expect the plaintiff to be liable, even though it is stretching the credulity of any sage of the law to put permission and right upon liability where a person gives a canine pet the right to perambulate and pounce unrestrained throughout the house. Such privileges, even to a poodle, seem more the part of valor than of wisdom, especially where the play pen is a $7,500 rug and expensive furniture and drapes.

The law has always allowed each dog its first bite, for then the owner is put on notice of its dangerous tendencies. I would even go one or two better in incidents such as this and would have allowed recovery for two or three incidents. This would give the insured some opportunity, through sight or smell, to discover the occurrence, prevent its repetition and make claim for that which seems a fortuitous circumstance or event. But, to allow for such prolific indiscretions, ad infinitum, is beyond credulity and borders onto wanton recklessness and disregard for which a person should not be rewarded.

While André might not be expected to know the terms and conditions of plaintiff's policy, it seems most fantastic that defendant should be able to contend that André's indiscretion was fortuitous. Judge Hand, in Mellon v. Federal Ins. Co., {citation omitted} said "* * *, even in an 'all risk' policy, there must be a fortuitous event—a casualty—to give rise to any liability for insurance."

In the law, "fortuitous" means "by chance" and "by accident." It seems to me that it is just "by accident" that André didn't do what he did, much before the alleged occurrence, and if "by chance" he didn't, it was just too much, and too often, to require plaintiff to pay for it.

One cannot stand by and see damage being done, allow it to be done and then collect for the total loss. In other words, one cannot be present and see a fire when it first originates and at a time when something could be done to extinguish it, then go off and allow the damage to be done and attempt to collect for the total damage. . . .

In the case at bar, defendant allowed and permitted the damage to become so extensive that he is now claiming a total loss, whereas plaintiff, if liable at all, should have been exposed only to a minimal loss.

I would say that defendant, because of such gross negligence and indiscretion in permitting André to roam the house at will, hoisting his leg at random, probably yipping and yiping in his canine Utopia, should not be allowed to recover. Certainly, a dog can be controlled by his master, and while a master cannot expect perfection from a dog, even a poodle, he should ever be aware to keep him from expensive parts of the house where he might do damage with either end. Further, defendant here should not be allowed to collect for a total loss which he himself could have kept at a minimum by the exercise of a little discretion, observance or care.

So, in the Eastern District of Missouri, while we love our dogs, let it be the law that we don't collect for so many puddles made by poodles, even under the "floater" provisions of a policy with "maritime" law as precedent. It is this Court's conclusion that judgment should be entered declaring the plaintiff is not liable under the terms and provisions of its policy of insurance for the damage caused to the carpeting in question under the circumstances proven and existing in this case. Further, that defendant should not be allowed to recover upon his counterclaim against the plaintiff.

In other words, I am saying to the defendant, "You cannot recover"; to the plaintiff, "You may continue your policy in peace"; and to the beloved little French poodle, the proximate cause of this litigation and discourse, I say, "*Paix à toi aussi, André* {Peace to you too, André}."

This Memorandum Opinion shall be filed as the findings of fact and conclusions of the Court herein and judgment will be entered in accordance herewith.

A lawsuit arising out of a dog fight in which one of the dogs was killed provided the basis for the following 1856 opinion in which the judge grappled with numerous convoluted issues of "dog" law.

WILEY v. SLATER

New York Supreme Court, Appellate Division
22 Barb. 506 (1856)

WILLIAM F. ALLEN, J.

... This is the first time I have been called upon to administer the law in the case of a pure dog fight, or a fight in which the dogs, instead of the owners, were the principal actors. I have had occasion to preside upon the trial of actions for assaults and batteries originating in affrays in which the masters of dogs have borne a conspicuous part, and acquitted themselves in a manner which might well have aroused the envy of their canine dependents. The branch of the law, therefore, applicable to direct conflicts and collisions between dog and dog is entirely new to me, and this case opens up to me an entire new field of investigation.

I am constrained to admit total ignorance of the *code duello* {dueling code} among dogs, or what constitutes a just cause of offense and justifies a resort to the *ultima ratio regum* {last resort of kings}, a resort to arms, or rather to teeth, for redress; whether jealousy is a just cause of war; or what different degrees and kinds of insult or slight, or what violation of the rules of etiquette entitle the injured or offended beast to insist upon prompt and appropriate satisfaction, I know not, and am glad to know that no nice question upon the conduct of the conflict on the part of the principal actors arises in this case.

It is not claimed, upon either side, that the struggle was not in all respects dog-like and fair. Indeed I was not before aware that it was claimed that any law, human or divine, moral or ceremonial, common or statute, undertook to regulate and control these matters, but supposed that this was one of the few privileges which this class of animals still retained in the domesticated institution, to settle and avenge, in their own way, all individual wrongs and insults, without regard to what Blackstone or any other jurist might write, speak or

7

think of the "rights of persons" or "rights of things." I have been a firm believer with the poet in the instructive if not semi-divine right of dogs to fight; and with him would say

> *Let the dogs delight to bark and bite,*
> *For God hath made them so;*
> *Let bears and lions growl and fight,*
> *For 'tis their nature to.*

It is possible that had the owners of both dogs been present the belligerents would have been charged and the familiar questions growing out of *son assault* {his own assault} and *molliter manus imposuit* {he gently laid hands upon} would have been presented, but no such questions are made here.

The defense is not rested upon the principle of self-defense, or defense of the possession of the master of the victorious dog. Had this defense been interposed, a serious and novel question would have arisen, as to the liability of the offending dog for excess of force, and whether he would be held to the same rules which are applied to human beings in like cases offending; whether he would be held strictly to the proof of the necessity and reasonableness of all the force exerted, under the plea that in defense of his carcase or the premises committed to his watch and care, "he did necessarily a little bite, scratch, wound, tear, devour and kill the plaintiff's dog, doing no unnecessary damage to the body or hide of the said dog."

Addressing myself to the question really made in the case then, the first difficulty I meet with is the want of proof of ownership by the defendant of the offending dog. The plaintiff made a *prima facie* case, by proving an apparent possession of the dog, but the appearances were entirely explained by the witness Nowell, who testifies that the dog was not owned by the defendant, nor kept nor harbored by him, but was really a trespasser on the premises, being kept at the shop adjoining. . . .

Whatever may have been the character and habits of the dog, there is no evidence that he was the aggressor, or in the wrong, in this particular fight. The plaintiff's dog may have provoked the quarrel and have caused the fight; and if so, the owner of the victor dog, whoever he may be, cannot be made responsible for the consequences. . . .

There is no evidence that the dog alleged to belong to the defendant was a dangerous animal, or one unfit to be kept. The cases cited, in which dogs have attacked human beings, although trespassers, and the owners have been held liable, are not applicable. It is one thing for a dog to be dangerous to human life, and quite another to be unwilling to have strange dogs upon the master's premises. To attack and drive off dogs thus suffered to go at large, to the annoyance if not to the detriment and danger of the public, would be a virtue, and that is all that can be claimed, upon the evidence, was done in this case. Owners of valuable dogs should take care of them proportioned to their value, and keep them within their own precincts or under their own eye.

It is very proper to invest dogs with some discretion while upon their master's premises, in regard to other dogs, while it is palpably wrong to allow a man to keep a dog, who may or will, under any circumstances, of his own volition, attack a human being. If owners of dogs, whether valuable or not, suffer them to visit others of their species, particularly if they go uninvited, they must be content to have them put up with dogfare, and that their reception and treatment shall be hospitable or inhospitable, according to the nature or the particular mood and temper at the time, of the dog visited. The courtesies and hospitalities of dog life cannot well be regulated by the judicial tribunals of the land. . . .

Evidence is slight that the dog died in consequence of this fight. I should infer, from the evidence, that he continued his annoying visitations until someone who did not own a white dog with black spots on his head, made use of a shot gun or "Sharpe's rifle," or some other substitute, to abate the nuisance. But as this question is left in doubt by the evidence, the judgment of the justice is conclusive as to the cause of death. I can, however, see no just grounds for the judgment. It can only be supported upon the broad ground that when two dogs fight and one is killed, the owner can have satisfaction for his loss from the owner of the victorious dog; and I know of no such rule. The owner of the dead dog would, I think, be very clearly entitled to the skin, although some, less liberal, would be disposed to award it as a trophy to the victor, and this rule would ordinarily be a full equivalent for the loss; and with that, unless the evidence differ materially from that in this case, he should be content.

The judgment of the county court, and of the justice, reversed.

The following case demonstrates what can happen when a bee gets loose inside a moving vehicle.

LUSSAN v. GRAIN DEALERS MUTUAL INSURANCE COMPANY

U.S. Court of Appeals, Fifth Circuit 280 F.2d 491 (1960)

JOHN R. BROWN, CIRCUIT JUDGE

This case presents the question whether an action which a human being would normally take may be considered by a jury to be that which the law's ordinary prudent person would have taken under such circumstances.

What brings this all about was a wasp—or a bee—it really doesn't matter for bees and wasps are both of the order Hymenoptera, and while a wasp, unlike the bee, is predacious in habit, both sting human beings, or humans fear they will. The wasp did not intrude upon a pastoral scene or disturb the tranquility of nature's order. What this wasp did—perhaps innocently while wafted by convection or the force of unnatural currents generated by the ceaseless motion of man's nearby machines—was to find itself an unwelcome passenger in an automobile then moving toward, of all places, Elysian Fields—not on the banks of Oceanus, but a major thoroughfare in the City of New Orleans on the Mississippi.

With the wasp was the defendant—owner and driver of the vehicle. Two others were with him in the front seat as his mobile guests. The wasp flew in—or his presence was suddenly discovered. Like thousands of others confronted with the imminent fear of a sting by such air-borne agents, the defendant driver swatted at the wasp. Whether he hit the wasp, no one knows. But momentarily the defendant driver apparently thought this menace had flown his coupe. The wasp, however, was not yet through. One of the passengers suddenly looked down and hollered out, "Watch out, it's still alive." Instinctively the defendant driver looked down at the floorboard and simultaneously made a sweeping swat at the wasp or where the wasp was thought to be. The wasp with all his capacity for harm scarcely could have thought itself so powerful. For without ever stinging anyone, or perhaps for that matter even being there at all, this anonymous bug brought substantial damage to one of the guests. Unconscious proba-

10

bly that it had set in motion the law's but-for chain reaction of causation, the wasp was the blame in fact. For when the driver by involuntary reflex took the swat, he lurched just enough to pull the steering wheel over to crash the moving car into a vehicle parked at the curb.

The traditional twelve good men performing their function in the jury system by which men drawn from all walks of life pass upon behavior of their fellow men, heard these uncontradicted facts. Instructed by the judge in a clear fashion on the law of due care in a charge to which no exception was taken, the jury in nine minutes returned a verdict for the driver. The plaintiff, appellant here, injured substantially by this combination of natural, human and mechanical forces, has a single aim, and hope and necessity: convincing us that the trial court erred in not granting the plaintiff's motions for instructed verdict and j.n.o.v.

His surprise or even disappointment in this adverse verdict, actually returned in favor of a direct action insurer-defendant, is not sufficient to give to this incident the quality essential to a directed verdict. Variously stated, restated, repeated and reiterated, the legal standard to be met is that no reasonable man could infer than the prudent man would have acted this way. Marsh v. Illinois Central R. {citation omitted}. In the determination of this, little instruction comes from prior cases involving a Connecticut bee in Rindge v. Holbrook {citation omitted} or a diversity Eighth Circuit Iowa wasp, Heerman v. Burke {citation omitted}.

Asserting this negative imperative—no reasonable man could hold as the jury did—inescapably puts the reviewing judge, trial or appellate, in the position of a silent witness in behalf of mankind. In assaying the scope of the specific record, we inevitably measure it in terms of the general experience of mankind including our own. Charles Alan Wright, The Doubtful Omniscience of Appellate Courts, 41 Minn.L.Rev. 751 (1957). We draw on what we and what all others constituting that composite reasonable man have come to know. The sources of this knowledge are as variable as are the subjects of inquiry.

In this simple case in the search for the negative limits of the inferences open to the so-called reasonable man, we deal with a situation known and experienced by all—the involuntary reflex responses by which nature protects life from harm or apprehended harm. In a philosophical way it may be that nature has here elevated the instinct of self-

11

preservation to a plane above the duty to refrain from harming others. It is here where man through law and ordered society steps in. But in stepping in, man, through law, has erected as the standard of performance, not what had to be done to avoid damage, but that which prudent human beings would have done or not done.

At times the judgment of the common man—voiced through the jury or other trier of fact—on what the prudent man should have done will be to deny to the individual concerned a legal justification for his perfectly human instinctive response. At other times what is actually usual may be equated with that which is legally prudent.

That is what occurred here. A wasp became the object of apprehended harm. Protective responses were instinctive and natural and swift. True, this diverted driver and his attention from other harm and other duties. But the jury in these circumstances under unchallenged instruction on legal standards concluded that this was normal and prudent human conduct. What better way is there to judge of this?

Affirmed.

A young bull strayed into the pen of a neighbor's expensive thoroughbred breeding heifer and promptly instigated a romantic "encounter." The result of this unanticipated communion was a calf of little value and lawsuit against the bull's owner for trespass.

KOPLIN v. QUADE
Supreme Court of Wisconsin
145 Wis. 454; 130 N.W. 511 (1911)

JOHN BARNES, J.

On September 14, 1907, the plaintiff was the owner of a thoroughbred Holstein-Friesian heifer, which was born on January 8, 1906, and had been thereafter duly christened "Martha Pietertje Pauline." The name is neither euphonious nor musical, but there is not much in a name anyway. Notwithstanding any handicap she may have had in the way of a cognomen, Martha Pietertje Pauline was a genuine "highbrow," having a pedigree as long and at least as well authenticated as that of the ordinary scion of effete European nobility who

12

breaks into this land of democracy and equality, and offers his title to the highest bidder at the matrimonial bargain counter.

The defendant was the owner of a bull about one year old, lowly born and nameless as far as the record discloses. This plebeian, having aspirations beyond his humble station in life, wandered beyond the confines of his own pastures, and sought the society of the adolescent and unsophisticated Martha, contrary to the provisions of section 1482, St. 1898, as amended by chapter 14, Laws 1903.

As a result of this somewhat morganatic mesalliance, a calf was born July 5, 1908. Plaintiff brought this action to recover resulting damages and secured a verdict for $75, upon which judgment was entered, and defendant appeals therefrom. . . .

The plaintiff offered testimony tending to show that he kept and intended to keep Martha for breeding purposes and for the milk which she might produce, and not for sale. It also showed that plaintiff was the owner of a blue blooded bull of the Holstein-Friesian variety, to which he intended to breed Martha some three months later than the date of the unfortunate occurrence related. There was evidence tending to show that a thoroughbred calf would be worth all the way from $22.50 to $150, depending on its sex, markings and other characteristics. Its sinister birth disqualified the hybrid calf born from becoming a candidate for pink ribbons at county fairs, and it was sold to a Chicago butcher for $7, and was probably served up as pressed chicken to the epicures in some Chicago boarding house. . . .

The true measure of damages was the difference between the value of the heifer to the plaintiff before and after the trespass, in view of the uses which the plaintiff intended to make of the heifer. . . .

Judgment affirmed.

Things other than soda occasionally get into beverage containers, despite rigorous bottling quality control efforts. Unfortunately, when the beverage is dark, the intruding matter sometimes cannot be seen until it is too late.

JACKSON COCA-COLA BOTTLING CO. v. CHAPMAN

Supreme Court of Mississippi
106 Miss. 864; 64 So. 791 (1914)

RICHARD F. REED, J.

A "sma' mousie" caused the trouble in this case. The "wee, sleekit, cow'rin,' tim'rous beastie" drowned in a bottle of Coca-Cola. How it happened is not told.

There is evidence for appellant that its system for cleansing and filling bottles is complete, and that there is watchfulness to prevent the introduction of foreign substances. Nevertheless the little creature was in the bottle. It had been there long enough to be swollen and undergoing decomposition when the bottle was purchased from the grocer and opened by appellee. Its presence in the bottle was not discovered until appellee had taken several swallows. An odor led to the discovery. Further events need not be detailed. Appellee says he got sick. Suffice it to say he did not get joy from the anticipated refreshing drink. He was in the frame of mind to approve the poet's[1] words:

> *The best-laid schemes o' mice an' men*
> *Gang aft aglay*
> *An' lea'e us nought but grief an' pain,*
> *For promis'd joy!"*

The record discloses sufficient evidence to sustain the jury's verdict for appellee. There is no error for reversal. Appellant company bottled the Coca-Cola for the retail trade to be sold to the general public as a beverage refreshing and harmless. The bottle in this case was purchased by the grocer from appellant.

We find the law pertinent to this case clearly stated ... in the

---

[1]{Ed. Note: The poem is "To a Mouse, on Turning Her Up in Her Nest, with the Plough, November 1785," by Robert Burns.}

14

case of Watson v. Augusta Brewing Company, {citation omitted} . . . as follows: "When a manufacturer makes, bottles and sells to the retail trade, to be again sold to the general public, a beverage represented to be refreshing and harmless, he is under a legal duty to see to it that in the process of bottling no foreign substance shall be mixed with the beverage, which, if taken into the human stomach will be injurious." . . .

The owner of an expensive Pomeranian dog brought this lawsuit when the dog was attacked and killed by a vicious Airedale owned by a neighbor. The plaintiff prevailed and was awarded $500, a considerable sum in 1919. The owner of the Airedale asked the court for a new trial and when the request was denied, filed an appeal.

ROOS v. LOESER
California Court of Appeals, First Appellate District
41 Cal. App. 782 (1919)

FRANK H. KERRIGAN, J.

The complaint alleges that on the sixteenth of May 1917, the plaintiff was the owner of a Pomeranian dog of the value of $1,000; that the defendant was the owner of an Airedale, of vicious disposition and dangerous character, which on said date and for a long time prior thereto was evilly disposed toward other dogs and was accustomed to attack them without provocation, all of which matters were well known to the defendant; that nevertheless, the defendant carelessly and negligently permitted said Airedale to go upon the public streets of San Francisco unleashed and free from restraint, and that on the day mentioned, without provocation and while the plaintiff's dog was proceeding peaceably along the public street, said Airedale attacked it from behind, the attack resulting in breaking the neck of the Pomeranian, from which its death immediately ensued.

From the evidence it appears that on said day the Pomeranian, attended by two maids, was pursuing the even tenor of its way upon the street, "tarrying" now and then and occupied with matters entirely its own, when the Airedale, an arrogant bully, domineering

15

and dogmatic, being beyond the reach of the sound of his master's voice and having evaded the vigilance of his keeper (for the maids and the man were vigilant), dashed upon the scene, and with destruction in his heart and mayhem in his teeth pounced upon the Pomeranian with the result already regretfully recorded; the plaintiff's dog had had its day. It crossed to that shore from which none, not even a good dog, ever returns.

Leaving this painful subject and turning to the considerations elaborately discussed in the briefs of able counsel, we remark that there was a time in history of the law when, as is said in one of the early cases, "dog law" was as hard to define as "dog Latin." As Blackstone puts it, dogs were the subject of property to a very limited and qualified degree, they had no intrinsic value, and were regarded as being kept only through the whim or caprice of their owner. They were not the subject of larceny, (2 Blackstone's Commentaries, 393). But that day has passed, and dogs now have a well-established status before the law. Considerable sums of money are invested in dogs, and they are the subject of extensive trade. Aside from their pecuniary value their worth is recognized by writers and jurists. Cuvier has asserted that the dog was perhaps necessary for the establishment of civil society, and that a little reflection will convince one that barbarous nations owe much of their subsequently acquired civilization to the dog. From the building of the pyramids to the present day, from the frozen poles to the torrid zone, wherever man has wandered there has been his dog.

In the case of State v. Harriman . . . he is eulogized in the following language: "He is the friend and companion of his master, accompanying him on his walks; his servant aiding him in his hunting; the playmate of his children, an inmate of his home, protecting it against all assailants."

In his well-known tribute to the dog, United States Senator Vest characterizes him as "the one absolutely unselfish friend a man may have in this selfish world, the one that never deserts him, never fails him, the one that never proves ungrateful or treacherous. . . ."

The Pomeranian was small, weighing about four and a half pounds, but history discloses that the small dog, perhaps oftener than his bigger brother, has rendered modest but heroic service and by his fidelity has influenced the course of history. . . .

16

As already indicated, the law now recognizes that dogs have pecuniary value, and constitute property of their owners, as much so as horses and cattle or other domestic animals. . . . The plaintiff's dog was the proud possessor of the kennel name Encliffe-Masterpiece; his pedigree and reputation entitled him to be regarded in dog circles as possessing the bluest of blood; in short, in canine society he belonged to the inner circle of the four hundred. In West and East he had won the first prize in every bench show at which he had been exhibited. He was middle-aged and in good health. Experts testifying placed his monetary value at $1,000.

The owner of a dog is not liable for the injuries caused by it unless it is vicious and the owner has notice of this fact. . . . But we think the evidence in this case shows, by inference at least, that while the defendant's dog was an estimable animal in many respects, he was, nevertheless, prone to attack without provocation other dogs irrespective of size, and that such an assault upon a dog of the weight and physical characteristics of that owned by the plaintiff was likely to prove harmful, if not fatal, to the object of the attack. As to the defendant's prior knowledge of the vicious propensities of his Airedale, while the evidence may not clearly show that he was personally aware of them, it sufficiently demonstrates that his employee, in charge of him at the time of the attack, and whose custom it was to exercise it on the public streets, knew of its dangerous character, which knowledge the law charges to the employer. The knowledge of a servant or agent of an animal's vicious propensity will be imputed to the master when such agent or servant has charge of or control over the animal. . . .

It is urged by the appellant that the court erred in refusing to instruct the jury, as requested, that the plaintiff was guilty of contributory negligence arising from the fact that her dog was upon the public streets without being licensed—unlike the defendant's Airedale, whose master had ornamented his favorite with a tag entitling him to roam the city's streets secure from interference by the poundkeeper or his myrmidons. The appellant's contention in this respect would be well grounded if the plaintiff's omission to comply with the ordinance requiring dogs to be licensed had contributed to the incident resulting in the Pomeranian's untimely end. But for aught that appears the absence of a tag from the collar of plaintiff's dog was unnoticed by the

Airedale, and was not the matter that aroused his ire or induced him to make the attack. His was the canine point of view and not that of the license collector. When the violation of an ordinance has no causal connection with the injury, as contributing thereto, the rule has no application. . . .

Judgment affirmed.

The owner of a now-deceased bull sued the defendant railroad company after a train collided with the animal.

GEORGIA SOUTHERN & FLORIDA RAILWAY COMPANY v. THOMPSON
Supreme Court of Georgia
111 Ga. 731; 36 S.E. 955 (1900)

SAMUEL E. LUMPKIN, J.

There was a head-end collision between a moving locomotive and a stationary bull, the latter showing fight and manifesting total ignorance of the doctrine of impenetrability. The company's servants in charge of the locomotive were better versed in the principles of natural philosophy, and according to their testimony, did their best to save the animal from the consequences of his rashness; but in spite of all their well-directed efforts, the crash came with its inevitable result. They were the only eye-witnesses. At the trial the plaintiff proved certain circumstances which were consistent with his contention that the defendant's witnesses did not state accurately the details of the catastrophe, but these circumstances were also perfectly consistent with the company's contention that its witnesses gave an entirely correct version of what occurred. Under the well-settled rules of evidence applicable to such a case, it must be held that the defendant's witnesses were in no legal or fair sense discredited, and that the verdict in the plaintiff's favor cannot lawfully stand.

Judgment reversed.

The judge in the following case presents an exhaustive, gushing anthology of laudatory and sympathetic references to the "dog" throughout history and literature, extolling the grand and noble canine "virtues" to an unprecedented degree, before actually ruling on the merits of a claim filed by the widow of a deceased dog-lover. Experienced judicial observers have little difficulty predicting how the court ultimately ruled.

MONTGOMERY v. MARYLAND CASUALTY COMPANY

Supreme Court of Georgia
169 Ga. 746; 151 S.E. 363 (1929)

STIRLING PRICE GILBERT, J.

{John Montgomery, a watchman for a boat repair business located on the Savannah River, drowned while attempting to rescue his dog. His widow applied to the Maryland Casualty Company for workman's compensation benefits. The insurance company denied the claim. Two higher courts took the side of the insurance company and the widow finally appealed to the Georgia Supreme Court.}

From the dawn of primal history the dog has loomed large in the art and literature of the world, including judicial literature. So it doubtless will be until the "crack of doom." In metal and in stone his noble image has been perpetuated, but the dog's chief monument is in the heart of his friend, "man." As a house pet, a watchdog, a herder of sheep and cattle, in the field of sport, and as the motive power of transportation, especially in the ice fields of the far north as well as in the Antarctics, the dog has ever been a faithful companion and helper of man. In the trackless forests of the new world he was on the firing line of civilization in the task of subduing all enemies, whether savage man or wild beast.

We find in astrology the dog star is "the brightest star in the heavens; the Alpha of the constellation Canis Major"; and in Greek mythology Cerberus is the watchdog at the entrance of the infernal regions. Diana, the goddess, had her deer-hounds, and literature is enriched by the story of Odysseus's (*Ulysses*) dog Argos. After twenty years of war and wandering this king of Ithaca returned, unrecognized in his beggar rags even by Penelope, but as he entered the courtyard, "Lo! a

19

hound raised up his head and pricked his ears. In times past the men used to lead the hound against wild goats and deer and hares, but as then despised he lay in the deep dung of mules and kine. There lay the dog Argos, full of fleas. Yet even now, when he was aware of Odysseus standing by, he wagged his tail and dropped both his ears, but nearer to his lord he had not strength to draw. Odysseus looked aside and brushed away a tear. Therewith he passed into the fairlying house and went straight to the hall, to the company of the proud wooers. But upon Argos came black death, even in the hour that he beheld his master again, in the twentieth year." Masters of the brush have pictured the dog on canvas everlasting, among them Landseer, Blake, Tracy and Andrea del Sarto. The last named painted "Tobias accompanied by the angel Raphael."

Among many of the most beautiful of nature's plants and trees, we have the dog-wood, dog-daisy, dog-laurel, dog-rose, dog-violet and the like; there are dog days, the dog watch (on ship board); there is dogma, doggery, dog-latin and the "dogged," as Shakespeare wrote: "Doth dogged war bristle his angry crest and snarl in the gentle eyes of peace" (*King John*, act IV, scene 3). Holy writ abounds with his mention, as "A living dog is better than a dead lion" (Ecclesiastes, IX:4). "Who loves me loves my dog" is a French proverb of the thirteenth century, and in substance has figured in the literature of many writers, including St. Bernard of Clairvaux and Erasmus. Poets great and small, their pens inspired by the Olympic maid, have paid tribute to the dog. Lord Byron, who was devoted to his Boatswain, wrote of him:

> *But the poor dog, in life the firmest friend,*
> *The first to welcome, foremost to defend,*
> *Whose honest heart is still his master's own,*
> *Who labors, fights, lives, breathes for him alone.*

And again:

> *'Tis sweet to hear the watch dog's honest bark.*
> *Bay deep mouthed welcome as we draw near home.*

The great Bard of Avon, in his *Julius Caesar*, makes Brutus say "I had rather be a dog and bay the moon, than such a Roman;" and in *Macbeth* Shakespeare gives us quite a catalogue of dogs: "hounds and greyhounds, mongrels, spaniels, shoughs, water-rugs and demi-wolves; the swift, the slow, the subtle, the housekeeper, the hunter;" and in *A Midsummer Night's Dream*, speaking of hounds, he says:

Their heads are hung
With ears that sweep away the morning dew;
Crook-knee'd and dew-lapp'd like Thessalian bulls;
Slow in pursuit, but match'd in mouth like bells, each unto each:

Such gallant chiding; for beside the groves,
The skies, the fountains, every region near
Seem'd all one mutual cry. I never heard
So musical a discord, such sweet thunder.

In modern times Thompson in "Major Jones' Courtship" makes his hero to boast of owning two of the best coon dogs in the settlement, describes the music they make in pursuit and concludes:

It puts me in mind of what Shakespeare sez about dogs:
I have herd sich powerful discord,
Sich sweet thunder.

Sir John Lucas in a poem "To a Dog" pictures his "wraith in a canine paradise" where the

. . . little faithful barking ghost
May leap to lick my phantom hand.

And so with other poets almost without number, among whom are Chaucer, Sir Walter Scott, Alexander Pope, Kipling, Trowbridge, Ruskin, and of course Stephen O. Foster, the author of so many beautiful southern melodies. It was he who wrote of old dog Tray:

Old dog Tray's ever faithful;
Grief can not drive him away;
He is gentle, he is kind—
I shall never never find
A better friend than old dog Tray.

Some three thousand years before Christ, Socrates[1] wrote: "When I see some men, I love my dog the more."

---

[1]{Ed. Note: According to our history books, Socrates was made to drink hemlock in 399 B.C. so this reference may be chronologically imprecise. Furthermore, the *Oxford Dictionary of Quotations*, 2nd ed., attributes the remark, or one similar to it, to Madame Roland, who died in A.D. 1793.}

Baron Curvier considered the dog "the most complete, the most singular, and the most useful conquest man has gained in the animal world."

Xanthippus, father of Pericles, had a dog, which leaped into the sea and swam along the galley side to follow his master, but finally fainted and died away near the island of Salamis; and Plutarch says: "That spot in the island which is still called the Dog's Grave is said to be his."

It is said that dogs bore their part in the siege of Troy, at Marathon, and in the battle of Salamis.

Herodotus said[2]: "In whatsoever house a cat has died by a natural death, all those who dwell in this house shave their eyebrows only; but those in whose house a dog has died shave their whole bodies."

Alcibiades' dog is now represented in marble at Duncombe Hall, England.

There was Prince Llewellyn and his greyhound Gelert; Sir Isaac Newton and his Diamond; Mirabeau and his Chico; Diomed, about whom his master, John S. Wise, wrote a book; Josephine and her Fortune that left a scar on Napoleon's leg; and Sir Walter Scott and his dozens of dogs.

Relics of dogs were found among the ruins of Herculaneum beside the forms of Roman sentries. In the late world war the dog shared the dangers of their soldier-masters in flood and field and trench.

Lord Byron had graven on a marble shaft his tribute to his dog: "Near this spot is deposited the remains of one who possessed beauty without vanity, strength without insolence, courage without ferocity, and all the virtues of man without his vices." This praise, which would be but meaningless flattery if inscribed over human ashes, is but a just tribute to the memory of Boatswain, a dog, who was born at Newfoundland, 1803, and died at Newstead Abbey, November 18, 1803.

In like vein Alexander H. Stephens wrote for his sagacious poodle Rio: "Here rest the remains of what in life was a satire on the human race, and an honor to his own—a faithful dog."

Senator George Graham Vest said: "The one, absolute, unselfish friend that man can have in this selfish world, the one that never deserts him, the one that never proves ungrateful or treacherous, is his dog."

---

[2]{Ed. Note: In his account of Egyptian customs.}

Tributes might be multiplied almost without number. Like man, not all dogs are good dogs. They have left behind them records showing every degree of good and bad. One poet's commentary has been judicially recognized in Woodbridge v. Marks, 36 N.Y. Supp. 82:

> *That dogs delight to bark and bite,*
> *For God hath made them so.*

In the case just cited it was said: "Conceding the highest place here or hereinafter to this companion of man which is claimed by any one, even to the faith of the Indian: *'That in the happy hunting grounds/His faithful dog shall bear him company.'* Still in the walks of life he must give way to the interests of man." . . .

For many of the facts stated above credit is due to "Pippa Passes, and Rather Doggily" (*Sewanee Review*), a little classic by William C. Jones, from which I quote as follows: "When the house is still and only the wind is abroad, Pippa muses by the fire at her master's feet, black muzzle on white paws, and in her eyes that question which troubled the soul of Tamas Carlyle, 'Is the universe friendly or nay?' The hearth is red, fleecy the rug, the shadows flickering warm; but Pippa is too staunch a terrier to leave danger or doubt unchallenged. She sniffs the unseen, then turns a more disquieted glance to the being in the chair. That damp, twitching nose senses truth beyond the oracle of his book, news beyond his radio's find. A growl, snarls, a rush to the window, a dash to the locked door. She lunges and scratches and leaps, back bristled, flanks heaving, teeth snapping, in her throat a hubbub that would rejoice the heart of three-headed Cerberus. The master is roused. What skulker, what power of darkness? A witch, perchance. Worse! It is that ancient anathema of a good dog's world, the dragon that would upset all seven of the tailwagging heavens; it is Grimalkin, the Stray Cat. A wild charge to the back fence, followed by a ferreting of every nook which might harbor the foe, so placates Pippa that she returns with tail as high as a bobbed tail well could be, and soon is aslumber on the rug. . . . When a dutiful fox dies, no epitaph is writ; rather he is flayed for the parsimonious tanner. When a mule goes the way of all flesh, no mound is reared, serviceful though his years have been. When a lambkin lies still and stark on the trencher, even the poet who was wont to rhyme on the pretty innocent will regale himself with one

23

of its chops. But when a certain little creature, having a bark at one end and a bit of tail at the other, with a flea or two between, takes leave for the isles of the blest, the lords of earth look foolish while their ladies weep, and humanity feels a tug at the heart."

A recent story, "Hound of Heaven," tells of a fox terrier after death, floating through the clouds, the cold winds blowing through his whiskers, finally landing at the pearly gates of canine heaven, and fresh upon his admission he is engaged in mortal combat with Hodge, the famous cat, pet of Samuel Johnson.

From what has been said it will not be difficult to ascertain where the sentiment and inclination of the court would lead. The court, however, is a court for the correction of errors, and we must be guided by law. The law of the case {is set forth below}:

Under the terms of the Workman's Compensation Act, in order for compensation to be due, the injury to the employee must arise both out of and in the course of the employment. Neither alone is enough. . . .

Under the law and the evidence of this case, the dog was not a part of the watchman's "equipment," even though it be conceded that the dog was useful as a watchdog and companion. . . .

The dog cannot legally be classified as a "fellow workman" falling under the principle ruled in Ocean Accident & Co. v. Evans (Texas) {citation omitted}. . . .

The act of the watchman in attempting to rescue the dog, which had jumped or fallen into the river, was not an emergency so as to constitute the act one performed in behalf of the employer, arising out of and within the scope of the employment. . . .

Judgment affirmed.

One summer afternoon in 1985, Mr. Sproed and his son were happily catching butterflies in Crater Lake National Park. To their surprise, by so doing, they were also committing a federal crime!

UNITED STATES v. SPROED
U.S. District Court, D. Oregon 628 F. Supp. 1234 (1986)

JAMES M. BURNS, DISTRICT JUDGE

Judges seldom get a chance to wax lyrical. Rarer still does a judge have an opportunity to see a case centered around a butterfly.[1] Those who read this opinion will, therefore, recognize that this case presented me with a temptation which I obviously could not resist. This case charges defendant Sproed with catching butterflies in a National Park.

Sproed and his son were at Rim Village of Crater Lake National Park on the afternoon of August 23, 1985, apparently doing just that—namely, catching butterflies! Along came a Park Ranger who had apparently taken keenly to heart the "Law and Order" rhetoric which some say has been a hallmark of the current administration. Responding to this Petty Offense[2] the Ranger issued to Sproed what became enshrined in judicial records as Citation P127482.

It would not be surprising to find that most of our citizens would be embittered if accused of such a heinous crime. Sproed is no exception. For reasons which appear below, I do not have to decide whether

---

[1] Butterflies are normally grist for the poet's mill, not that of the judge. Occasionally, even the august Court of Appeals finds itself cerebrating over butterfly-related causes, Friends of the Endangered Species v. Jantzen, 760 R.2d 976 (9th Cir. 1985).

[2] Petty offenses, a species of criminal offense established by the Congress (18 U.S.C. §1) used to carry a maximum penalty of six months in jail or a $500 fine or both. (Actually, the maximum fine for the offense charged here would have been $5,000; last year in the comprehensive Crime Control Act of 1984, Congress "upped the ante" for petty offense fines to $5,000.) Under applicable statutes, regulations are promulgated by the various federal agencies—Department of Interior and so forth; violation of such regulations—after they are published in the Code of Federal Regulations is a petty offense. When a Park Ranger—or some other agency enforcement officer—comes across a violation, a citation is issued. The citation normally provides a specified sum as collateral, i.e. bail. If the accused does not wish to contest the matter, he or she sends in the bail amount and the matter is closed. The accused may demand a trial, usually before a U.S. Magistrate; the accused, however, as a matter of right, can have the case heard by a District Judge. Occasionally a sort of third option is chosen by the accused, as happened here. He will send in a letter of explanation with a request, usually explicit, that the matter be dismissed, or otherwise be disposed of.

Sproed was, in fact, guilty of a crime. If his letter is to be believed, he and his young son may well have been moved by somewhat the same poetic spirit as the "aged, aged man" invented and immortalized by Lewis Carroll:

> *I saw an aged, aged man,*
> *A-sitting on a gate.*
> *'Who are you, aged man?' I said,*
> *'And how is it you live?'*
> *And his answer tickled through my head*
> *Like water through a sieve.*
> *He said, 'I look for butterflies*
> *That sleep among the wheat;*
> *I make them into mutton-pies,*
> *And sell them in the street.'*
> —Through the Looking Glass, *Ch. 8.*

Or Mr. Sproed may have believed, along with the German poet Heine, that:

> *With the rose the butterfly's deep in love*
> *A thousand times hovering round;*
> *But round himself, all tender like gold,*
> *The sun's sweet ray is hovering found.*

Mr. Sproed may even have been mulling over the lines written by Oregon's own "poet," Joaquin Miller.

> *The gold-barr'd butterflies to and fro*
> *And over the waterside wander'd and wove*
> *As heedless and idle as clouds that rove*
> *And drift by the peaks of perpetual snow.*

In any event, alas, no trial will ever occur to sort these things out. The reader should be made aware of why the judicial machinery never geared up for a full trial of this case. When Sproed's letter[3] arrived at the Clerk's office, it was referred to Magistrate Hogan, along with a touching note suggesting this might be a case in which Judge Hogan would want to exercise his judicial discretion. Shortly thereafter, Assistant U.S. Attorney Kent filed a motion to dismiss pursuant to Rule 48(a) of the Federal Rules of Criminal Procedure. Judge Hogan dis-

---

[3]I have reproduced, in typewritten form, Mr. Sproed's handwritten letter received by the Clerk's office on September 9, 1985, and it is attached as Appendix A to this opinion.

26

missed the case. Fortunately (or otherwise), I became aware, shortly afterward, of this case of lepidopteral *lese majeste* {injured majesty, i.e., high treason}. I chose to exercise my supervisory power as a District Judge to review the ruling of the Magistrate, 28 U.S.C. §636.[4]

In his letter to the Court, Sproed says that he and his son "have always loved and enjoyed the out-of-doors and never knowingly disregard laws. . . . [W]e were out catching butterflies. We have a collection and wherever we go we try to add to it. It never entered my mind that it was unlawful to catch a butterfly in the park."

Sproed said he and his son "saw no signs and there was nothing even hinting {that butterfly catching was a crime} in the paper given to us when we entered the park." Thus, he felt "that a friendly explanation and a warning was all that was necessary—it would have made this a learning experience instead of a bitter remembrance." He said that "it will take some time for me to restore my boy's previous respect for park rangers. I trust that your decision will make that job easier for me."

---

[4]Judge Hogan had no need, in view of the government's motion, to look more closely at the citation. The Park Ranger may have been on shaky legal as well as entomological grounds. The description of the violation alleged was "Preservation of Natural, Cultural and Archeological Resources." The Ranger filled in, as the regulation he felt had been trampled upon, 36 C.F.R. 2.1(a)(1). That section provides as follows:

    2.1 Preservation of Natural, Cultural and Archeological Resources:
        (a) Except as otherwise provided in this chapter, the following is prohibited:
            (1) Possessing, destroying, injuring, removing, digging, or disturbing its natural state:
                (i) Living or dead wildlife or fish, or the parts of products thereof, such as antlers or nests.
                (ii) Plants or the parts of products thereof.
                (iii) Nonfossilized and fossilized paleontological specimens, cultural or archeological resources, or the parts thereof.

Wildlife is defined by 36 C.F.R. §1.5 to mean: "any member of the animal kingdom and includes a part, product, egg or offspring thereof, or the dead body or part thereof, except fish."

Actually, one could read Mr. Sproed's second paragraph as the functional equivalent of a Rule 12 Motion to Dismiss on the ground that the citation fails to state a claim. Under well-settled constitutional principles, a criminal charge, under the Fifth Amendment, must be specific enough in its charging language to notify the accused of the nature of his alleged offense so he may prepare a defense and plead double jeopardy in the event of conviction or acquittal. Under these circumstances, however, I doubt that the Park Ranger would want to pursue the charge. He would presumably take to heart Wordsworth's dictum in his poem "To a Butterfly," which may not be entirely inapplicable here:

Much converse do I find in thee, / Historian of my infancy! / Float near me; do not yet depart! / Dead times revive in thee; / Thou bring'st, gay creature as thou art!/a solemn image to my heart. . . .

27

The Sproeds' experience exemplifies the axiom "Nature Imitates Art," as one can see from Appendix B. It is a copy of a recent strip from the widely syndicated comic "Bloom County." Permission to reproduce this copyrighted strip has been graciously granted by the *Washington Post* Writers' Group, which syndicates this comic strip.

Judge Hogan, AUSA Kent, the sharp-eyed young lady in the Clerk's office and I have now done our bit. Restoring the younger Sproed's respect—if this will help somewhat in achieving that worthy aim— seems, somehow, a fitting way to close the year 1985. It is a small victory, perhaps, but well worth the effort.

Mr. Sproed's young son, as a part of the process of having his respect restored, is urged not to take too literally the accompanying panel strip of "Bloom County."

For the foregoing reasons, I approve, affirm and adopt the Magistrate's order of dismissal.

APPENDIX A

Your Honor:

Since it is neither reasonable nor practical to appear in court, I am writing this letter of explanation. I don't like to use the courts time on such matters but $50 represents a lot of time and hard work to me and more important is this decision in my boys mind.

I plead not guilty to the charge of "Destruction of Natural Cultural & Archeological Resources." The park ranger spent about 30 minutes on his C.B. and looking through his book but never did find anything against collecting insects. So he just included it in the above class.

My boy and I have always loved and enjoyed the out-of-doors and never knowingly disregard laws. In this case we were out catching butterflies. We have a collection and wherever we go we try to add to it. It never entered my mind that it was unlawful to catch a butterfly in the park. We saw no signs and there was nothing even hinting at such a thing in the paper given to us when we entered the park (which I have enclosed). It does state that it is o.k. to catch fish.

It is this kind of incident that destroys young peoples' respect for the law. I felt that a friendly explanation and a warning was all that was necessary—it would have made this a learning experience instead of a bitter remembrance. We do not have the opportunity to travel a lot and I am afraid this "special occasion" may be remembered only by the outcome of this incident.

It will take some time for me to restore my boy's previous respect for park rangers. I trust that your decision will make that job easier for me.

Very Sincerely,
[s]
David Sproed

The following opinion was authored by Logan E. Bleckley, an esteemed judge and one of the great judicial humorists of the nineteenth century. Judge Bleckley was entirely self-educated, rising from obscurity in rural Georgia to eventually occupy the highest judicial post in the state, Chief Justice of the Georgia Supreme Court.

STEVENS v. THE STATE OF GEORGIA
Supreme Court of Georgia
7 Ga. 310 (1886)

LOGAN E. BLECKLEY, CHIEF JUSTICE

{*The defendant, Stevens, was indicted for the larceny of a black sow-hog, the property of Roland. At trial, the following facts emerged: The hog was a pet, and was in the habit of going up to the house and did not run away. It was found missing from Roland's*

29

property on Sunday, and he suspected the defendant, who lived about three hundred yards away. With two others, Roland went to the Stevenses' house, looking for his hog as a "stolen hog." He asked Stevens to allow him to search the house, but the defendant declined. Roland then went to town to obtain a search warrant. After he was gone, the defendant said he, too, was going to town to see if the owner had a right to a warrant. He did not return. On searching Stevens's premises, some hog bones were found in the house; hog hair and entrails were found buried in one hole in the garden and fresh hog meat in another. The meat was equivalent in size and the hair was the same color as that of the missing hog. Stevens was found and arrested several years later at a place more than fifty miles away. The jury convicted the defendant.}

In the house hog bones, in the garden hog hair, hog entrails, hog meat, buried in the earth, refusal of the occupant of the premises to permit a search without legal warrant, his abrupt departure from home whilst the warrant was being procured, his flight or retreat to a point more than fifty miles distant, and his continuous absence until arrested and brought back for trial, are strongly suggestive of a suspicious intercourse on his part with some hog or other. The jury were of opinion that it was the hog described in the indictment; and as he was a near neighbor to that hog, and as it disappeared about that time and its owner went in search of it as a stolen hog, and as the hair and the meat found buried in the garden looked like the hair and meat of that hog, it is highly probable that the jury were not mistaken.

Complaint is made that a witness was allowed to testify that the owner was hunting for the animal "as a stolen hog." And so he was, undoubtedly. He would not want to look in a dwelling-house, or under the ground in a garden, for a strayed hog; and such were the places searched. How the witness ascertained that the owner regarded it as stolen, whether from acts alone, or from declarations and acts together, does not appear; but if the prisoner or his counsel had wanted to learn this, the witness ought to have been interrogated on the sources of his knowledge. . . .

Any man who inters his pork may expect the late departed hog to be hunted for as stolen, if it is hunted for at all, on his premises.

Judgment affirmed.

Carl and Elaine Miles, the owners and promoters of a talking cat named Blackie, were forced by the city of Augusta, Georgia, to purchase a business license for Blackie's commercial activities. The Mileses brought a federal lawsuit against the city alleging, among other things, that Augusta's business ordinance violated their right of free speech.

MILES v. CITY COUNCIL OF AUGUSTA, GEORGIA

U.S. District Court, S.D. Georgia
551 F. Supp. 349 (1982)

DUDLEY H. BOWEN, DISTRICT JUDGE

... In this case, the attack upon the power of the City of Augusta to levy an occupation tax arises under somewhat unusual circumstances. The pertinent facts, as gleaned from the record, are as follows:

A. THE CAT

Carl and Elaine Miles are an unemployed, married couple who own "Blackie, the Talking Cat." Trained by Carl Miles, Blackie allegedly is able to speak several words and phrases of the English language. On June 22, 1981, plaintiffs were required by defendant to obtain a business license. From May 15 to June 22, 1981, plaintiffs had accepted contributions from pedestrians in the downtown Augusta area who wanted to hear the cat speak. People would stop the plaintiffs, who strolled the streets with the cat. Upon being stopped, plaintiffs would ask for a contribution. There is, however, evidence of the plaintiffs soliciting an off-duty policeman for money in exchange for a performance. Plaintiffs dispute this allegation. It is undisputed that plaintiffs would ask for, and lived off, the contributions received for Blackie's orations. Several complaints were received by the Augusta Police Department regarding the plaintiffs' solicitations. Plaintiffs were warned by the police not to solicit unless they first obtained a business license.

Through their exploit of his talents, Blackie has provided his owners with at least the minimal necessities of life.[1] Plaintiff Carl Miles has entered into several contracts with talent agents in Georgia, South Carolina and North Carolina. These agents have paid, at least in part, the Mileses' living expenses over a period of time. The evidence does not clearly show that this support was provided during the relevant time period of May 15 to June 22. It does, however, permit the inference that prior to the plaintiffs' arrival in Augusta, they intended to commercially exploit Blackie's ability.[2]

---

[1]That a talking cat could generate interest and income is not surprising. Man's fascination with the domestic feline is perennial. People of western cultures usually fall into two categories. Generally, they are ailurophiles or ailurophobes. Cats are ubiquitous in the literature, lore and fiber of our society and language. The ruthless Garfield commands the comic strips, the Cat in the Hat exasperates even Dr. Seuss, and who hasn't heard of Heathcliff, Felix or Sylvester? Historically, calico cats have eaten gingham dogs, we are taught that "a cat can look at a king" and at least one cat has "been to London to see the Queen."

It is often said that imitation is the sincerest form of flattery. To the animal world, I am sure that the sincerest form is anthropomorphosis. The ailurophobes contend that anthropomorphosis abounds, and that it is the work of ailurophiles. The ailurophiles say that they do not anthropomorphize cats but, rather, that cats have such human qualities as they may condescend to adopt for their own selfish purposes. Perhaps such was the case with Saki's ill-fated Tobermory, the cat who knew too much and told all; who, when asked if the human language had been difficult to learn, ". . . looked squarely at [Miss Resker] for a moment and then fixed his gaze serenely on the middle distance. It was obvious that boring questions lay outside his scheme of life."

For hundreds, perhaps thousands of years, people have carried on conversations with cats. Most often, these are one-sided and range from cloying, mawkish nonsense to topics of science and the liberal arts. Apparently Blackie's pride does not prevent him from making an occasional response to this great gush of human verbiage, much to the satisfaction and benefit of his "owners." Apparently, some cats do talk. Others just grin.

[2]In ruling on the motions for summary judgment, the Court has considered only the evidence in the file. However, it should be disclosed that I have seen and heard a demonstration of Blackie's abilities. The point in time of the Court's view was late summer 1982, well after the events contended in this lawsuit. One afternoon when crossing Greene Street in an automobile, I spotted in the median a man accompanied by a cat and a woman. The black cat was draped over his left shoulder. Knowing the matter to be in litigation, and suspecting that the cat was Blackie, I thought twice before stopping. Observing, however, that counsel for neither side was present and that any citizen on the street could have happened by chance upon this scene, I spoke, and the man with the cat eagerly responded to my greeting. I asked him if his cat could talk. He said he could, and if I would pull over on the side street he would show me. I did, and he did. The cat was wearing a collar, two harnesses and a leash. Held and stroked by the man Blackie said, "I love you" and "I want my Mama." The man then explained that the cat was the sole source of income for him and his wife and requested a donation, which was provided. I felt that my dollar was well spent. The cat was entertaining as was its owner. Some questions occurred to me about the necessity for the multiple means of restraint and the way in which the man held the cat's paw when the cat was asked to talk. However, these are not matters before the Court and are beyond the purview of a federal judge. I do not know if the man whom I saw with the cat was the plaintiff Mr. Miles.

This sequence has not been considered as evidence or as an uncontroverted fact in the case. It is simply stated for the purpose of a disclosure to the parties of the chance contact.

B. THE ORDINANCE

Under its charter the City of Augusta is empowered to impose license taxes. Section 139 of the charter states, in pertinent part:

> The City Council of Augusta, by ordinance, may require any person, firm or corporation to pay a license tax upon any occupation, trade or business followed or carried on within the corporate limits of the City of Augusta. . . .

Pursuant to this enabling provision, the City Council enacted Ordinance No. 5006, the 1981–1982 business license ordinance. The ordinance exhaustively lists the trades, businesses and occupations subject to the ordinance and the amount of tax to be paid. Although the ordinance does not provide for the licensing of a talking cat,[3] section 2 of the ordinance does require any "Agent or Agency not specifically mentioned" to pay a $50 tax.

C. THE ATTACK

Plaintiffs attack the ordinance as being unconstitutionally vague and overbroad in contravention of the Due Process clauses of the Fourteenth Amendment to the United States Constitution and of the Georgia Constitution. They contend they are not required to obtain a license and that requiring them to do so before they may solicit on the streets violates their First Amendment rights of speech and association as well as the right to equal protection secured by the Fourteenth Amendment. . . .

The power of the defendant to levy an occupation tax is unquestionable. The city charter authorizes the very ordinance passed by the defendant council. The taxing power, as embodied in a municipality's charter, is well recognized as a means for raising revenue. The ordinance is not one designed to regulate speech or association, but merely to raise revenue. The ordinance does not subject anyone's speech or associational activity to any penalty unless committed within the context of one's occupation for which a tax has not been

---

[3]It seems doubtful that the city fathers would anticipate the need for a specific category of this sort.

paid. Thus, the ordinance does not tread upon plaintiffs' fundamental constitutional rights. . . .

Plaintiffs cannot reasonably argue that before the defendant can require a business license for a talking cat, it must specifically provide for such an occupation in its ordinance. The self-evident thrust of the ordinance is to tax occupations, businesses and trades that derive income from the practice of that occupation, business and trade in the marketplace.

Plaintiff's contention that they are not required to obtain a license carries the implication that they are not engaged in an occupation. In their brief, plaintiffs cite several definitions of the terms "occupation" and "business." The general import of these definitions is that one is engaged in an occupation or business when that work or activity occupies one's time or attention on a regular basis for profit or support. Inasmuch as the ordinance does not define "occupation" or "business," the common definition cited above applies. Plaintiffs' activity, regardless of its peculiarity, falls within this definition.

Carl Miles, in his deposition of April 23, 1982, stated at pages 35–36 that prior to June 22, 1981, he would ask for a contribution when people asked to hear his cat talk. From May 15, 1981, to June 22nd, he received enough contributions, usually 25 cents or 50 cents each, to pay his weekly rent of $35 and purchase other necessities, except for a two-week period in which he used money from his savings (Miles's Deposition, at p. 38). He and his wife were otherwise unemployed, with no other income. Plaintiffs would walk, with the cat, in the vicinity of Broad and Greene streets, major avenues of motorized and pedestrian traffic, for several hours a day (Deposition of Elaine Miles, at p. 13). Thus, they were regularly engaged in a pursuit yielding income however small.

The plaintiffs' commercial interest in Blackie is well established. It is undisputed that before they moved to Augusta and after the business license was obtained, Carl Miles entered into several agreements with talent, or booking, agencies in South Carolina, North Carolina and Georgia (Carl Miles's Deposition, at pp. 6–7, 21–23). Prior to June 22, Blackie appeared on television and radio. For example, in 1980 Blackie appeared on "That's Incredible," a nationally televised program, for $500. Also, plaintiffs' living expenses have been paid in part by at least one promotional agency who had contracted with Carl

34

Miles. Although the activity recounted here occurred either prior to the plaintiffs' move to Augusta or after June 22, it is relevant to show the interest plaintiffs had in exploiting Blackie on a commercial basis. This interest, coupled with the near daily receipt of contributions requested by the plaintiffs for performances by the cat, brings them well within the definition of occupation.

Furthermore, the question of obtaining a business license was not new to Carl Miles. He had on previous occasions, in Charlotte and Columbia, inquired as to the necessity of a license (Deposition, at pp. 19–20). He therefore viewed his exploitation of the cat as a business activity for which a license might be required. The fact that those cities did not require a license does not alter the nature of his activity or prevent the City of Augusta from requiring one. Since they did not hold themselves out as a charity, the plaintiffs cannot persuasively argue that their activity did not require a license. The ordinance is not impermissibly vague. . . . Accordingly, in consideration of the foregoing findings and conclusions, plaintiffs' motion for summary judgment is DENIED. Judgment is, however, granted in favor of the defendant City Council of Augusta on all issues.

Mr. Hampton, a commercial fisherman, owned two parcels of land, one on each side of the Roanoke River in North Carolina, making his fishing operation especially valuable due to yearly upriver spawning migrations. He filed a lawsuit against the defendant pulp manufacturer, North Carolina Pulp Company, alleging that the poisonous discharge from the factory polluted the water and destroyed the fish, costing him $30,000 in losses over a period of three years. The court dismissed Mr. Hampton's complaint (environmental law not being well recognized in 1943) and Mr. Hampton appealed. The same judge who presided over the original dismissal heard Mr. Hampton's appeal and wrote the following opinion.

HAMPTON v. NORTH CAROLINA PULP CO.
U.S. District Court, E.D. North Carolina
49 F. Supp. 625 (1943)

ISAAC M. MEEKINS, DISTRICT JUDGE

Well, . . . Fish is the subject of this story. From the fifth day of the Creation down through the centuries, some of which lie behind us like a hideous dream, fish have been a substantial factor in the affairs of men. After giving man dominion over all the Earth, God gave him dominion over the fish in particular, naming them first in order, reserving unto Himself only one certain fruit tree in the midst of the Garden,[1] and Satan smeared that—the wretch! Whatever else we may think of the Devil, as a business man he is working success. He sat in the original game, not with one fruit tree, but with the cash capital of one snake, and now he has half the world grabbed and a diamond hitch on the other half.[2]

Great hunters lived before Nimrod, who was a mighty one before the Lord,[3] and great fishermen before Izaak Walton, whose followers are as numberless as the sands of the sea—not counting the leaves of the forest, as if anybody ever did, or could, except the quondam *Literary Digest*, which polled itself to death in the late summer and middle fall of 1936.

The most notable group of fishermen of all time was that headed

---

[1] Gen. 1:26, 28; 2:17; 3:3, 4.
[2] The eminent American Modernist.
[3] Gen. 10:9.

by Peter, the impulsive Apostle, and his followers Thomas, Nathaniel, the sons of Zebedee, and two other Disciples, seven fishermen in all—a working majority of The Twelve.[4]

Considered solely as a food product, fish have unlimited possibilities—quantitative and qualitative. We are told that a few little fishes and seven loaves, five loaves and two fishes, according to St. Luke, were more than sufficient to feed a hungry multitude of four thousand men, together with the women and children present, and of the fragments there were seven baskets full of fish.[5] Quantitative.

Professor Agassiz, the eminent Harvard scientist said: "Fish is a good brain food." One wrote to know "in what quantities should it be taken?" The great scientist wrote back: "In your case, a whale a day for thirty days." Qualitative.

Fish have their place in song and story. In song, from the nursery rime: "Little Fishes in the Brook," to the huge leviathans that forsake unsounded deeps to dance on sands.[6] In story, since the dawn of civilization and the imagination of man began to build romances and tall tales, full and fruity. He was more wag than skeptic who said: "In all the world there are only three really great fish stories—Admiral Noah, Commodore Jonah and Captain John Smith." Herbert Hoover added the fourth when, fishing in Nevada, he pulled a twenty-five-pound trout from the green waters of Pyramid Lake.[7]

Noah built an ark so many cubits high, wide and long. It had one door in the side, and one window in the top twenty-two inches square.[8] What ventilation! We are told it rained forty days and forty nights and all the mountains were covered with water.[9] We know that Mount Everest is 29,140 feet high.[10] Since it was covered by the flood, the water reached an altitude of more than 29,140 feet. Divide the altitude by forty and we find that the average rainfall was more than 700 feet per day. How's that for dampness!

Apart from the biblical account of the flood, many nations have

---

[4]John 21:2, 3.
[5]Matthew 15:36.
[6]*Two Gentlemen of Verona*.
[7]*Desert Challenge*, Lillard.
[8]Gen. 6:14, 15, 16.
[9]Gen. 7:12, 20.
[10]*Encyclopedia Brittanica*.

vivid accounts of floods in which all the people except a chosen few were destroyed. One account, that points this story, is a fable about a flood in ancient India. A fish warned Manu that a flood was coming. Manu built a ship and the fish towed it to a mountain and thus saved everybody.[11] We can laugh at this fable without fear of condemnation here and damnation hereafter. That was not *our* flood.

Jonah, like all the orthodox Jews of his time, thought Jehovah was a local Deity. Jonah did not like his assignment to Nineveh and in an effort to side-step it he took passage on a ship at Joppa for Tarshish and fled from the presence of the Lord.[12] The Prophet thought that if he could get into another jurisdiction he would be safe. However, before he crossed the boundary line into Tarshish, Jehovah pulled down on him with a double-barrel tempest and a muzzle-loading leviathan.[13] When he found himself a prisoner, for three days and three nights, in the belly of the great fish that the Lord had prepared, Jonah began to think things over. We all do when our "take a chance" does not pan out as we hoped. The net result was that the Prophet, after repenting of his disobedience and praying forgiveness, was allowed to go ashore. "The Lord spake unto the fish, and it vomited out Jonah upon the dry land."[14] This was before the advent of the camera enthusiast, else we might have been fortified with an authentic photograph of the minor Prophet walking ashore with the lower jaw of the whale for gang-plank. The eminent American Modernist said he was rather inclined to think that Jonah proved too tough for his whaleship's digestion and that in a fit of acute ptomaine poisoning, the cantankerous old Prophet was cast forth.

Captain John Smith, in the minds of many people, is more a joke than a myth. However, patient and interesting investigation has led me to the conclusion that he was not only a great Englishman, but a very great Englishman; that he was not only a great man, but a very great man; that he was good, useful and sane and did a very great World Service. Measured by all the standards of constructive achievement he was essentially a World Man. That Captain John

---

[11] *Encyclopedia Brittanica.*
[12] Jonah 1:3.
[13] Jonah 1:4, 17.
[14] Jonah 2:10.

Smith is less a myth than a joke is one of the glaring anomalies of history. Perhaps the raconteur had it in mind to emphasize his facetiousness by fact; to contrast his shadow with substance—his fancy with truth.

The Skeptic may scoff and the Modernist may moderate, but the story of Noah and the story of Jonah are enduring torches that lighted the way of man in his struggle upward through the immensity of the Shadow, and now as then guide the fumbling fingers of the trembling hand as with the establishment and strength of Jachin and Boas.[15]

Divested of the insistence of the Fundamentalists on the Verbal Inspiration and Infallibility of the Bible, and accepted in the light of reason, which examines and explains, the story of Noah is the greatest statement on the importance of preparation ever penned by mortal hand. In thunder tones we are warned; in time of peace, prepare for war; in the days of ease and luxury and laissez-faire, remember that evil days are ahead; in the fat years, prepare for the lean ones just around the corner—always be ready "to flee from the wrath to come!"[16]

Likewise, the story of Jonah is the greatest statement on fidelity to duty, hard and inexorable, that ever fell from the lips of man. It shouts forth the consequences that follow lapses from duty through wilful disobedience or otherwise. "Duty," said General Lee, "is the most sublime word in the English language."

The fish industry is among the foremost in World Trade. Indeed, in some countries it is the chief occupation of the people and the main source of national income. Through the ages it has developed a lore and nomenclature peculiar unto itself. What is more expressive of failure than "A Water Haul"? What more charming password for an Ananias Club than "What a Whopper"? What better synonym for discomfort and disgust than "Fisherman's Luck," though coarse in translation—classic in application? And where is the Lawyer who has never gone on a "Fishing Expedition"? Who wants to "Fish in Troubled Waters"? A whale of a bargain is a big one. Land Shark suggests Shylock, and Shylock is a type. They are synonymous and offer a per-

---

[15]I Kings 7:21.
[16]Matthew 3:7.

fect illustration of a distinction without a difference. "It sounds Fishy," means "It's a Lie on Its Face," and much more diplomatic. Everybody knows that "Fishy Smell" as well as the man "With the Codfish Eye." All these terms are as well understood by the Public as are the terms Bulls and Bears of the Stock Exchange. Codfish Tongues and Codfish Sounds mean one and the same thing and are interchangeable terms in the Trade.

As it is the biggest fish that always breaks the hook or bites the line in two, so, here, the huge sum of thirty thousand dollars is asked as compensation for fish that were never caught. I can remember when that sum would buy a lot of fish. I have seen six-pound roe shad retail for five cents apiece and cured herrings sell for two dollars a thousand—one hundred and twenty pounds of shad for one dollar and five herrings for one cent.

And this large sum is now asked for whose Fish? Certainly not the plaintiff's because he never owned them. I repeat the question, *whose* Fish? The answer is plain: they belonged to the Public.

Yes, I am fully aware that my fall from the Woolsack, and my break over time's old barrier growth of right and fit;[17] my reluctance to plod on with the solemn brood of care,[18] and my impatience of professional solemnity,[19] may cause the Big Wigs of the Bar to scowl down their displeasure. So be it. Permit me to interrupt myself:

Wigs were introduced in the Courts of England in 1670. A little more than a century ago the modern article was invented, and is made of the manes and tails of horses in the ratio of five white strands to one of black. The advantage is that it maintains its permanent wave without the aid of curling irons and oil. The disadvantage is that they are almost prohibitively expensive.[20] I resume.

I have often observed that the bigger the wig, the smaller the wigger, and the louder the roar and thunder in the index.[21] With majestic mien, wrinkled front and prone brow, oppressive with its mind,[22] one Big Wig, with a slight shiver, asks another: "Influenza?" Then another

---

[17]Browning.
[18]Gray.
[19]Chesterton.
[20]Newton on Blackstone.
[21]*Hamlet.*
[22]Browning.

with emphatic sniff asks: "John Barleycorn?" The answer is, "Neither!" I am sound in limb, wind and withers and as dry as Shadrach, Meshach and Abednego when, with their hair unsinged and with no smell of fire passed on them, they walked out of Nebuchadnezzar's burning fiery furnace and were each forthwith raised to an high estate in the Province of Babylon.[23]

Oh, well, now, yes, of course, the Circuit Court gives me a lot of trouble. But "hit ain't as bad as it mought be." If I am not reversed in more than nine cases out of ten, I feel from fair to middling. And if I draw ten straight, that does not send me to bed as even one reversal does some of the gentlemen of the Bench, State and Federal, so I have heard. Nor do I waste time explaining how and wherein the Circuit Court "got all balled up" and reversed me. That is what Circuit Courts are for—to correct the mistakes of District Judges—otherwise there would have been no compelling need to justify their establishment, except the need to protect the Supreme Court against a deluge of appeals.

When I see a Big Wig infused with self and vain conceit, as if this flesh which walls about our life were brass impregnable,[24] I think of Charles James Fox, who, when looking at a portrait of Lord Chancellor Thurlow, his full-bottomed wig falling bountifully to his shoulders and giving him that appearance of sagacity for which he is remembered, said: "No man ever was so wise as Thurlow looks," and but for the unimpeachable integrity of Charles Lamb I might well doubt his observation that "lawyers were children once. . . ."[25]

Far be it from me to bandy civilities with my superiors in learning, but after a round with the May Act I think a Judge is entitled to chuckle if he can; that it is pardonable now and then to intersperse a little human interest in the tedious search for judicial maxims and precedents that bind. "One laugh," said Charles Lamb, "is worth a hundred groans in any state of the market."

I invoke Equity, which does not depend upon the length of the chancellor's foot, notwithstanding the learned John Selden said it did, and set up: the weight of years and the weariness of service, and that this remains a fish story whichever way it is twisted. I shall not further

---

[23]Daniel 3:26, 27, 30.
[24]*Richard II.*
[25]Newton on Blackstone.

prolong this prologue, but here upon this bank and shoal of time, I'll jump the life to come[26] and proceed to consider the questions involved in the cause before me for determination.

The plaintiff, in substance, alleges that he is now, and has been since 1911, the owner and in possession of those two certain tracts of land, situated on opposite sides of the Roanoke River, and known respectively as the "Kitty Hawk" and "Slade" Fisheries; that the properties are ideally located for the business of fishing, and have for a number of years, during the fishing season, been operated for that purpose by the plaintiff and his ancestors in title, expensive equipment having been placed and maintained thereon for the proper and profitable conduct of such business; that, from time immemorial, great quantities of fish of the kinds specified have been accustomed, during the spring of each year, to make their way from the Ocean through Albemarle Sound, and thence into the fresh-water spawning grounds in the upper reaches of the Roanoke River; and that, by reason of this annual migration of fish, plaintiff's fishing business, and his "Kitty Hawk" and "Slade" Fisheries, have been "principally and particularly valuable."

It is alleged that the defendant is the owner of a boundary on the Roanoke River situate below the plaintiff's property which the fish, entering the river in their annual migration to the spawning grounds, are compelled to pass before reaching that portion of the river running between the plaintiff's properties; that, during the period referred to in the complaint, the defendant has maintained upon the boundary a plant for the manufacture of sulphate pulp, bleached and unbleached; that, in the course of the manufacturing operation, during the three years immediately preceding the institution of this action, the defendant has from day to day discharged into the waters of the Roanoke River, opposite its plant, a large volume of poisonous and deleterious waste and matter injurious to the fish then in passage to the spawning grounds, with the result that the annual migration of the fish upstream has been interrupted or diverted and large quantities of them have been destroyed; and that, as a natural consequence thereof, the plaintiff's business, and the usufruct of his property, during each of the three years have greatly

---

[26]*Macbeth.*

diminished—all to the plaintiff's great and lasting damage in the sum of $30,000. . . .

I am of the opinion the motion should be allowed and the action dismissed. It is so ordered and judgment will be entered accordingly.

N.B. The footnotes are merely references and are not intended to indicate quotations.

{ *Judge Meekins affirmed his original decision and the dismissal of Hampton's lawsuit was upheld.* }

Jordache, the famous jeans maker, brought a trademark infringement action against Hogg Wyld, a tiny New Mexico manufacturer of jeans for larger women called "Lardashe."

JORDACHE ENTERPRISES, INC. v. HOGG WYLD, LTD.

U.S. Court of Appeals, Tenth Circuit
828 F.2d 1482 (1987)

DEANELL REECE TACHA, CIRCUIT JUDGE

This case, a trademark infringement action brought against a manufacturer that identifies its blue jeans for larger women with a smiling pig and the word "Lardashe" on the seat of the pants, reminds us that "you can't make a silk purse out of a sow's ear."[1] Appellant Jordache Enterprises, Inc., alleges error in a district court decision finding no likelihood of confusion between the Jordache and Lardashe trademarks and finding no violation of New Mexico's antidilution statute. We affirm.

Appellant, a New York corporation formed by three immigrant brothers in 1978, is the fourth largest blue jeans manufacturer in the United States. It produces and markets all types of apparel for men, women and children, the principal product being designer blue jeans. Most items are identified by one of appellant's several registered trademarks, including the word "Jordache" printed in block letters,

---

[1]The first appearance of this proverb in its present form is attributed to Jonathan Swift. See J. Swift, *A Complete Collection of Genteel and Ingenious Conversation, According to the Most Polite Mode and Method Now Used at Court, and in the Best Companies of England* 181 (London, 1738).

the word "Jordache" printed in block letters and superimposed over a drawing of a horse's head, and a drawing of a horse's head alone. Some products are identified by the word "Jordache" written in script letter, a mark which has not been registered.

An intensive advertising campaign has created great customer awareness of Jordache products. In 1984, for example, appellant spent about $30 million annually on television, radio, newspaper and magazine advertisements and other promotional efforts. The message of this advertising has been that Jordache jeans convey "the look of the good life." Jordache jeans are now sold in retail outlets throughout the world.

Appellant has licensed Shaker Sport to manufacture and market Jordache jeans for larger women. Shaker Sport has expended substantial resources in advertising these jeans, and it had sold between 33,000 and 60,000 pairs by 1985.

In 1984, appellees Marsha Stafford and Susan Duran formed Hogg Wyld, Ltd., now Oink, Inc., for the purpose of marketing designer blue jeans for larger women. In an operation conducted out of their homes in New Mexico, the two women designed a product, selected a manufacturer, and ultimately sold over 1,000 pairs of jeans. Sales were limited to specialty shops in several southwestern states and to acquaintances or others who heard of the product. The women have not directly advertised their jeans, although several retailers have done so.

The name of the Oink, Inc., blue jeans gave rise to this suit. Names suggested at one time or another for the jeans by Stafford, Duran or others, included "Thunder Thighs," "Buffalo Buns," "Seambusters," "Rino Asirus," "Hippo Hoggers," "Vidal Sowsoon," and "Calvin Swine." Other names and marks were suggested as a take-off on Stafford's childhood nickname, "Lardass." This nickname inspired ideas such as "Wise-ashe" with a picture of an owl, "Dumbashe" with a picture of a donkey, "Horseashe" with a picture of a horse, and "Helium Ash" with a picture of a balloon. The women decided to name their jeans "Lardashe."

Appellant first became aware of Lardashe jeans after an Albuquerque TV station broadcast a news segment, which was also broadcast nationally by NBC, highlighting the new product. Jordache brought suit against Stafford, Duran and their corporation, alleging trademark infringement in violation of the Lanham Trade-Mark Act,

15 U.S.C. §§1051–1127, the new Mexico Trademark Act, N.M.Stat.Ann. §§57-3-1 to -14 (1987) and common law. The district court, after a three-day bench trial, held that no trademark infringement had occurred on any of the alternative claims. . . . Jordache now appeals this court.

I.

The Lanham Act prohibits the unauthorized use of a reproduction, copy or imitation of a registered trademark in a way that "is likely to cause confusion" with the registered mark . . . (similar test for infringement of an unregistered trademark by a junior user). "Confusion occurs when consumers make an incorrect mental association between the involved commercial products or their producers." . . . This court has identified several factors, originally set forth in Restatement of Torts §729 (1938), that are relevant to whether there is a likelihood of confusion between two marks:

(a) the degree of similarity between the designation and the trade-mark or trade name in
    (i)   appearance;
    (ii) pronunciation of the words used;
    (iii) verbal translation of the pictures or designs involved;
    (iv) suggestion;
(b) the intent of the actor in adopting the designation;
(c) the relation in use and manner of marketing between the goods or services marketed by the actor and those marketed by the other;
(d) the degree of care likely to be exercised by purchasers. . . .

This list is not exhaustive. All of the factors are interrelated, and no one factor is dispositive. . . . The party alleging infringement has the burden of proving likelihood of confusion. . . .

The district court found that the Jordache mark and the Lardashe mark are not confusingly similar. Appellant argues that the court employed an improper legal construction . . . in reaching this result. . . .

Trademarks may be confusingly similar if they suggest the same

45

idea or meaning. For example, this court has held that a trademark consisting of an overflowing stein with the words "Brew Nuts" conveys the same meaning as a trademark consisting of the words "Beer Nuts" {citation omitted}.

The court found the *words* "Jordache" and "Lardashe" similar, but not the horse and pig *designs*. The court did not find the word "Jordache" has an inherent meaning. Rather the "meaning" described by the court referred to the "relatively subtle and refined" horse design that is employed in the Jordache trademarks. The district court did not attach an improper "meaning" to the Jordache marks.

Appellant further argues that the district court erred in finding the trademarks are not confusingly similar. Similarities between trademarks are to be given more weight than differences. . . . The district court found that "[t]he overall differences between the two marks greatly overcomes the similarity in spelling and pronunciation of the names Jordache and Lardashe." . . .

Our review of the evidence shows that the marks, and their suggested images, are obviously different. Many of the Jordache jeans are identified by a small brown patch with the word "Jordache" written in white in block letters with a gold horse's head superimposed over the lettering. In other instances, the patch is white with blue block lettering and no horse. Sometimes "Jordache" is written in script or only the horse's head is used.

In contrast, the Lardashe jeans have a large, brightly colored pig head and two hooves, giving the appearance that a pig is peering over the back pocket. The word "Lardashe" is written in script beneath the pig's head, below which is an upside down embroidered heart. We agree with the district court that the "striking, brightly colored, and far from subtle" pig design is "humorous, or 'cute,' or facetious" . . . we agree with the district court's finding that the striking dissimilarities in the designs used in the marks greatly outweigh any similarities. . . .

The district court found the appellees' "intent was to employ a name that, to some extent, parodied or played upon the established trademark Jordache"; appellees "did not intend to 'palm off' their jeans as Jordache jeans; that is, to confuse the public into believing it was buying a Jordache product." . . . Appellants contend the court erred in its analysis of intent and the relevance of parody.

46

The "deliberate adoption of a similar mark may lead to an inference of intent to pass off goods as those of another which in turn supports a finding of likelihood of confusion." ... "The proper focus is whether defendant had the intent to derive benefit from the reputation or goodwill of plaintiff." ...

Given the unlimited number of possible names and symbols that could serve as a trademark, it is understandable that a court generally presumes one who chooses a mark similar to an existing mark intends to confuse the public. However, where a party chooses a mark as a parody of an existing mark, the intent is not necessarily to confuse the public but rather to amuse ... the purpose of a parody is "to create a comic or satiric contrast to a serious work."

In one sense, a parody is an attempt "to derive benefit from the reputation" of the owner of the mark ... if only because no parody could be made without the initial mark. The benefit to the one making the parody, however, arises from the humorous association, not from public confusion as to the source of the marks. A parody relies upon a difference from the original mark, presumably a humorous difference, in order to produce its desired effect.

"Now everything is funny as long as it is happening to somebody Else, but when it happens to you, why it seems to lose some of its Humor, and if it keeps on happening, why the entire laughter kinder Fades out of it" (W. Rogers, "Warning to Jokers: Lay Off the Prince," in *The Illiterate Digest, 1-3: The Writings of Will Rogers,* 75 ([1974]). The same is true in trademark law. As McCarthy writes, "No one likes to be the butt of a joke, not even a trademark. But the requirement of trademark law is that a likely confusion of source, sponsorship or affiliation must be proven, which is not the same thing as 'right' not to be made fun of" (2 J. McCarthy, *Trademarks and Unfair Competition* §31:38 at 670 [2d ed., 1984]). ...

The district court found the appellee's explanation for their adoption of the Lardashe mark not credible.[2] The court found that their real intent was to parody Jordache. ...

---

[2]Stafford and Duran testified at trial that they had not heard of Jordache jeans when they selected the Lardashe name. Stafford explained that "Lardashe" was meant to be a more polite version of "lardass," her childhood nickname. She testified to the meaning of "ashe" as an alternative spelling by saying that "if you'll look in your Bible, it's the goddess of fertility. It's the goddess of womanhood which I've known about for a long time and which meant quite a bit to me."

C.

Another factor to be considered in determining whether there is a likelihood of confusion is "the degree of care likely to be exercised by purchasers." . . . The district court found that customers are likely to exercise a high degree of care in purchasing clothing that costs between fifteen and sixty dollars. . . . Appellant says that "[o]ne can just as easily surmise" that a lesser degree of care will be used in selecting a pair of blue jeans (Brief of Appellant at 27). Appellant has offered only a guess, not any evidence of the degree of care that would satisfy its burden of proof. The district court's finding of a high degree of care is not clearly erroneous.

D.

Obviously, the best evidence of a likelihood of confusion in the marketplace is actual confusion. . . . Appellant offered evidence that it believed showed actual confusion, but the district court did not find this evidence compelling. Appellant challenges the court's findings.

Further testimony revealed that Stafford was referring to several goddesses, but was unable to locate any of them in the Bible. {Ed. Note: Stafford perhaps was thinking of Ashtoreth, a fertility goddess also known as Astarte and Ishtar.} Finally, Stafford testified that the "e" at the end of "Lardashe" is meant to appear like a pig's tail when the word is written in script.

"In cases where defendant concocts an elaborate fantastic and strained scenario of how it 'coincidentally' hit upon its symbol, judges are not amused when asked to swallow fantastic fabrications about coincidental, unknowing usage" (2 J. McCarthy, *Trademarks and Unfair Competition* §23:35 at 156 [2d ed., 1984]). (See cases cited in n. 8 and in 1986 supplement.) In one case, Sears, Roebuck & Co., the owner of the trademark "SEARS" for its Sears Financial Network, sued an individual who had established a corporation called Sears Financial Services. The defendant explained how he had chosen that particular name: "Realizing that the Corporation needed a name, I began considering my options. I had long ago been smitten with a Miss Patricia Sears and, upon parting, promised to memorialize her through one of my endeavors. Remembering this promise, I named the company Sears Financial Services" (Sears, Roebuck & Co. v. Sears Fin. Network, 576 F. Supp. 857, 863 [D.D.D.1983]). The court said that it had difficulty in accepting this story, and "it can thus be preliminarily inferred that the defendant's intent was to trade off the plaintiff's well-known name and marks SEARS." *Id.*

Similarly, the district court in this case correctly looked beyond appellees' stated explanation in determining their true purpose in selecting the Lardashe mark. Indeed, Duran testified that the reason for rejection of "Horseashe" with a picture of a horse's head as a possible mark was that the appellees wanted to stay away from Jordache's horse mark. This awareness of the Jordache mark belies Stafford's explanation for choosing "Lardashe" and supports the district court's finding that "Lardashe" was intended to be a parody.

Paul Ornstein, Executive Vice President of Shaker Sports, testified that he was called by associates who asked whether Lardashe jeans were affiliated with Jordache. The district court ruled that this testimony was hearsay and that even if it was admissible, it was not evidence of actual confusion by consumers in the marketplace. . . . We hold that Ornstein's testimony was admissible because it was offered to show the then existing state of mind of Ornstein's associates. See Fed.R.Evid. 803(3).

Although Ornstein's testimony was admissible, the district court correctly gave it little weight. . . .

Dilution of a trademark can also occur if the challenged mark blurs the mental image conveyed by the original mark. The statutorily protective distinctive quality of a trademark is diluted as the mark's propensity to bring to mind a particular product or source is weakened. . . .

In the present case, the district court found that "[b]ecause of the parody aspect of Lardashe, it is not likely that public identification of JORDACHE with the plaintiff will be eroded; indeed, parody tends to increase public identification of a plaintiff's mark with the plaintiff" {citation omitted}. The court further found that "[u]nder all the circumstances, the continued existence of LARDASHE jeans imply will not cause JORDACHE to lose its distinctiveness as a strong trademark for jeans and other apparel." *Id.* We hold these findings are not clearly erroneous.

The third element of dilution law is tarnishment. A mark can be tarnished if it is used in an unwholesome context. Precisely what suffices as an unwholesome context is not immediately evident {citation omitted}. (use of "Bagzilla" mark on garbage bags not "unsavory or degrading") {citation omitted}; ("Petley Flea Bags" does not tarnish "Tetley Tea Bags") {citation omitted}; (use of "Be Prepared" slogan on poster portraying a pregnant girl in a Girl Scout uniform does not injure the Girl Scouts) {citation omitted}; (use of Dallas Cowboys Cheerleaders uniforms in "sexually depraved" movie improperly injures plaintiff's business reputation) {citation omitted}; and (use of Coca-Cola design in "Enjoy Cocaine" poster improper tarnishment). The district court found that while LARDASHE "might be considered to be in poor taste by some consumers . . . it is not likely to create in the mind of consumers a particularly unwholesome, unsavory, or degrading association with plaintiff's name and marks" {citation omitted}.

This argument presumes that the public will associate the manufacturer of Lardashe jeans with the manufacturer of Jordache jeans, thereby causing damage to the high-quality image of Jordache. Because we find that the Lardashe mark was an intentional parody of the Jordache mark, we assume that the public will to some extent associate the two marks. To be actionable, however, the association of the two marks must tarnish or appropriate the good will and reputation of the owner of the mark. If the public associates the two marks for parody purposes only and does not associate the two sources of the products, appellant suffers no actionable injury. . . . Association of marks for parody purposes without corresponding association of manufacturers does not tarnish or appropriate the good will of the manufacturer of the high-quality similar product. . . .

The cases finding a trademark had been tarnished even though there was no unwholesome context all involve the use of identical, or almost identical, trade names on different products {citation omitted}; (Steinway pianos and Stein-Way clip-on beverage can handles) {citation omitted}; (Cartier jewelry, china and silver and Cattier cosmetics and toiletries) {citation omitted}; (Black Label beer and Black Label cigarettes) {citation omitted}; (Tiffany jewelry, china, silverware and glassware and Tiffany's Restaurant and Lounge) {citation omitted}; (Yale locks and Yale flashlights) {citation omitted}. In each of these cases the public could readily associate one product with the manufacturer of the other product on the assumption that the manufacturer is in the business of producing two separate and distinct products. This is not the case here. It is unlikely that the public would assume that the same manufacturer would use quite different marks on substantially the same product. . . . Our review of the records convinces us that the public will not associate Lardashe jeans with the appellant or, if they do, they will only make the association because they believe Jordache Enterprises, Inc., manufactures Lardashe jeans. Therefore, there is no likelihood of an injury to appellant, and its dilution claim must fail.

III.

'If it had grown up,' she said to herself, 'it would have been a dreadfully ugly child; but it makes rather a handsome pig, I think'" (L. Carroll, *Alice's Adventures in Wonderland*, 78–79 [1892]).

The judgment of the district court is affirmed.

APPENDIX

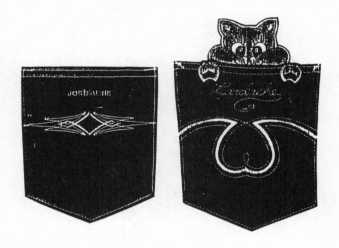

CHAPTER II
Law, Lawyers, Judges, Legal Procedures, Processes, Interpretations, Subtleties, Distinctions, Loopholes, Technicalities, Nuances and Intricacies

Mr. Leach made a speech,
Angry, neat, but wrong;
Mr. Hart, on the other part,
Was prosy, dull, and long.
 Mr. Bell spoke very well,
 Though nobody knew about what;
 Mr. Trower talk'd for an hour,
 Sat down, fatigued, and hot.
  Mr. Parker made the case darker,
  Which was dark enough without;
  Mr. Cooke quoted his book,
  And the Chancellor said, I doubt.
         —Anonymous[1]

... I should apologize, perhaps, for the style of this bill. I dislike the
verbose and intricate style of the English statutes, and in our revised
code I endeavored to restore it to the simple one of the ancient statutes,
in such original bills as I drew in the work. I suppose the reformation
has not been acceptable, as it has been little followed. You, however,
can easily correct this bill to the taste of my brother lawyers, by
making every other word a "said" or "aforesaid," and saying everything
over two or three times, so that nobody but we of the craft can untwist
the diction, and find out what it means; and that, too, not so plainly
but that we may conscientiously divide one half on each side....
         —Thomas Jefferson[2]

---

[1]Anon. poem, in *A Second Miscellany at Law,* Sir Robert Megarry, ed. p. 4 (1973), quoting from *Oxford Book of Light Verse,* p. 272 (1938).

[2]Thomas Jefferson, Letter to Joseph Carrington Cabell (1778–1856), dated Sept. 9, 1817, written from Poplar Forest (regarding a plan for elementary schools). From *The Writings of Thomas Jefferson,* Vol. XVII, *Definitive Edition,* pp. 417–418 (1905).

An attorney has a duty to argue "zealously" on behalf of his client in the courtroom, but may risk incurring the wrath of the judge if the boundaries of courtesy and decorum are exceeded, even in the face of an obviously "questionable" ruling.

IN RE JESUS RAMIREZ
Justice Court of California, Tuolumne County
Case No. 516 (1851)

R. C. BARRY, J.P.

This is a suit fore Mule Steeling in which Jesus Ramirez is indited for steeling one black mare mule, branded 0 with a 5 in it from Sheriff Werk. George swares the mule in question is hisn and I beleeve so to on hearing the caze I found Jesus Ramirez gilty of feloaniusly and against the law made and provided and the dignity of the people of Sonora steelin the aforesade mare mule sentenced him to pay the costs of Coort $10 and fined him $100 more as a terrour to all evil dooers. Jesus Ramirez not having any munney to pay with I rooled that George Werk shuld pay the costs of coort, as well as the fine, and in defalt of payment that the said one mare mule be sold by the Constable John Luney or other officer of the Court to meet the expenses of the Costs of the Coort, and also the payment of the fine aforesaid.

H. P. Barber the lawyer for George Werk insolently told me there were no law for me to rool so, I told him that I didn't care a damn for his booklaw, that I was the law myself. He continued to jaw back I told him to shut up but he wouldn't I fined him $50 and committeed him to gaol for 5 days for comtempt of Coort in bringing my roolings and dississions into disreputableness end as a warning to unrooly persons not to contradict this Coort.

Aug. 21, 1851
John Luney, Constable.

———————————

Judges frequently complain that attorneys file too much paperwork with the courts. As the following case demonstrates, this complaint is not new, and the sanctions imposed against the offending attorney were particularly mortifying.

MYLWARD v. WELDON

Chancery Court of England
Reg Lib-A 1596, fol. 672 (1596)
Reprinted in Monroe's Acta Cancellariae
1545–1625, vol. 1, p. 692

ANONYMOUS, JUDGE

Forasmuch as it now appeared to this court by a report made by the now Lord Keeper being then Master of the Rolls, upon consideration had of the plaintiff's Replication[1] according to an order of the 7th of May, of Anno 37 Reginæ, that the said Replication doth amount to six score[2] sheets of paper, and yet all the matter thereof which is pertinent might have been well contrived in sixteen sheets of paper, wherefore the plaintiff was appointed to be examined to find out who drew the same Replication, and by whose advice it was done, to the end that the offender might, for example's sake, not only be punished, but also be fined to her Majesty for that offence; and that the defendant might have his charges sustained thereby. . . .

And for that it now appeared to his Lordship, by the confession of Richard Mylward, alias Alexander, the plaintiff's son, that the said Richard himself did both draw, devise, and engross the same Replication, and because his Lordship is of opinion that such an abuse is not in any sort to be tolerated—proceeding of a malicious purpose to increase the defendant's charge, and being fraught with much impertinent matter not fit for the court;

It is therefore ordered, that the warden of the Fleet shall take the said Richard Mylward, alias Alexander, into his custody, and shall bring him into Westminster Hall on Saturday next, about 10 of the clock in the forenoon, and then and there shall cut a hole in the midst of the same engrossed Replication which is delivered unto

---

[1]{Ed. Note: A "replication" is a reply made by the plaintiff to the defendant's answer in a suit in chancery.}

[2]{Ed. Note: One hundred twenty.}

him for that purpose, and put the said Richard's head through the same hole, and so let the same Replication hang about his shoulders with the written side outward, and then, the same so hanging, shall lead the said Richard bareheaded and barefaced round about Westminster Hall, whilst the Courts are sitting, and shall shew him at the Bar of every of the three Courts within the Hall, and then shall take him back again to the Fleet, and keep him prisoner until he shall have paid £10 to her Majesty for a fine, and 20 nobles to the defendant for his costs in respect of the aforesaid abuse, which fine and costs are now adjudged and imposed upon him by this court for the abuse aforesaid.

Ms. Lavinia Goodell, one of the very few female lawyers in America during the 1800s, had been admitted to local practice in the Circuit Court of Rock County, Wisconsin, in June 1874. However, one of her cases was appealed to the Wisconsin Supreme Court the following year, and since she had not been admitted to the bar of that court, was prevented from arguing the case. Her application to practice before Wisconsin Supreme Court was denied in a particularly florid and patronizing Victorian fashion by Justice Ryan, a vociferous opponent to women's suffrage.

IN THE MATTER OF THE MOTION
TO ADMIT MISS LAVINIA GOODELL
TO THE BAR OF THIS COURT
Supreme Court of Wisconsin
39 Wis. 232 (1875)

EDWARD G. RYAN, C. J.

... This is the first application for admission of a female to the bar of this court. And it is just matter for congratulation that it is made in favor of a lady whose character raises no personal objection; something perhaps not always to be looked for in women who forsake the ways of their sex for the ways of ours. ...

So we find no statutory authority for the admission of females to the bar of any court of this state. And, with all the respect and sympathy for this lady which all men owe to all good women, we cannot

56

regret that we do not. We cannot but think the common law wise in excluding women from the profession of the law. The profession enters largely into the well being of society; and, to be honorably filled and safely to society, exacts the devotion of life. The law of nature destines and qualifies the female sex for the bearing and nurture of the children of our race and for the custody of the homes of the world and their maintenance in love and honor. And all life-long callings of women, inconsistent with these radical and sacred duties of their sex, as is the profession of the law, are departures from the order of nature; and when voluntary, treason against it.

The cruel chances of life sometimes baffle both sexes, and may leave women free from the peculiar duties of their sex. These may need employment, and should be welcome to any not derogatory to their sex and its proprieties, or inconsistent with the good order of society. But it is public policy to provide for the sex, not for its superfluous members; and not to tempt women from the proper duties of their sex by opening to them duties peculiar to ours. There are many employments in life not unfit for female character. The profession of the law is surely not one of these.

The peculiar qualities of womanhood, its gentle graces, its quick sensibility, its tender susceptibility, its purity, its delicacy, its emotional impulses, its subordination of hard reason to sympathetic feeling, are surely not qualifications for forensic strife. Nature has tempered woman as little for the juridical conflicts of the court room, as for the physical conflicts of the battle-field. Womanhood is moulded for gentler and better things. And it is not the saints of the world who chiefly give employment to our profession. It has essentially and habitually to do with all that is selfish and malicious, knavish and criminal, coarse and brutal, repulsive and obscene, in human life.

It would be revolting to all female sense of the innocence and sanctity of their sex, shocking to man's reverence for womanhood and faith in woman, on which hinge all the better affections and humanities of life, that woman should be permitted to mix professionally in all the nastiness of the world which finds its way into courts of justice; all the unclean issues, all the collateral questions of sodomy, incest, rape, seduction, fornication, adultery, pregnancy, bastardy, legitimacy, prostitution, lascivious cohabitation, abortion, infanticide, obscene publications, libel and slander of sex, impotence, divorce: all the nameless catalogue of indecencies, *la chronique scandaleuse* {the scandalous chronicle} of all the vices and all the infirmities of all society, with which the profession has to deal, and which go towards filling judicial reports which must be read for accurate knowledge of the law. This is bad enough for men.

We hold in too high reverence the sex without which, as is truly and beautifully written, *le commencement de la vie est sans secours, le milieu sans plaisir, et le fin sans consolation* {the beginning of life is without assistance, the middle is without pleasure, and the end without consolation}, voluntarily to commit it to such studies and such occupations. *Non tali auxilio nec defensoribus istis* {Not with such help or with those defenders}, should judicial contests be upheld. Reverence for all womanhood would suffer in the public spectacle of woman so instructed and so engaged. . . .

By the Court.—The motion is denied.

{*Ms. Goodell was eventually admitted to the bar of the Wisconsin Supreme Court in 1879, following legislative reform, over Judge Ryan's dissent, and she continued to practice brilliantly until her death of sciatic rheumatism in 1880.*}

The law usually permits a judge on his or her "own motion" to review any case being considered and, if appropriate, to dismiss it. Here, Judge Cristol brought such a "motion" and ruminated over whether or not to dismiss the debtor's Chapter 7 bankruptcy petition, setting forth his opinion in POE-etically rhymed verse.

IN RE ROBIN E. LOVE
U.S. Bankruptcy Court, S.D. Florida
61 B.R. 558 (1968)

A. JAY CRISTOL, BANKRUPTCY JUDGE

This cause came on to be heard sua sponte upon the court's own motion to dismiss this chapter 7 petition pursuant to 11 U.S.C. §707(b) and the court having received the inspiration for the motion from a little old ebony bird and not from any party in interest or any other person and having considered the presumption in favor of debtor provided in 11 U.S.C. §707(b) and not deeming it appropriate to take evidence, the court finds:

Once upon a midnight dreary, while I pondered weak and weary
Over many quaint and curious files of chapter seven lore
While I nodded nearly napping, suddenly there came a tapping
As of someone gently rapping, rapping at my chamber door,

"'Tis some debtor," I muttered, "tapping at my chamber
*   door—*
Only this and nothing more."

Ah distinctly I recall, it was in the early fall
And the file still was small
The Code provided I could use it
If someone tried to substantially abuse it

No party asked that it be heard.
"Sua sponte" whispered a small black bird.
The bird himself, my only maven, strongly looked to be a raven.

Upon the words the bird had uttered
I gazed at all the files cluttered
"Sua sponte," I recall, had no meaning; none at all.

And the cluttered files sprawl, drove a thought into my brain.
Eagerly I wished the morrow—vainly I had sought to borrow

From BAFJA, surcease of sorrow—and an order quick and plain
That this case would not remain as a source of further pain.
The procedure, it seemed plain.

As the case grew older, I perceived I must be bolder.
And must sua sponte act, to determine every fact,
If primarily consumer debts, are faced,
Perhaps this case is wrongly placed.
This is a thought that I must face, perhaps I should dismiss this case.

I moved sua sponte to dismiss it for I knew
*   I would not miss it*
The Code said I could, I knew it.
But not exactly how to do it, or perhaps someday I'd rue it.

I leaped up and struck my gavel.
For the mystery to unravel.
Could I? Should I? Sua sponte, grant my motion to dismiss?
While it seemed the thing to do, suddenly I thought of this.

Looking, looking towards the future and to what there was to see
If my motion, it was granted and an appeal came to be,
Who would file, but pray tell me, a learned brief for the appellee
The District Judge would not do so
At least this much I do know.
Tell me raven, how to go.

As I with the ruling wrestled
In the statute I saw nestled
A presumption with a flavor clearly in the debtor's favor.
No evidence had I taken
Sua sponte appeared foresaken.
Now my motion caused me terror
A dismissal would be error.
Upon consideration of §707(b), in anguish, loud I cried
The court's sua sponte motion to dismiss under §707(b) is denied.

A local justice of the peace in Georgia exceeded the scope of his judicial authority while presiding over a jury trial, by actually telling the jury how and what to decide. The disgruntled losing party appealed.

BENDHEIM BROTHERS & COMPANY v. BALDWIN
Supreme Court of Georgia
73 Ga. 594 (1884)

M. H. BLANDFORD, JUSTICE

. . . His honor charged the jury as follows: "Gentlemen, this is a case which has been tried by me before, and I decided in favor of defendant; I further charge you, gentlemen, that if you find that any settlement has been made, you find for defendant; retire and make up your verdict."

The law does not require a justice of the peace to charge the jury at all; his ignorance of the law, as well as propriety, would seem to demand that he should not, but if he undertakes to instruct the jury, he must do it correctly and in accordance with law. A justice of the peace is generally a man of consequence in his neighborhood; he writes the wills, draws the deeds and pulls the teeth of the people; also he performs divers surgical operations on the animals of his neighbors.

The justice has played his part on the busy stage of life from the time of Mr. Justice Shallow down to the time of Mr. Justice Riggins. Who has not seen the gaping, listening crowd assembled around his honor, the justice, on tiptoe to catch the words of wisdom as they fell from his venerated lips?

> *And still they gazed,*
> *and still the wonder grew,*
> *that one small head*
> *Could carry all he knew.*

The instructions given in this case exercised an undue and unwarrantable influence upon the jury. Such is to be inferred from the fact that they found for defendant, when the evidence was overwhelmingly in favor of the plaintiff. The judge of the superior court should have granted the writ of *certiorari* in this case, and it was error to have refused the same.

Judgment reversed.

Serving a subpoena can be a hazardous undertaking, especially when the person to be served is dangerous and violent.

WILLIAMS v. JOHNS
Chancery Court of England
21 E.R. 355; Dick. 477 (1773)

SIR HENRY BATHURST, J.

This was an application without notice, to commit the defendant for a contempt, in making the person, who served him with a subpoena to appear and answer, eat the same, and otherwise ill treating him; the defendant ordered to stand committed, unless cause; but by reason of his ferocious, and terrible disposition, no one being willing to hazard serving him, leaving the order at his house, was to be deemed good service.

Brevity is a rare and highly cherished commodity in the law. The following is one of the shortest opinions on record.

DENNY v. RADAR INDUSTRIES, INC.

Court of Appeals of Michigan
28 Mich. App. 294; 184 N.W.2d 289 (1970)

JOHN H. GILLIS, JUDGE

The appellant has attempted to distinguish the factual situation in this case from that in Renfroe v. Higgins Rack Coating and Manufacturing Co., Inc. (1969) {citation omitted}. He didn't. We couldn't.

Affirmed. Costs to appellee.

Lawsuits for "alienation of affections" typically involved heart-wrenching tales of shame and woe, including breaches of agreements to marry and charges of seduction. Such lawsuits were more common historically than today and often provoked a great deal of emotion, not only by the parties, but also by their lawyers.

FERGUSON v. MOORE

Supreme Court of Tennessee
98 Tenn. 342; 39 S.W. 341 (1897)

JOHN S. WILKES, J.

... {Defendant} further assigned as error that plaintiff's counsel, in his closing argument, called defendant hard names, such as "villain," "scoundrel," "fiend," "hell hound," etc., which, it is alleged, was calculated to prejudice defendant before the jury. It must be admitted these are rather harsh terms, and other language could have been used, no doubt, equally as descriptive, and not so vituperative; but it does not appear that defendant asked the court to interpose, and we cannot put the trial judge in error under these circumstances.

It is true the trial judge, in his discretion, might have checked the counsel on his own motion; but, inasmuch as defendant and his counsel did not object, the court did not probably feel called upon to act. It is not reversible error.

It is next assigned as error that counsel for plaintiff, in his closing argument, in the midst of a very eloquent and impassioned appeal to the jury, shed tears, and unduly excited the sympathies of the jury in favor of the plaintiff, and greatly prejudiced them against defendant. Bearing upon this assignment of error we have been cited to no authority, and after diligent search we have been able to find none ourselves.

The conduct of counsel in presenting their cases to juries is a matter which must be left largely to the ethics of the profession and the discretion of the trial judge. Perhaps no two counsel observe the same rules in presenting their cases to the jury. Some deal wholly in logic,—argument without embellishments of any kind. Others use rhetoric, and occasional flights of fancy and imagination. Others employ only noise and gesticulation, relying upon their earnestness and vehemence instead of logic and rhetoric. Others appeal to the sympathies—it may be the passions and peculiarities—of the jurors. Others combine all these with variations and accompaniments of different kinds. No cast-iron rule can or should be laid down.

Tears have always been considered legitimate arguments before a jury, and, while the question has never arisen out of any such behavior in this court, we know of no rule or jurisdiction in the court below to check them. It would appear to be one of the natural rights of counsel which no court or constitution could take away. It is certainly, if no more, a matter of the highest personal privilege. Indeed, if counsel has them at command, it may be seriously questioned whether it is not his professional duty to shed them whenever proper occasion arises, and the trial judge would not feel constrained to interfere unless they were indulged in to such excess as to impede or delay the business of the court. This must be left largely to the discretion of the trial judge, who has all the counsel and parties before him, and can see their demeanor as well as the demeanor of the jury.

In this case the trial judge was not asked to check the tears, and it was, we think, an eminently proper occasion for their use, and we cannot reverse for this. But for the other errors indicated the judgment must be reversed, and the cause remanded for a new trial. Plaintiff will pay the costs of the appeal.

In the following lawsuit for securities violations, the plaintiff filed so many lengthy and confusing pleadings that the judge had difficulty understanding what the case was all about. The action was dismissed because it violated one of the Federal Rules of Civil Procedure requiring that a litigant's statement of the claim be "short" and "plain."

GORDON v. GREEN
U.S. Court of Appeals, Fifth Circuit
602 F.2d 743 (1979)

JOHN R. BROWN, CHIEF JUDGE

As we see it, the only issue currently before the Court in these five consolidated cases is whether verbose, confusing, scandalous, and repetitious pleadings totaling into the thousands of pages comply with the requirement of "a short and plain statement" set forth in F.R.Civ.P. 8. We think that the mere description of the issue provides the answer:[1] we direct the District Court to dismiss the complaints—with leave to amend—because of appellant's failure to comply with F.R.Civ.P. 8(a) and (e).

THE PLEADINGS:
GOBBLEDYGOOK

The appellant, Edwin F. Gordon, invested several million dollars in a series of Florida real estate syndications. When the promises of substantial profits failed to materialize, appellant filed suit against the sellers and promoters of the syndications, claiming various violations of the federal securities laws.

Under F.R.Civ.P. 8, a party seeking relief must submit a pleading containing "a short and plain statement of the grounds upon which the court's jurisdiction depends," F.R.Civ.P. 8(a)(1), and "a short and plain statement of the claim showing that the pleader is entitled to relief," F.R.Civ.P. 8(a)(2). In addition, F.R.Civ.P. 8(e)(1) states that "[e]ach averment of a pleading shall be simple, concise, and direct." As

---

[1]The trial judge apparently did not, since he struggled and strained to decipher plaintiff's mountain of papers, ultimately holding that the Court lacked jurisdiction.

the following factual account demonstrates, nothing was further from the minds of the appellant and his lawyer than the clear directions contained in F.R.Civ.P. 8(a) and (e).

These five consolidated cases were originally brought in the Southern District of New York in March and April of 1976. At this initial stage, appellant filed five separate long, verbose and confusing verified complaints containing a total of 165 typewritten pages and an additional 413 pages of exhibits. In one of the five cases, appellant filed an amendment to the verified complaint (8 pages plus 39 pages of exhibits). . . .

In September 1976 . . . appellant filed an "Amendment to Verified Complaint" for each of the actions. Each "Amendment to Verified Complaint" was 19 pages. On September 30, 1976, the Trial Court dismissed the action, but not for failure to comply with Rule 8. Rather, after combing through the mountain of pages before him, the Trial Judge concluded that appellant failed to establish federal court jurisdiction. Subsequently, appellant topped his mountain of legal papers with a fourth set of complaints and a motion for leave to amend. The motion was summarily denied.

"LET THY SPEECH BE SHORT, COMPREHENDING MUCH IN FEW WORDS"[2]

The various complaints, amendments, amended amendments, amendments to amended amendments and other related papers are anything but short, totaling over 4,000 pages, occupying 18 volumes and requiring a hand truck or cart to move.[3] They are not plain, either. The Trial Court described the pleadings as being "extremely long and combin[ing] into single counts detailed recitation of evidence and legal arguments complete with extensive citations of authority." The

---

[2]Ecclesiasticus 32:8.

[3]Appellant's filings demonstrate once and for all that history does in fact repeat itself. In discussing Dr. J. H. Baker's second volume of Spelman's Reports, the 1978 Report of the Council and Abstract of the Accounts of the Selden Society reveals (p. 6): "It is in the 16th century that the sheer physical bulk of the [plea] rolls [became] truly daunting, with a mile or two of parchment used in a term." If every party filed the massive pleadings submitted here, we would only hasten the speed at which our country's trees are being transformed into sheets of legal jargon. Moreover, we would need to build another courthouse simply to store legal documents.

Court also observed that a paragraph from one typical complaint was single spaced, "extend[ed] the full length of a legal page and constitute[d] a single sentence." Much of the pleadings are scandalous as well.[4] Moreover, we cannot tell whether complaints filed earlier in time are to be read in conjunction with those filed later or whether the amended versions supersede previous pleadings.

One option before us is to struggle through the thousands of pages of pleadings in an effort to determine (assuming we possibly could) whether the Trial Court correctly dismissed for lack of jurisdiction. However, such a course of action would be unwise from the standpoint of sound judicial administration. All would know that there is no longer any necessity for paying the least bit of heed to F.R.Civ.P. 8(a) in its demand for "a short and plain statement" reiterated by the 8(e) requirement that each averment "be simple, concise, and direct." Lawyers would see that in the face of even gross violations of Rule 8, we would undertake the burden of trying to parse out 18 volumes of words, disorganized and sometimes conflicting, with a mish-mash of so-called evidentiary materials, citations of authority, and other things that a pleader, aware of and faithful to the command of the Federal Rules of Civil Procedure, knows to be completely extraneous. And the District Courts who come on the firing line are the first victims of this paper mill. We think that the Trial Court should have dismissed the complaints with leave to amend. While a Trial Court is and should be given great leeway in determining whether a party has complied with Rule 8, we think that as a matter of law, verbose and scandalous pleadings of over 4,000 pages violate Rule 8.

---

[4]At the risk of further polluting the legal waters by immortalizing this gibberish in the annals of the *Federal Reporter,* we quote some typically scandalous language from one of appellant's many filings: Green and Broberg worked closely together to keep their grandiose "Money making monster" scheme in operation. . . . This scheme can only be described as diabolical and monstrous . . . by not only failing to register this securities investment scheme to bring it under the supervision and censure of the S.E.C. but to openly operate in what was, in fact, an outlaw fashion, based on the spurious so-called legal opinion of Attorney Broberg, rendered to investors and potential investors, to the effect that this scheme did not constitute securities but that, on the contrary, it was simple country-style real estate with lots of country-style profit in it for all collaborators, but destruction for the defector who will be cannibalized by the rest of the group, again based on the so-called legal opinion of Broberg to the effect that the failure to make payments for whatever reason constitutes a breach of the so-called trust agreement and subjects the defector to losing his entire interest and having it assumed (cannibalized) by the remaining investors. . . .

In finding a violation of Rule 8, we do not recede even one inch from the position expressed by this Court in {citations omitted} and a host of other cases sounding an approach of liberality under F.R.Civ.P. 12 in reading a pleading as an adequate statement or claim. Appellant asks not that we adopt a liberal approach, but that we stand liberality on its head by accepting 4,000 pages of chaotic legal jargon in lieu of a short and plain statement. We would be hindering, not promoting, the underlying purpose of Rule 8, which is "to eliminate prolixity in pleading and to achieve brevity, simplicity, and clarity." ... We fully agree with the observation of the District Court for the Eastern District of Michigan that "the law does not require, nor does justice demand, that a judge must grope through [thousands of] pages of irrational, prolix and redundant pleadings. ..." {citation omitted}.

Our view—that flagrant violations of Rule 8 should not be tolerated—is shared by Courts throughout the country. There are numerous cases in which complaints have been dismissed as being contrary to the letter and spirit of the Rule. ...

As previously stated, in ordering the suits dismissed we do so with leave to amend. Appellant may file a short and plain statement in lieu of the 18 volumes of papers currently before us. ...

If our holding results in more time and expense to appellant, that would be fair recompense for these marked, unjustifiable violations of the letter and spirit of the Federal Rules of Civil Procedure and an indifference as though they had never been adopted 41 years ago.[5]

... VACATED and REMANDED.

---

[5]Counsel as scrivener would have been fair game for the discipline meted out by the Chancellor in 1596. As Professor Richard C. Wydick of Davis Law School reports:

In 1596 an English chancellor decided to make an example of a particularly prolix document filed in his court. The chancellor first ordered a hole cut through the center of the document, all 120 pages of it. Then he ordered that the person who wrote it should have his head stuffed through the hole, and the unfortunate fellow was led around to be exhibited to all those attending court at West Minster Hall.

{Ed. Note: See Mylward v. Weldon on page 53.}
—Wydick, Plain English for Lawyers, 1978, 66 Calif.L.Rev. 727
Obviously this applies only to counsel who filed the papers, not to the appellate counsel who briefed and argued the case here.

CHAPTER III

Alcohol, *Drugs, Gambling,* Vice, *Profanity, Lewdness, Obscenity,* Indolence, *Sloth,* Vagrancy and Other Assorted *Prevalent Evils*

Now of all the laws, by which the Kingdoms of the Earth are governed, no Law so near this Law of Nature and the Divine Pattern, as the Law of England; a System of Laws, so Comprehensive, so Wise, so favourable to the Subject, and yet so strongly guarding the Prerogatives of the Prince, that no Nation upon Earth does enjoy the like.
—Fortesque[1]

It has now been said that the law of the land in countries under the Common Law of England is a "rubbish-heap which has been accumulating for hundreds of years, and ... is ... based upon feudal doctrines which no one (except professors in law schools) understands"—and rather with the implication that even the professors do not thoroughly understand them or all understand them the same way.
—J. Riddel[2]

---

[1]The Right Honorable John Lord Fortesque, *Reports of Special Cases in All the Courts of Westminster Hall.* From preface, p. ii (1748).
[2]From Miller v. Tipling, 43 Ontario Law Reports 88 (1918).

In the following case, defendant Jacob Waddel was arrested, tried and convicted on the charge of criminal vagrancy. When he requested a new trial on the grounds that there was no evidence supporting the conviction, it was denied. He appealed the matter to the Georgia Supreme Court.

WADDEL v. THE STATE OF GEORGIA

Supreme Court of Georgia
27 Ga. 262 (1859)

JOSEPH H. LUMPKIN, J.

... I was never more impressed with the folly of sticking to forms, than when reading the presentment of the grand jury in this case. Jacob is accused of having with force and arms &c., doing what? Knocking some one down? No, but with force and arms, doing nothing; strolling about in idleness. He is not indicted for being a *know*-nothing,[1] but a *do*-nothing. The offence itself is somewhat anomalous. Every other in the Code charges the defendant with doing something. This for doing nothing.

Is the offence sufficiently sustained by the proof? The grand jury presented Jacob, and the traverse jury convicted him upon the testimony, notwithstanding Jacob was seen ploughing a potato patch, and doing some other small jobs, within the last two years. His fancy seems to have been mostly to walk the highways. The case is not a very strong one, still there was proof enough to warrant a conviction. And the jury are peculiarly the judges of the proof.

So Jacob will have to go to work; and not only work, but to *hard work*. So says the Code. We fear this will go *hard* with Jacob at first. It will be a great change in his habits. Might not the law, in this humanitarian age, have condemned the vagrant the first year, to work only; and the second year to *hard* work? Ought not a portion of the vagrant's *hard* earnings to be appropriated to his family, provided he have one?

I am quite satisfied that a large portion of the population of our towns could be convicted upon stronger proof than this. It is time, perhaps, to give them a scare; to admonish them of the old adage, that

---

[1]{Ed. Note: The "Know-Nothings" were members of a secret political organization (anti-Catholic and anti-immigrant) in America from 1843 to 1861.}

a bird that can sing, and won't sing, must be *made* to sing. That able-bodied man must not cumber the ground, living on the sweat of the other men's toil. "Why stand ye here all the day idle?"[2] is a question which the master of the vineyard propounds, and which the Penal Code will have answered.

Judgment affirmed.

It is not a wise bet for an attorney to complain too vociferously about the outcome of the case after the judge has decided against him.

KROBRE v. HEED
Justice Court of California, Tuolumne County
Case No. 606 (1851)

R. C. BARRY, J.P.

This was a suit between two Gamboleers E. Krobre the gamboleer who sooed Sam Heed the gamboleer to recover 3000 dolers wun at Keards. After much swarin one way and another the lawyers H. P. Barber and Leeander Quint argooed the caze which after a long while they got through with I discided that Barber was right whereupon Quint said please your honor I never can get justice in your coort putting out his finger and thum i told him the likes of him in my country often lost their fingers stealing corn or chickens and that if I had anything to say he never shood have justice here i ordered him to hold his tung and shetup when he went out of coort he began to grumble again i ordered John Luney the constable to arrest him and bring him into coort before me which he done I then fined him $25 for contempt of Court.

Cost of Court $10 which was pade.

September 10, 1851

John Luney, Constable.

---

[2]{Ed. Note: Matthew 20:6.}

The defendant, Mitchell Sentovich, was arrested and convicted for possession of marijuana as a result of the peculiar "scentsory" talents of a gifted DEA agent. On appeal, the question centered on whether the drug seizure occurred before or after a search warrant was properly issued.

UNITED STATES v. SENTOVICH
U.S. Court of Appeals, Eleventh Circuit
677 F.2d 834 (1982)

FRANK M. JOHNSON, JR., CIRCUIT JUDGE

The ubiquitous DEA Agent Paul Markonni once again sticks his nose into the drug trade. This time he is on the scent of appellant Mitchell Sentovich's drug courier activities. We now learn that among Markonni's many talents is an olfactory sense we in the past attributed only to canines. Sentovich argues that he should have been able to test, at a magistrate's hearing on issuance of a search warrant, whether Markonni really is the human bloodhound he claims to be. Sentovich's claims, however, have more bark than bite. In fact, they have not a dog's chance of success. Zeke, Rocky, Bodger and Nebuchadnezzar,[1] and the drug dogs of the southeast had best beware. Markonni's sensitive proboscis may soon put them in the dog pound.

I.

An anonymous telephone caller told a Florida Sheriff's department that three males carrying seven suitcases full of marijuana would leave the Fort Myers airport at seven the next morning. The next day local police, proving they had their noses to the grindstone, telephoned Atlanta police detective James Burkhalter and informed him that they had dogged Sentovich and two other men, Mark Diefenthaler and Randall Alander, at the airport. The men had purchased tickets for flights from Fort Myers to Montana, via Atlanta. Police located a cart with luggage to be put on the flight to Atlanta. Not having Drug Enforcement Agency Agent Paul Markonni about, they had to fall back on a mere canine, Rocky, with 50—60 hours training in marijuana

---

[1] The court understands that Bodger and Nebuchadnezzar are in training.

detection, who sniffed the bags on the cart as well as other bags nearby. Rocky alerted strongly to two bags belonging to Diefenthaler. Police detained Diefenthaler. Alander, without being asked to do so, left the plane and proceeded to a security lounge. Before the plane left, police found and seized seven pieces of luggage, including two carry-on bags, belonging to the two men. Sentovich, showing what a dog-eat-dog world this is, abandoned the men to their fate and flew on to Atlanta with his two suitcases and shoulder-type bag.

Burkhalter informed the Drug Enforcement Agency of the information he had received. Agent Paul Markonni had the airline on whose flight Sentovich had arrived in Atlanta nose around and locate Sentovich's bags. Markonni, who stated in an affidavit that he had smelled marijuana more than 100 times over the past eleven years, applied his proboscis to the three bags and alerted to two of them because of the odor of marijuana. Not willing to have Sentovich depart from under his very nose, Markonni told Burkhalter of his discovery. Burkhalter stopped Sentovich as he was boarding a flight to Montana and asked him to consent to a search. Sentovich initially consented but, after talking to an attorney, changed his mind and refused to allow a search.

Markonni doggedly went to obtain a search warrant for the two bags that smelled of marijuana. He presented to a magistrate an affidavit containing the information obtained from Florida police and stating that he had detected the nose-tickling odor of marijuana emanating from the luggage. The magistrate issued the warrant after refusing to have the bags taken to the courthouse to be smelled by him or by another neutral party and after refusing to allow counsel for Sentovich to cross-examine Markonni. The counsel asked to be allowed to be present when the bags were opened. Markonni advised that counsel could be present but that he would not allow counsel to ride with him to the airport and would open the bags immediately. Markonni returned to the airport. Before defense counsel arrived, he opened the two bags in which he had detected the odor and found marijuana in them. Sentovich was convicted of possession of marijuana with intent to distribute, in violation of 21 U.S.C.A. §841(1)(1).

II.

Sentovich argues that he should have been able to cross-examine Markonni before a search warrant was issued. Unless some compelling reason requires an ex parte hearing, he asserts that a police officer will be able to obtain a warrant too dog-cheaply unless the hearing on whether to issue a search warrant is adversarial. The Supreme Court has ruled otherwise. "To mandate an evidentiary hearing [with respect to a request for a search warrant], the challenger's attack must be more than conclusory and must be supported by more than a mere desire to cross-examine. There must be allegations of deliberate falsehood or of reckless disregard for the truth, and those allegations must be accompanied by an offer of proof. . . . Allegations of negligence or innocent mistake are insufficient." Franks v. Delaware {citation omitted}.

Sentovich asserts that cross-examination would have provided an opportunity to test Markonni's ability to discern the odor of marijuana. Neither on appeal nor below does he allege that Markonni deliberately lied or recklessly disregarded the truth in stating that he nosed out marijuana. Without a claim of such doggery, the magistrate was on the nose in finding that no adversarial hearing was necessary.

Sentovich next asserts that the magistrate should have ordered the bags to be brought to the court or that Markonni should have awaited the arrival of Sentovich's counsel before opening the bags. Because of the absence of third-party confirmation, he argues that important evidence was destroyed. Sentovich suggests several remedies: exclusion of the alleged odor of the luggage from a determination of whether probable cause for the warrant existed, suppression of the evidence of the marijuana discovered in the bags, or dismissal of the indictment.

We find no error by the magistrate or misconduct by the government. We address first Sentovich's arguments concerning the need to exclude the evidence from a finding of probable cause for a warrant and concerning the suppression of the evidence of marijuana. He raised neither argument in his motion to suppress. A party not raising an argument below waives his right to raise it on appeal absent plain error. . . .

Indeed, reaching the merits, we find no error at all. The magistrate need not have required a neutral party to smell the luggage. As we noted above, *Franks* supplies the standard for determining when an evidentiary hearing is necessary. Since there was no allegation of deliberate falsehood or reckless disregard of the truth by Markonni, here was no reason for the magistrate to hold a hearing allowing third-party confirmation of Markonni's sense of smell.

There was also no misconduct by Markonni in failing to delay opening the luggage until Sentovich's counsel arrived at the airport. Police with a search warrant simply need not await the arrival of counsel before executing that warrant. Moreover, the inability of counsel to smell marijuana would have no bearing on the validity of the warrant. Even if Markonni was wrong in thinking that he smelled marijuana, his misstatement would invalidate the warrant only if it was intentional or made in deliberate disregard of the truth. ... We note again that Sentovich never alleges any malodorous motive or activity by Markonni that was intentional or in reckless disregard of the truth.[2]

Sentovich did seek dismissal of the indictment against him because of the alleged destruction of the evidence of the odor of the marijuana. At the very least, Sentovich must make some showing of the materiality of the evidence the government suppressed. ... The standard for determining materiality varies somewhat with the situation at issue {citation omitted}. Here, however, we need not inquire into the exact applicable standard. Whatever the standard may be, Sentovich has not met it. The odor of the marijuana—as opposed to the marijuana itself—was of no relevance to Sentovich's conviction.

Markonni emerges with his nose unbloodied and his tail wagging. Sentovich's claims are without merit. Having also reviewed the evidence, we find it sufficient for his conviction. The judgment of the district court is AFFIRMED.

---

[2]Sentovich also alleges that there was insufficient evidence of the reliability of the dog smelling the bags at Fort Myers for the dog's reaction to be used as a basis for the search warrant. His argument is that a mere statement that the dog had been trained in drug detection was not enough without an accompanying statement that the dog had proved reliable in the past and that an experienced handler was with the dog. Since we believe Markonni's statement concerning his detection of an odor of marijuana was sufficient alone for a finding of probable cause, the adequacy of the proof of the reliability of the dog is not essential to our holding. We believe, in any event, that his argument is without merit. The case on which Sentovich relies, United States v. Klein {citation omitted}, does state that statements that a dog had had training and had proved reliable in the past were sufficient indicia of the dog's reliability. The court did not, however, state that the handler had to be trained or that training alone was insufficient to show reliability. Two other circuits have held that training of a dog alone is sufficient proof of reliability. ...

In the following case, a bookseller loaned out a particularly scandalous book which was passed from hand to hand, and was eventually kept by an unintended party. The merchant subsequently filed a lawsuit for its recovery.

CATLING v. BOWLING
King's Bench, Easter Term, 26 George II
96 E.R. 810; 1 Sayer 80 (1753)

SIR WILLIAM LEE, CHIEF JUSTICE

Upon a motion for leave to bring a book into court, for the conversion of which an action of Trover was brought, it appeared; that the book, entitled *Memoirs of a Woman of Pleasure*, had been lent by a bookseller to some young ladies at a boarding school; that the defendant's wife, who was mistress of the school, took it from them and sent it to the bookseller, with a request that it might not be again sent to the young ladies; and that the book being afterwards found in the possession of one of the young ladies, the defendant's wife took it from her and kept it.

A rule was made to shew cause, why, upon bringing the book into court, the proceedings should not be stayed; and it is probable, that the plaintiff there-upon agreed to drop his action; for the court never heard any more of the rule.

Illicit gambling activities are difficult to conceal, particularly when one is caught red-handed at one o'clock in the morning.

PACETTI v. THE STATE OF GEORGIA
Supreme Court of Georgia
82 Ga. 297; 7 S.E. 867 (1888)

LOGAN E. BLECKLEY, C.J.

A social, genial gentleman, fond of company and a glass, by occupation a cigar-maker, who keeps his sleeping apartment with the doors "blanketed" in a fit condition for privately gaming therein, and who invites his friends at night to refresh themselves with beer, but has in the room, besides barrel and bottles, a table suitable for gaming, together with eleven packs of cards and two boxes of "chips," one containing eighty chips and the other three hundred, and a memorandum book with names and numbers entered in it, and whose guests, or some of them, retire hurriedly under the bed on being surprised by a visit from the police at one o'clock in the morning, may or may not be guilty of the offence of keeping a gaming-house. A verdict of guilty based on these and other inculpatory facts, such as the rattle of chips and money, and some expressions about seven dollars and twelve dollars heard by the police on approaching the premises, is warranted by the evidence, and is not contrary to law.

Judgment affirmed.

In the marketing of alcoholic products, adherence to general principles of "good taste" has not always been universal. In this case, Hawkeye Distilling Company's application for registration of its M*A*S*H vodka was flatly denied by the New York Liquor Authority. Hawkeye appealed the ruling, which resulted in the following opinion.

HAWKEYE DISTILLING COMPANY
v. NEW YORK STATE LIQUOR AUTHORITY
New York Supreme Court, Special Term
118 Misc.2d 505; 460 N.Y.S.2d 696 (1983)

RICHARD W. WALLACH, JUSTICE

This is a CPLR Art. 78 application by the Hawkeye Distilling Co. for a judgment annulling a determination of respondent New York State Liquor Authority (SLA) denying to Hawkeye brand label registration for its alcoholic beverage known as M*A*S*H vodka. The determination is annulled and the court grants judgment in favor of petitioner.

Doubtless to bask in the afterglow left by the 4077th Mobile Army Surgical Hospital as it strikes its tents and steals away from the Korean and golden TV hills, petitioner Hawkeye Distilling Co. obtained a license from Twentieth Century—Fox Film Corp. to use the name and logos of the popular television series "M*A*S*H" in marketing its "M*A*S*H Vodka." To get the full benefit of the "tie-in" with the show, the distiller devised a rather special marketing technique: it packages its clearly labelled domestic vodka in the form of an intra-venous (IV) feeding device. Sold together with the liquor is a metal contrivance permitting hookup of the bottle in the inverted position above the patient's head so familiar to experienced viewers of "General Hospital" and "Marcus Welby, M.D."

The liquid can be drunk by placing the tube in the imbiber's mouth. Presumably the gaiety of many a suburban rumpus room will be enhanced as the harried commuter drags himself inside the door of his home after a hard day at the office to obtain the dramatic resuscitation available from an oral "transfusion" of the vodka.

The whimsical features of the promotion, however, were entirely lost upon respondent SLA when petitioner applied to register its Hawkeye brand for sale in New York State. The SLA found that "the proposed label and bottling is misleading, deceptive, offensive to the commonly and generally accepted standards of fitness and good taste, is not dignified. . . . approval would not be conducive to proper regulation and control. . . ."

The decision of the authority cannot be upheld on the ground that the label of the product is misleading. . . . The court has inspected the bottle produced in open court and finds that it unmistakably labels the contents as 80-proof vodka manufactured in Skokie, Illinois. No rational person could believe that a serious medicinal application of the product was intended, certainly no more so than a buyer who might be induced to purchase an alcoholic beverage known as "Dr. Funk" or "MD 20/20" (both of which are distributed in New York) in the supposed belief that a medically or ophthalmologically beneficial result might ensue. Once it appears that neither the bottle nor its label are misleading, the Authority's writ runs no farther, certainly not so far as to empower it to reject a bottle (as opposed to a label) simply on the ground that it offends good taste.

Although the problem has not arisen in this form before in New York, a New Jersey decision under a similar regulatory scheme points to the correct result. In Boller Beverages, Inc. v. Davis {citation omitted}, the director of the New Jersey alcoholic beverage control authority had refused to sanction the sale of "Georgia Moon Corn Whiskey" in what appeared to be an ordinary home canning Mason jar. This determination rested in part upon lack of good taste. The court held that in the absence of any legislative mandate

78

empowering the director to approve of bottling as such, his ruling could not be sustained simply as a matter of aesthetics. Although some jurisdictions empower their liquor authorities to regulate bottling {citation omitted}, New York (like New Jersey) is pointedly not one of them.

It further appears that 39 other states, including some who are the exclusive purveyors, have approved the product for distribution (which surely says something, either praiseworthy or deplorable, about the good taste of this product). Be that as it may, this is a case for application of the maxim: *"de gustibus non disputandum"* {There is no disputing over personal tastes}. One of the prized qualities of vodka is its tastelessness. Insofar as good taste may be relevant at all, it is worth recalling that the last public official who held the undisputed title of "Arbiter Elegantiae" (supreme judge of taste) was Gaius Petronius. He worked for the Emperor Nero. Both came to a bad end.

It follows that the decision of the SLA is found to be arbitrary and capricious, and that if the ruling is defended as discretionary, such discretion was exercised in an area where the authority has no jurisdiction to act. Its determination must be annulled. . . .

Let petitioner settle a judgment in its favor accordingly.

The following is the earliest recorded drunk driving case under English law that we have yet been able to locate.

IN RE GILBERT COLT
Assize Court of Northumberland County
Northumberland Assize Rolls, 40 Henry III (1256)

ANONYMOUS, JUDGE

Gilbert Colt, a servant of the parson of Brombury, while driving a certain wagon with a large container of wine, as a result of excessive intoxication fell beneath this same wagon and was crushed under the wheel of this same wagon. No one is suspected in this incident. Verdict: misadventure. Value of the wine, oxen, and wagon: 8 marks, 2 shillings, for which the sheriff will be answerable. Also, John of

Kestern and Gilbert of Worton falsely assessed the value of the aforesaid deodand*; accordingly, they are to be fined.

When Henry Miller's book *The Tropic of Cancer* was published in 1961, it was considered by Pennsylvania authorities to be legally obscene, thereby meriting restraint of its commercial distribution. Pennsylvania banned the sale of the book by means of an injunction against the publisher and bookseller. The bookseller appealed and the Supreme Court of Pennsylvania decided that *Cancer* could not be banned or enjoined in any manner, based upon a precedent set by a similar U.S. Supreme Court case. Justice Musmanno, the judge who authored the following dissenting opinion, vociferously disagreed with his brethren on the Pennsylvania Supreme Court.

COMMONWEALTH OF PENNSYLVANIA v. ROBIN
Supreme Court of Pennsylvania
421 Pa. 70; 218 A.2d 546 (1966)

MICHAEL A. MUSMANNO, JUSTICE *(dissenting)*

The decision of the Majority of the Court in this case has dealt a staggering blow to the forces of morality, decency and human dignity in the Commonwealth of Pennsylvania. If, by this decision, a thousand rattlesnakes had been let loose, they could not do as much damage to the well-being of the people of this state as the unleashing of all the scorpions and vermin of immorality swarming out of that volume of degeneracy called *The Tropic of Cancer*. Policemen, hunters, constables and foresters could easily and quickly kill a thousand rattlesnakes but the lice, lizards, maggots and gangrenous roaches scurrying out from beneath the covers of *The Tropic of Cancer* will enter into the playground, the study desks, the cloistered confines of children and immature minds to eat away moral resistance and wreak damage and harm which may blight countless lives for years and decades to come.

---

*{Ed. Note: Under ancient English law, "deodand" was the term used to identify personal property directly causing a death, which had to be forfeited to the Crown, ostensibly for use in connection with pious or charitable purposes.}

From time immemorial civilization has condemned obscenity because the wise men of the ages have seen its eroding effects on the moral fiber of a people; history is replete with the decadence and final collapse of mighty nations because of their descent into licentiousness and sloth. . . .

What is obscenity? Rivers of ink have flowed in an attempted definition of this word, and, more often than not, the greater the attempt at specificity, the more ambiguous has been the resulting language. The fact of the matter is that there is nothing complicated or puzzling about the word *obscenity.* It is a word as simple as *cat.* No person with reasonable intelligence and a modicum of human decency and dignity has any trouble in determining what is obscene. The determination does not require any long study in the laboratory, no working out of a mathematical formula. One sees at a glance whether a given exhibit or situation is obscene or not. . . . In the case of Roth v. United States, the Supreme Court . . . defined obscenity as follows:

> [W]hether to the average person, applying contemporary community standards, the dominant theme of the material taken as a whole appeals to prurient interest * * * and if it goes substantially beyond customary limits of candor in description or representation of such matters.

To say that *Cancer* has no social importance is like saying that a gorilla at a lawn party picnic does not contribute to the happiness of the occasion. *Cancer* is a definite sociological evil. It is not to be described negatively. It is a positive menace to the well-being of the community in which it contaminates the air it displaces. It condemns, outrages and ridicules the most fundamental rules of good society, namely, honesty, morality and obedience to law. It encourages anti-Semitism and racial conflict. It incites to disorder. . . .

Who is the author of this monstrous work, as described by the witnesses in Court? Henry Miller, who identifies himself in the book as a thief, an adulterer and a "hopeless lecher." He is irreverent, profane and blasphemous. He lauds harlots and glorifies a sinful career. . . .

. . . Henry Miller himself proclaims the degenerate character of his work in the introduction where he says:

> This then? This is not a book. This is libel, slander, defamation of character. This is not a book in the ordinary sense of the word. No, this is a prolonged insult, a gob of spit in the face of Art, a kick in the pants

to God, Man, Destiny, Time, Love, Beauty * * * what you will. I am going to sing for you, a little off key, perhaps, but I will sing. I will sing while you croak, I will dance over your dirty corpse.

A *favorable* review of *Cancer* describes it in the following language:

> * * * Lice, bedbugs, cockroaches, and tapeworms crawl across its pages; they are spattered with spittle, pus, vomit, scum, and excrement; blood, bile, semen, and sewers flow through them. Women, most of them prostitutes, throng *Tropic of Cancer.* Miller and his pals lust after them daily, and perform feats of satyriasis; but in their thoughts and talk a woman is seldom a "woman"—she is a name for a portion of her anatomy. . . .

The defendants argued that under the Roth case only hard-core pornography comes within the ban of obscenity, and this would exclude *Cancer.* The defendant would have reason to say that *Cancer* is not hard-core pornography; it is, in fact, *rotten*-core pornography. No decomposed apple falling apart because of its rotten core could be more nauseating as an edible than *Cancer* is sickening as food for the ordinary mind. *Cancer* is dirt for dirt's sake, or, more appropriately, as Justice Frankfurter put it, dirt for money's sake.

Then the defendants say that *Cancer* is entitled to immunity under the First Amendment because court decisions have declared that only worthless trash may be proscribed as obscene. To say that *Cancer* is worthless trash is to pay it a compliment. *Cancer* is the sweepings of the Augean stables, the stagnant bile of the slimiest mudscow, the putrescent corruption of the most noisome dump pile, the dreggiest filth in the deepest morass of putrefaction.

Falling back from position to position, arguing merit where none exists and claiming immunity which no law upholds, the defendants maintain that even if *Cancer* can be regarded filthy, obscene and rotten, it nevertheless qualifies for legal guardianship, if it possesses the slightest literary value. In effect, they say that if a fresh maple leaf should fall into a sewer, the sewage could then be run into a swimming pool to refresh and engladden the bathers disporting therein. The law is not so foolish.

And then, standing at the very last ditch, the apologists for *Cancer* glibly assert that there is no proof anywhere that *Cancer* or any work of that character has any bearing on human conduct. Of course, scientific research, sociological study and juvenile and criminal court records, as well as the realities of life are all to the contrary. . . .

Rape represents the most depraved animalistic aberration in the whole catalogue of offenses against society. For a youth or grown-up man to cast away the last modicum of social restraint and bestially inflict injury and irreparable harm on an innocent girl or woman means that the attacker has been prodded into primitive violence by a force of extraordinary excitation long continued. . . .

A tide of printed filth is driving across the land at such height and volume as to cause wholesome-thinking people to wonder and worry whether it may not impair the very foundations of the basic morality upon which our nation and our Constitution were founded. In bookstores, railroad stations, air terminals, drug stores, everywhere that print is displayed and pictures revealed, there stand pyramids of smut, pornography and obscenity.

Language that would be too raw and grating for the dives of opium-smoking debauchees degrades and defaces the paper that carries it. Magazines with pictures and sketches that would disgrace oriental harems are sold to children as if they were innocuous bags of popcorn. Exotic rites that would raise the blush of shame to the faces of the most primitive tribes are described with nonchalance in high-priced books, medium-priced books and low-priced books. Themes that should be the subject only for clinical studies in the hospitals for the criminal insane are turned into scarifying stories that inflict untold harm to the youths into whose hands they fall.

Acts of degeneracy and unnatural conduct are being portrayed in contemporary literature as if they were normal and accepted practice in civilized life. Adultery and every other type of illegal and sinful conduct is being depicted glamorously, inviting emulation. The healthful, romantic and poetic relationship between man and woman is being treated in the basest and grossest of terms.

It used to be that pornographic literature, to the extent that it existed, was trafficked in clandestinely. The secrecy and the furtiveness with which it was sold and circulated was an indication that the public looked upon it as something improper and not in consonance with the morals of the community. But now the most salacious books,

83

the most degrading publications are sold openly practically everywhere. It is difficult to think of a mart where print appears that one's eyes and spirits will not be assailed by pornography of the vilest character. And it is impossible to believe that over a sufficient period of time, this situation can do other than deleteriously affect the moral standards of the nation.

So far as youth and immature minds are concerned, pornographic literature can do as much harm as narcotics. Of course, no one dares to defend illicit traffic in narcotics, but a thousand tongues will wag to protect filthy books and magazines. Pornography is big business. It is conservatively estimated that the traffic in pornography in the United States amounts yearly to several billion dollars. Naturally the tycoons who can light cigars with hundred dollar bills as they ride in their luxurious yachts which cruise over rivers of printed filth will resist every effort to curb their deluxe and malodorous voyages.

And so, the false cry of censorship is heard in the land. But there is no censorship involved in banning pornography. The Supreme Court of the United States declared emphatically in the *Roth* case, as already stated, that "implicit in the history of the First Amendment is the rejection of obscenity as utterly without redeeming social importance."

There can be no more false notion than the one that the First Amendment protects everything that may be uttered orally or in print. We have laws that prohibit false advertising of food and drugs. If law will protect people from poison that may enter their systems through the throat, why may law not protect children from poison that may enter their minds, and do far more harm than any extra grain of aspirin? The constant fare of dirty books, to the exclusion of good literature, will eventually produce a sick mind. The mind governs the body and if the mind becomes sick, the body will become sick. . . .

The contention that anything printed is protected by the Constitution is arrant nonsense. It is the most bizarre notion imaginable that a printing press constitutionalizes every paper that passes between and beneath its rollers. Filth does not lose its stench or its bubonic characteristics because it is formed into letters of the alphabet. If everything that is printed or written is presumed to be good and incapable of evil, then correspondence on conspiracy to overthrow the government, ransom notes or even counterfeit money could not become the basis for prosecution of those who engage in its dissemination or use.

World War II, which filled the universe with graves, cripples, devastation and ruin, began with a *book*! Hitler's *Mein Kampf* fired Germany with a bellicose spirit, a hatred for minority and helpless peoples, and whipped the nation into a global conflict which almost drove civilization to the very brink of destruction, where indeed it even teeters today. . . .

The preface to *Cancer* characterizes its worthlessness when it tells the reader:

> Let us try to look at it with the eyes of a Patagonian for whom *all that is sacred and taboo in our world is meaningless.*

Cancer is not a book. It is a cesspool, an open sewer, a pit of putrefaction, a slimy gathering of all that is rotten in the debris of human depravity. And in the center of all this waste and stench, besmearing himself with its foulest defilement, splashes, leaps, crawls and wallows a bifurcated specimen that responds to the name of Henry Miller. One wonders how the human species could have produced so lecherous, blasphemous, disgusting and amoral a human being as Henry Miller. One wonders why he is received in polite society.

I would prefer to have as a visitor in my home the most impecunious tramp that ever walked railroad ties, a tramp whose raggedy clothes are held together by faith and a safety pin, a tramp who, throughout his entire life, always moved at a lazy pace, running only to avoid work, a tramp who rides the rods of freight cars with the aplomb of a railroad president in his private train, a tramp who knows as much about Emily Post's etiquette as a chattering chimpanzee and who couldn't care less; I would prefer to invite that lazy, bewhiskered cavalier of the road to my residence for a short visit, than even to see on the highway that hobo of the mind, that licentious nomad called Henry Miller, whose literary clothes are plastered with filth, whose language is dirtier than any broken sewer that pollutes and contaminates a whole community—Henry Miller who shuns a bath of clean words as the devil avoids holy water, who reduces human beings to animals, home standards to the pigsty, and dwells in a land of his own fit only for lice, bedbugs, cockroaches and tapeworms.

So far as American standards are concerned, I would regard Henry Miller as Moral Public Enemy No. 1, doing more damage to the ethic foundations of our Republic than any criminal whose picture appears in the lobby of post offices under the heading: "Wanted by the Police!" Those criminals have warred on society but Henry Miller's works, with those of his brother pornographic writers, unless curbed by the law, may eventually undermine the moral foundations of our nation because they are aimed at the youths of today who eventually will be the citizens of tomorrow.

Cancer is not a book. It is malignancy itself. It is a cancer on the literary body of America. I wonder that it can remain stationary on the bookshelf. One would expect it to generate self-locomotion just as one sees a moldy, maggoty rock move because of the creepy, crawling creatures underneath it.

Henry Miller is not the only foul-minded pornographic writer. There are others whose gangrenous productions raise a stench that would make polecats smell like new-mown hay in comparison. *Cancer* was published by the Grove Press, whose printing presses must by now be corroded with the festering mildew emanating from the accounts of human depravity, abnormal relations and Satanic perversion which have passed over its purulent type. Recently it advertised *Cancer* as a "classic!" . . .

In view of these fundamental rules in the interpretation of judicial decisions, it is obvious that the Supreme Court of the United States, in the *Gerstein* case, left the door open as wide as the horizon for the State courts to determine for themselves whether so loathsome a beast as *Cancer* should enter into the ark of the First Amendment protection. But this court refused to see the door; instead, it looked out the narrow window of a restricted interpretation and declared that the *Gerstein* case locked our hands, fettered our minds, bound our conscience, gagged our expression and compelled us, with blindfolded eyes, to follow a path that has no guidelines, no traveled surface and skirts the precipice of chaotic license. I refuse to go along. I prefer to follow the broad clean highway of decent literature, inspirational books, wholesomely entertaining stories, uplifting essays, enlightening histories and novels that one can read as easily as riding comfortably in a gondola—books that do not require one to don hipboots to slosh through muck, mire and filth that would make the pornographers of the early ages seem like a board of censors in comparison.

The Majority has missed a great opportunity to ring the Liberty Bell again for high moral standards. This was a case where the Court did not have to balance between literary excellence and moral turpitude in a book. It did not have to consider what the public might lose in being deprived of a work with some social value as against obscenity, because *Cancer* has no social worth whatever, it has no literary merit and no information value. It is a scabious toad croaking obscene phrases in a pestiferous swamp of filth and degradation.

And then, the Majority Opinion speaks of *Gerstein* as if it were the last unchangeable word to be spoken on the subject of obscenity in literature. I refuse to accept the thought that once a decision is rendered on any particular subject, this means that the last bell has rung, the last whistle has blown, the last nail has been driven, the last rivet has been hammered, the last bus has departed, and all that is left to do is wait until Judgment Day. Particularly on the subject here involved is there is no such fatalism as would appear in the short ambit of the short Majority Opinion. . . .

The Majority seems to overlook the fundamental observation that the long-honored standards of American decency are part of our national heritage. The patriots of the Revolutionary War fought just as bravely, and the colonial statesmen who built our structure of government labored just as earnestly and valiantly for moral cleanliness as they did to destroy political tyranny.

I regret that the action of the Supreme Court of Pennsylvania, the oldest Supreme Court in the nation, should result, not in *Cancer's* being consigned to the garbage can malodorously yawning to receive it, but, instead, in *Cancer's* being authorized unquestioned entry into the Public Library in Philadelphia within ringing distance of Independence Hall where the Liberty Bell rang out joyously the proclamation of the freedom, independence and *dignity of man*.

I would recoil in dismay if I attempted to visualize the reaction of the founding fathers if they could see this, one of the foulest books that ever disgraced printer's type, now taking a place on the library shelves with the Bible, *Pilgrim's Progress*, Shakespeare's *Works*, Plutarch's *Lives*, Homer's *Iliad*, Sir Thomas More's *Utopia*, Cervantes' *Don Quixote*, Thomas Paine's *Common Sense* and the other immortal books that inspired the brilliant architects, the brave leaders, the kneeling prayers and the heroic soldiers who fashioned the United States of America.

From Pittsburgh to Philadelphia, from Dan to Beersheeba, and from the ramparts of the Bible to Samuel Eliot Morison's *Oxford History of the American People*, I dissent!

A Nashville, Tennessee bar, the *Classic Cat II*, received two citations and had its beer permit suspended for thirty days as a result of allegedly permitting a drunken patron to loiter about its premises. Such loitering was a prohibited activity under local statute, which the Davidson County Beer Board investigated and attempted to prosecute.

METRO. GOV'T OF NASHVILLE
v. MARTIN
Supreme Court of Tennessee
584 S.W.2d 643 (1979)

JOSEPH W. HENRY, CHIEF JUSTICE

The Metropolitan Beer Permit Board of Nashville and Davidson County suspended the beer permit of Classic Cat II, pursuant to two citations. The Davidson County Circuit Court, pursuant to statutory writs of certiorari and a *de novo* hearing as provided in {Tenn. Code, Sec. 57-209} reversed. . . .

III.
The Second Citation

The second citation was properly certified by the Beer Board and is included in the record. It charges the permittee with allowing "an[y] intoxicated person to loiter on or about the premises," on April *14*, 1978.

All the proof was directed to activities occurring on April *16*, 1978; however, counsel makes no issue of this discrepancy. Therefore, we do not treat it as being of critical significance. It is but another of many instances of sloppy Beer Board procedure.

The proof presented to the Beer Board was meager and marginal. If there were no other proof in the record we unhesitatingly would affirm the Trial Judge and hold that the Beer Board acted arbitrarily; however, upon the *de novo* hearing before the Trial Judge additional proof was presented which placed the matter in an entirely different light. . . .

. . . Before the Trial Court the Beer Board presented the deposition of the "loitering drunk" and his cohort and companion. This proof was not presented to the Beer Board.

He is a member of the regular army stationed at Fort Campbell. He and his companion, another soldier, arrived in Nashville in the early afternoon of April 16, 1978, and took a room at a local motel.

About mid-afternoon they wended their way to the Classic Cat II, where they stayed several hours imbibing seven and sevens,[1] "[m]aybe 10 to 15." Thereafter, they left, bought a bottle of Seagrams V.O. and settled down to some serious drinking—"drinking out of the bottle."

Around 9:30 or 10:00 P.M. they returned to the Classic Cat and the seven and sevens. While he denies that his first 10 to 15 drinks caused him to be "smashed," he admits that after his interlude with Seagrams V.O. and after topping that off with more seven and sevens, he was drunk.

He says that every time he drinks "hard liquor" he gets drunk or tries to. He admits that he was in Nashville to get "bombed," and that he went to the Classic Cat to get drunk and "watch the women." Of course, he denies that he has a drinking problem; he says he just likes to drink.

They apparently remained at the Classic Cat for some two or three hours on their second visit.

When we analyze this soldier's actions in terms of his stated intention "to get bombed," the conclusion is inevitable that success crowned his efforts. While he lolled, loafed and loitered about the Classic Cat satisfying his lickerish craving for liquor by lapping up lavish libations, he fell from his chair, clutching his drink in his hand, into the waiting hands of vice squad officer McElhaney, who helped him up and took him to jail.

---

[1]Seagrams and 7-Up.

We subject his conduct to the most liberal standard that has come to the attention of the author of this opinion.

> *Not drunk is he who from the floor*
> *Can rise alone and still drink more;*
> *But drunk is he, who prostrate lies,*
> *Without the power to drink or rise.*[2]

This soldier fails the test. He was drunk—openly, visibly, notoriously, gloriously and uproariously drunk.

The Classic Cat II violated one of the great commandments by which "beer joints" must live. In summary and in short, in paraphrase and in idiom, the law "don't allow no [drunken] hanging around" beer establishments.

We do not deal with an isolated case of a drunk who came in from the cold and was drunk on arrival, or with a customer who consumed beer and became intoxicated as a result of that consumption under circumstances where the management reasonably could not be expected to realize that the customer had reached the point of intoxication. We deal purely and simply with permitting a drunk to "hang around" a beer joint under circumstances that were known, or should have been known to the permittee, or her employees.

We find no reported cases wherein the courts have attempted to define the offense of drunken loitering about premises where beer was sold. However, Hopper v. State {citation omitted} deals with an analogous prohibition against permitting minors to loiter about such premises. There, this Court quoted with approval the definition of "loitering" as contained in a decision of the Connecticut Supreme Court:

> To be slow in moving; to delay; to linger; to be dilatory; to spend time idly; to saunter; to lag behind ...

See also McCoy v. State {citation omitted} where the Court approved a definition from *Black's Law Dictionary:*

> To be dilatory, to be slow in movement, to stand around, to spend time idly, to saunter, to delay, to idle, to linger, to lag behind ...

We approve these definitions; they accord with the common understanding of the term "loiter" or "loitering."

---

[2]Thomas L. Peacock, *The Misfortunes of Elphin* (1827). Translated from the Welsh.

90

Appellants' assignment . . . is sustained and the action of the Beer Board in suspending Classic Cat II's license for a period of thirty (30) days is upheld. . . .

. . . Affirmed in part; reversed in part; remanded.

Gambling has been the source of many disputes throughout history, often requiring calm and reflective judicial intervention in order to unravel the controversy and keep the peace. In the following case, both participants were found to be in the wrong.

IN RE T. SMITH AND FELIPE VEGA
Justice Court of California, Tuolumne County
Case No. 60 (1850)

R. C. BARRY, J.P.

This was a gambling scrape in which T. Smith the monte deeler, shot and wounded Felipe Vega. After heering the witnesses on both sides, I adjudged Smith guilty of the shooting and fined him 10 dolars and Vega guilty of attempting to steele 5 ounces. I therefore fined him 100 dolars, and costs of coort.

Costs of Coort 3 ounces.

Sept. 4, 1850

U. H. Brown, Constable

CHAPTER IV

Business, *Trade, Commerce, Contracts, Property, Professions, Corporations, Regulation, Taxation* and *Related Mercantile Matters*

The true law, everywhere and at all times, delighteth in the payment of just debts. Blessed is the man that pays. The practice of paying promptly, and to the last cent, tends to the cultivation of one of the most excellent traits of human character. If debtors were guided by their own true interest, on an enlarged scale, they would be even more clamorous to pay than creditors are to receive. Tender would be more frequent than calls for money. Debt is the source of much unhappiness. The best possible thing to be done with a debt is to pay it. . . .

—Logan E. Bleckley, J.[1]

---

[1]From Robert v. N. & A. F. Tift, 60 Ga. 566 (1878).

Although competition is necessary to sustain the free enterprise system, our courts have always been ready to intervene and protect the mercantile competitors from any unfair tactics utilized by their overzealous colleagues.

IN RE W. T. BULL
Justice Court of California, Tuolumne County
Case No. 859 (1851)

R. C. BARRY, J.P.

W. T. Bull in this caze is charged of attempting to murther R. F. Cole by shooting at him with a riffle loded with powder and ball wilst working in his clame. I examined a large number of witnesses, each contradicting the other flatly. After much patient hearing and taking time to think over it I concluded that R. F. Cole had jumped ½ of W. T. Bull's clame and that he was only defending his justs & rites which he probably was only doing. Therefore after long studdy and thinking it just and proper I ordered Cole to restore to Bull the part of the clame and to pay Bull $500 for the dammage he has done to it in so jumping it.

Cost of Court $40.

Sonora, Oct. 31, 1851

John Luney, Constable

Whether or not a new hat was paid for was the simple question posed in the following case. The judge also had to grapple with deeper issues of fashion, social propriety and sartorial chic.

MRS. AGNES GARNER
v. JOSEPH BURNSTEIN
Louisiana Court of Appeals
1 La. App. 19 (1924)

WESTERFIELD, J.

Plaintiff purchased a hat from the defendant, who conducts a millinery establishment in this city, for the sum of $20. The hat was to be paid for on delivery or, as it is termed commercially, C.O.D. The hat was delivered as agreed upon by the porter employed by defendant and according to the positive testimony of plaintiff and a lady friend of hers, whom she was visiting, was paid for by handing the porter two ten-dollar bills. The porter returned to defendant's place of business and upon being asked for the money stated that no money had been paid him, and that he was induced to leave the hat by plaintiff stating that she had called at the hat shop of defendant earlier in the day and paid for the hat. Whereupon the porter was told to return to plaintiff's residence and get the hat or the money.

The porter returned and finding plaintiff absent persuaded the servant to give him the hat and returned same to his employer. Upon plaintiff returning home and discovering her hat was gone she immediately repaired to the hat shop and demanded the hat, which the defendant refused to surrender unless she paid him the price. This plaintiff refused to do upon the ground that she had already paid for it. Thereupon plaintiff entered suit against defendant for $270, twenty dollars of which sum she claims to have paid defendant and $250 as consequential and punitive damages.

The first question for our consideration is whether the porter of defendant was paid for the hat and we have no difficulty in concluding that he was. Plaintiff is corroborated in this regard by another lady and both swear positively and circumstantially that the hat was paid for with two ten-dollar bills given the porter of defendant. Payment to defendant's agent was payment to him and whether he got the money or not plaintiff should have had her hat. His refusal to give her the hat renders him liable to pay any damages which might be reasonably contemplated as resulting from his refusal to do so. . . .

The damages claimed here are, so far as we can consider them (punitive damages not being allowable at all), said to be due to mental anguish caused by disappointment due to the fact that the hat was bought to be worn with a certain dress to a dinner party on the very evening it was to be delivered. Plaintiff went to the party, though she alleges in her petition that she was unable to do so because of the lack of a proper hat, but says she was unable to wear the dress for which the hat was bought, causing her deep humiliation, disappointment and distress.

We are not inclined to treat her alleged state of mind on this occasion jocosely. It is said, "The apparel oft proclaims the man."[1] It more often proclaims the woman. Nature seems to have intended that the male should be more pulchritudinous. Witness the majestic beauty of the male lion as compared with the plainness of its mate and the beauteous plumage of the mallard drake as compared with the drab appearance of the duck. But man, at least modern man, has decreed otherwise and countless industries and hosts of individuals are devoted to the production of clothing, jewelry, feathers, powders and, we regret to say, paints designed exclusively for the ornamentation of the female form in an effort to "paint the lily." No Rubens or Van Dyke ever studied the colors of their masterpieces with greater care than the modern woman studies the color scheme of her costume, for the laws of modern convention, though subject to frequent change, are inexorable.

Therefore, when the plaintiff in this case tells us that the yellow hat bought of defendant and that yellow hat alone was suitable for her new dress which she had bought for the dinner party and that not having the hat she was compelled to wear an inappropriate costume, to her great embarrassment, mortification and, yes, mental anguish, we believe her. The only question is, could the defendant reasonably contemplate the result of his refusal to surrender the hat? He might be charged with knowledge of the intricate rules of feminine attire; indeed, his business is largely based upon the rigidity of these rules, and he must be held to be familiar with them, but he could not know the condition of the plaintiff's wardrobe, and since the record does not disclose that he was advised of the dinner dance and the special purpose for which the hat was intended, he cannot be charged with such knowledge, for it might well be, so far as defendant knew anything to the contrary, that plaintiff possessed a number of hats suitable for the occasion.

In the case of Lewis v. Holmes {citation omitted}, the defendant was held liable for damages caused by the disappointment of a bride in not having her trousseau properly made in time for the wedding and for social functions incident thereto. Holmes made the dresses, but they were four inches too short and the bride could not wear them without embarrassment and mortification, thus preventing her from being properly attired at social functions given in her honor. But

---

[1]{Ed. Note: Shakespeare, *Hamlet*, Act I, Scene 3.}

in the instant case we are not dealing with bridal robes, which in themselves impart a warning of their importance, but with a hat in itself suggestive of none of the consequences that have resulted here.

We conclude, therefore, that the judgment appealed from must be amended by reducing the amount awarded plaintiff to twenty dollars, and it is so ordered.

On occasion, almost every judge has utilized the time-honored "Wisdom of Solomon" method of allocating an award to the parties in a difficult case. (See Holy Bible, I Kings 3:16–27.)

IN RE JAMES TOVER
Justice Court of California, Tuolumne County
Case No. 500 (1851)

R. C. BARRY, J.P.
This was a caze in which James Tover had jumped a peece of grund that the Wideawake company claimed as part of thear clame. Upon hearing the evidence of all the witnesses on boath sides, and taking the caze under avisement I came to the following conclusion that boath parties is in falt. I therefore decree that the ground be equally divided, and one haf be returned to James Tover and one half to the Wideawake Company and that each pay one haf of the Costs of Coort share and share alik.

Costs of Coort 6 ounces, and that each stand committed until each of them pays there amount.

Sonora, Aug 14, 1851

U. H. Brown, Constable

Physicians and most other professionals generally find it more difficult to collect their fees when the services rendered have been unsuccessful.

HALL v. MOORING
Court of Appeals of Georgia
12 Ga. App. 74; 76 S.E. 759 (1912)

JAMES ROBERT POTTLE, J.

This was a contest between two members of the gentler sex. The plaintiff was a practitioner of the art or science of osteopathy, and the defendant either needed, or thought she did (which is the same thing), the services of the plaintiff. Several visits were made at $3.10 per visit, the ten cents being added for street-car fare, and the whole bill amounted to $27.90. The defendant says she paid all she really owed, and that the plaintiff charged her for a number of social calls, during the course of which the defendant was importuned to continue the treatment. The defendant says that she declined to do so, and that the services rendered by the doctor gave her no relief, and were so unsatisfactory that she was forced to resort to a physician of the allopathic school, who administered pills and mixtures in the good old-fashioned way.

On the issues of fact the plaintiff outswore the defendant, or at least the jury in the justice's court thought she did, and the judge of the superior court refused to interfere. This is the end of the law so far as this branch of the case is concerned.

It would never do to hold that a doctor is entitled to recover only where he cures the patient. If we did, the members of this learned profession might hesitate to respond in extreme cases where the chances were against them. So far as we are concerned the doctors may continue to bury their mistakes and recover for their services as they have always done. If we were dealing with lawyers, the rule might be different, but sufficient unto the day is the evil thereof.

The defendant says she ought not to pay the extra ten cents per visit, because the doctor usually walked. However, the plaintiff testified that the charge was usual and reasonable. If so, she had a right to walk and save the ten cents.

It appears from the record that the trial waxed warm, and, during the testimony of the defendant, the plaintiff became excited and exclaimed, "liar, liar, liar"; and while the defendant's counsel was endeavoring to persuade the jury to accept his client's theory of the case, the plaintiff did, at intervals, "yell out in court that the defendant was a liar and had lied." Complaint is made that this conduct of the plaintiff humiliated and embarrassed the defendant and prejudiced the jury against her, and that the verdict ought to be set aside because the magistrate failed to punish the plaintiff for contempt.

Doubtless the conduct of the plaintiff overawed the chivalrous young justice and embarrassed him quite as much as it did the defendant, and we are not disposed to criticize too harshly his exhibition of judicial timidity. At any rate the failure of the magistrate to punish the contumelious plaintiff must be allowed to rest upon his judicial conscience. If we had any means of knowing that the plaintiff's conduct terrorized the jury and coerced the verdict in her favor, we would, in the interest of a fair and impartial trial, direct another hearing. But the jury doubtless felt secure under the protection of the bailiff and the sacred precincts of the court-room; and if they had returned a verdict adverse to the plaintiff, there was, no doubt, some rear door through which they might have dispersed and thus have escaped violence at the hands of a litigant outraged at the injustice which had been meted out to her. Viewing the matter from this safe distance, we are inclined to think that the unseemly conduct of the plaintiff would more likely have prejudiced her own cause than it did the defendant's. . . .

Judgment affirmed.

It takes a unique and arguably perverse talent to transform an opinion devoted exclusively to the droll topic of laundry detergent labeling requirements into a humorous, entertaining and legally cogent recitation of law. The venerable Judge John R. Brown was more than ready to meet this challenge.

CHEMICAL SPECIALTIES MANUFACTURERS ASSOCIATION, INC. v. CLARK

U.S. Court of Appeals, Fifth Circuit
482 F.2d 325 (1973)

PER CURIAM {JOHN R. BROWN, HOMER THORNBERRY, LEWIS R. MORGAN, JJ.}

{A Florida county amended its municipal code to require every detergent product to bear a label showing its ingredients in descending order of presence by weight. Plaintiff, an association consisting of detergent manufacturers and marketers, brought this action on the grounds that a similar, but less rigorous, federal act preempted the local ordinance. The U.S. Court of Appeals agreed that the Dade County regulation must give way to the supremacy of federal law.}

JOHN R. BROWN, CHIEF JUDGE *(concurring)*

As soap, now displaced by latter-day detergents, is the grist of Madison Avenue, I add these few comments in the style of that street to indicate my full agreement with the opinion of the court and to keep the legal waters clear and phosphate-free.

As *Proctor* of this dispute between the representative of many manufacturers of household detergents and the Board of Commissioners of Metropolitan Dade County, Florida, who have promulgated regulations which seek to control the labeling of such products sold within their jurisdiction (largely to discourage use that pollutes their waters), the Court holds that Congress has specifically preempted regulatory action by Dade County. Clearly, the decision represents a *Gamble* since we risk a *Cascade* of criticism from an increasing *Tide* of ecology-minded citizens. Yet, a contrary decision would most likely have precipitated a *Niagara* of complaints from an industry that justifiably seeks uniformity in the laws with which it must comply. Inspired by the legendary valor of *Ajax*, who withstood

Hector's lance, we have *Bold*ly chosen the course of uniformity in reversing the lower Court's decision upholding Dade County local labeling laws. And, having done so, we are *Cheer*ed by the thought that striking down the regulation by the local jurisdiction does not create a void which is detrimental to consumers, but rather merely acknowledges that federal legislation has preempted this field with adequate labeling rules.

Congress, of course, has the *Cold Power* to preempt. Of the three situations discussed by the Court, the first (direct conflict) is easy, for it is *Crystal Clear* that the state law must yield. The third, in which the ordinance may *supplement* the federal law and thereby extend or increase the degree of regulation, is more troublesome. For where Congress has chosen to fashion a regulatory scheme that is only the *Head and Shoulders,* but has not opted to regulate every aspect of the area, the states have implied power to flesh out the body. It is where Congress fails to clearly signify, with an appropriate preemption clause, its intent to fully occupy the area regulated that the problem arises. With some *Joy,* the Court finds there is such a clause.

Concerning the precautionary labeling aspect, this is *SOS* to consumers. If we *Dash* to the heart of the question, it is apparent, as the Court points out, that the 1966 Amendments to FHSA indicate an explicit congressional purpose to preempt state regulation of the labeling of these substances. Undoubtedly, this unequivocal congressional *Salvo* was directed at such already existing regulations as those of the Fire Department of New York City relating to pressurized containers. . . .

Indeed, Congress intended to wield its *Arm and Hammer* to *Wisk* away such local regulations and further, to preclude the growing *Trend* toward this proliferation of individual community supervision. Its purpose was at least two-fold: (i) to put day-to-day responsibility in the hands of local government, but (ii) at the same time to impose detailed identical standards to eliminate confusion or overlapping.

With this clear expression of congressional intent to create some form of preemption, the only thing remaining was whether the meaning of the term "precautionary labeling" is sufficiently broad to embrace the words of the Dade County ordinance, *Vel* non. In making this determination, the Court is furnished with a *Lever* by our

Brothers of the Second Circuit {citation omitted}. And so we hold. This is all that need be said. It is as plain as *Mr. Clean* the proper *Action* is that the Dade County ordinance must be superseded, as *All* comes out in the wash.

{REVERSED AND REMANDED}

A native New Englander, Mrs. Webster, ordered a bowl of fish chowder while dining with relatives at the Blue Ship Tea Room, a Boston restaurant. A fish bone lodged in her throat, resulting in two esophagoscopies at Massachusetts General Hospital, and one lawsuit against the operator of the restaurant. The following opinion is considered to be a "classic" exposition on both the gastronomic traditions of New England and the implied warranty of fitness and merchantability under the Uniform Commercial Code.

WEBSTER v. BLUE SHIP TEA ROOM, INC.
Supreme Judicial Court of Massachusetts
347 Mass. 421; 198 N.E.2d 309 (1964)

PAUL CASHMAN REARDON, JUSTICE

This is a case which by its nature evokes earnest study not only of the law but also of the culinary traditions of the Commonwealth which bear so heavily upon its outcome. It is an action to recover damages for personal injuries sustained by reason of a breach of implied warranty of food served by the defendant in its restaurant....

On Saturday, April 25, 1959, about 1:00 P.M., the plaintiff, accompanied by her sister and her aunt, entered the Blue Ship Tea Room operated by the defendant. The group was seated at a table and supplied with menus.

This restaurant, which the plaintiff characterized as "quaint," was located in Boston "on the third floor of an old building on T Wharf which overlooks the ocean."

The plaintiff, who had been born and brought up in New England (a fact of some consequence), ordered clam chowder and crabmeat salad. Within a few minutes she received tidings to the effect that "there was no more clam chowder," whereupon she ordered a cup of fish chowder. Presently, there was set before her "a small bowl of fish chowder." She had previously enjoyed a breakfast about 9:00 A.M. which had given her no difficulty. "The fish chowder contained haddock, potatoes, milk, water and seasoning. The chowder was milky in color and not clear. The haddock and potatoes were in chunks" (also a fact of consequence). "She agitated it a little with the spoon and observed that it was a fairly full bowl * * *. It was hot when she got it, but she did not tip it with her spoon because it was hot * * * but stirred it in an up and under motion. She denied that she did this because she was looking for something, but it was rather because she wanted an even distribution of fish and potatoes." "She started to eat it, alternating between the chowder and crackers which were on the table with * * * [some] rolls. She ate about three or four spoonfuls, then stopped. She looked at the spoonfuls as she was eating. She saw equal parts of liquid, potato and fish as she spooned it into her mouth. She did not see anything unusual about it. After three or four spoonfuls she was aware that something had lodged in her throat because she couldn't swallow and couldn't clear her throat by gulping and she could feel it." This misadventure led to two esophagoscopies at the Massachusetts General Hospital, in the second of which, on April 27, 1959, a fish bone was found and removed. The sequence of events produced injury to the plaintiff which was not insubstantial.

We must decide whether a fish bone lurking in a fish chowder, about the ingredients of which there is no other complaint, constitutes a breach of implied warranty under applicable provisions of the Uniform Commercial Code, the annotations to which are not helpful on this point. As the judge put it in his charge, "Was the fish chowder fit to be eaten and wholesome? * * * [N]obody is claiming that the fish itself wasn't wholesome. * * * But the bone of contention here—I don't mean that for a pun—but was this fish bone a foreign substance that made the fish chowder unwholesome or not fit to be eaten?"

The plaintiff has vigorously reminded us of the high standards imposed by this court where the sale of food is involved . . . and has made reference to cases involving stones in beans . . . trichinae in pork . . . and to certain other cases, here and elsewhere, serving to bolster her contention of breach of warranty.

The defendant asserts that here was a native New Englander eating fish chowder in a "quaint" Boston dining place where she had been before; that "[f]ish chowder, as it is served and enjoyed by New Englanders, is a hearty dish, originally designed to satisfy the appetites of our seamen and fishermen;" that "[t]his court knows well that we are not talking of some insipid broth as is customarily served to convalescents." We are asked to rule in such fashion that no chef is forced "to reduce the pieces of fish in the chowder to minuscule size in an effort to ascertain if they contained any pieces of bone." "In so ruling," we are told (in the defendant's brief), "the court will not only uphold its reputation for legal knowledge and acumen, but will, as loyal sons of Massachusetts, save our world-renowned fish chowder from degenerating into an insipid broth containing the mere essence of its former stature as a culinary masterpiece." Notwithstanding these passionate entreaties, we are bound to examine with detachment the nature of fish chowder and what might happen to it under varying interpretations of the Uniform Commercial Code.

Chowder is an ancient dish preexisting even "the appetites of our seamen and fishermen." It was perhaps the common ancestor of the "more refined cream soups, purées, and bisques" (Berolzheimer, *The American Woman's Cook Book* [Publisher's Guild Inc., New York, 1941], p. 176). The word "chowder" comes from the French "chaudière," meaning a "cauldron" or "pot." "In the fishing villages of Britany * * * 'faire la chaudière' means to supply a cauldron in which is cooked a mess of fish and biscuit with some savory condiments, a hodge-podge contributed by the fishermen themselves, each of whom in return receives his share of the prepared dish. The Breton fishermen probably carried the custom to Newfoundland, long famous for its chowder, whence it has spread to Nova Scotia, New Brunswick, and New England" (*A New English Dictionary* [Macmillan and Co., 1893], p. 386).

Our literature over the years abounds in references not only to the delights of chowder but also to its manufacture. A namesake of the plaintiff, Daniel Webster, had a recipe for fish chowder which has survived into a number of modern cookbooks[1] and in which the removal

---

[1] "Take a cod of ten pounds, well cleaned, leaving on the skin. Cut into pieces one and a half pounds thick, preserving the head whole. Take one and a half pounds of clear, fat salt pork, cut in thin slices. Do the same with twelve potatoes. Take the largest pot you have. Fry out the pork first, then take out the pieces of pork, leaving in the drippings. Add to that three parts of water,

of fish bones is not mentioned at all. One old-time recipe recited in the *New English Dictionary* study defines chowder as "A dish made of fresh fish (esp. cod) or clams, stewed with slices of pork or bacon, onions, and biscuit. 'Cider and champagne are sometimes added'" (Hawthorne, in *The House of the Seven Gables* [Allyn and Bacon, Boston, 1957], p. 8), speaks of "[a] codfish of sixty pounds, caught in the bay, [which] had been dissolved into the rich liquid of a chowder." A chowder variant, cod "Muddle," was made in Plymouth in the 1890s by taking "a three or four pound codfish, head added. Season with salt and pepper and boil in just enough water to keep from burning. When cooked, add milk and piece of butter."[2] The recitation of these ancient formulae suffices to indicate that in the construction of chowders in these parts in other years, worries about fish bones played no role whatsoever.

This broad outlook on chowders has persisted in more modern cookbooks. "The chowder of today is much the same as the old chowder * * *" (*The American Woman's Cook Book*, supra, p. 176). The all-embracing Fannie Farmer states in a portion of her recipe, fish chowder is made with a "fish skinned, but head and tail left on. Cut off head and tail and remove fish from backbone. Cut fish in 2-inch pieces and set aside. Put head, tail, and backbone broken in pieces, in stewpan; add 2 cups cold water and bring slowly to boiling point * * *." The liquor thus produced from the bones is added to the balance of the chowder (Farmer, *The Boston Cooking School Cook Book* [Little Brown Co., 1937], p. 166).

Thus, we consider a dish which for many long years, if well made, has been made generally as outlined above. It is not too much to say that a person sitting down in New England to consume a good New England fish chowder embarks on a gustatory adventure which may entail the removal of some fish bones from his bowl as he proceeds.

---

a layer of fish, so as to cover the bottom of the pot; next a layer of potatoes, then two tablespoons of salt, 1 teaspoon of pepper, then the pork, another layer of fish, and the remainder of the potatoes. Fill the pot with water to cover the ingredients. Put over a good fire. Let the chowder boil twenty-five minutes. When this is done have a quart of boiling milk ready, and ten hard crackers split and dipped in cold water. Add milk and crackers. Let the whole boil five minutes. The chowder is then ready to be first-rate if you have followed the directions. An onion may be added if you like the flavor." "This chowder," he adds, "is suitable for a large fishing party" (Wolcott, *The Yankee Cook Book* [Coward-McCann, Inc., New York City, 1939], p. 9).

[2]Atwood, *Recipes for Cooking Fish* (Avery & Doten, Plymouth, 1896), p. 8.

We are not inclined to tamper with age-old recipes by any amendment reflecting the plaintiff's view of the effect of the Uniform Commercial Code upon them. We are aware of the heavy body of case law involving foreign substances in food, but we sense a strong distinction between them and those relative to unwholesomeness of the food itself, e.g., tainted mackerel {citation omitted}, and a fish bone in a fish chowder. Certain Massachusetts cooks might cavil at the ingredients contained in the chowder in this case in that it lacked the heartening lift of salt pork. In any event, we consider that the joys of life in New England include the ready availability of fresh fish chowder. We should be prepared to cope with the hazards of fish bones, the occasional presence of which in chowders is, it seems to us, to be anticipated, and which, in the light of a hallowed tradition, do not impair their fitness or merchantability. While we are buoyed up in this conclusion by Shapiro v. Hotel Statler Corp. {citation omitted}, in which the bone which afflicted the plaintiff appeared in "Hotbarquette of Seafood Mornay," we know that the U.S. District Court of Southern California, situated as are we upon a coast, might be expected to share our views.

We are most impressed, however, by Allen v. Grafton {citation omitted}, where in Ohio, the Midwest, in a case where the plaintiff was injured by a piece of oyster shell in an order of fried oysters, Mr. Justice Taft (now Chief Justice) in a majority opinion held that "the possible presence of a piece of oyster shell in or attached to an oyster is so well known to anyone who eats oysters that we can say as a matter of law that one who eats oysters can reasonably anticipate and guard against eating such a piece of shell * * *" {citation omitted}

Thus, while we sympathize with the plaintiff, who has suffered a peculiarly New England injury, the order must be

Exceptions sustained.

Judgment for the defendant.

In this case, the plaintiff, Mr. Vann, went to his local barber-shop for a quiet, relaxing shave and instead received a severe razor injury to his hand. He sued the owner of the shop for the employee's negligence.

VANN v. IONTA

Municipal Court of City of New York, Borough of Queens
157 Misc. 461; 284 N.Y.S. 278 (1935)

NICHOLAS M. PETTE, JUSTICE

... Plaintiff, who is a businessman in the neighborhood, sat in Jimmie's chair to be shaved. He testified that Jimmie had shaved him twice before without trouble, but that this time Jimmie "started to fool around" and began "wisecracking and tickling" him. Plaintiff claims that he told Jimmie to stop, that he was very ticklish, but Jimmie persisted. He says that Jimmie made wisecracks and "poked him in the ribs" at the same time, causing plaintiff, as he says, to be in a "continuous state of laughter, uncontrolled." About the time plaintiff had been shaved over once, he claims that Jimmie again tickled him, and that this time he (plaintiff) jumped up, his hand caught the razor, and a severe cut resulted, requiring fourteen surgical sutures.

Jimmie testified that he has been a barber for ten years and had been working for defendant about two years. He admits talking to the customer, but denies that he poked or tickled him. When plaintiff came in this time, they got to talking "about things" and the customer started laughing. Jimmie says that he does not recall the object of conversation, but that he went right on with his task and got through shaving once over; but that as he was about to wipe the razor on the tissue paper which was resting upon the customer's chest, the razor "must have tickled him," so that plaintiff jumped up and grabbed the razor.

The question is one of negligence on two theories: (1) In the operation or handling of the razor by the employee, and (2) in employing a helper with "an unusual propensity for fooling around with customers."

With respect to the first ground of negligence, I am inclined to find for defendant for the reason that the facts seem to support the view that this was an unavoidable accident, as to which there can be no recovery. I do not believe that this barber of ten years' experience, with razor in hand, intentionally poked and tickled the plaintiff with the other hand. My observation of the witnesses rather impresses me that owing to plaintiff's easily excitable ticklishness, when the back of the razor struck his stomach or chest, he instinctively caught hold of the razor, thereby unfortunately sustaining the injuries.

The second theory of negligence requires a determination of what constitutes an "unusual propensity" on the part of a barber "for fooling around with customers." This very theory presupposes that barbers *usually* have a tendency to "fool around with customers."

In order to ascertain what conduct is to be classified as unusual on the part of a barber, we are first to see what is usual. There is no testimony either way, and the court is called upon to fix the usual rule of conduct substantially by resorting to judicial notice. There being no reported precedent, we are free to inquire into what is the common practice, as one of first impression. Considerable significance is to be attached to the fact that no similar case appears to have reached the courts heretofore, that is, at least the higher courts, so that there might be a record thereof.

The presiding judge may have personal knowledge of the adaptability of some barbers to jest and humor so as to entertain their patrons, but that would not permit the taking of judicial notice. The custom must be so widespread that it can be said that the tribunals will take cognizance thereof without special proof, and accept it as an established fact. What, then, is a barber's habit of "fooling around" with customers? The answer may have equal application to ladies' beauty parlors, which are closely related to the barbershop in primary and ultimate purpose.

A passage in Jimmie's testimony is a guide to an examination of the subject. He was asked by the court whether he was not "usurping the functions of a comedian," that is, whether he was "pulling an Eddie Cantor" on plaintiff, by "wisecracking," to which he, wistfully enough, replied: "Well, when a customer comes in he doesn't like to sit in the chair and be still, he wants you to talk to him."

So that, while admitting the talking, Jimmie tenders the proposition that barbering and talking go hand in hand, and that although the conversation evokes laughter, there can be no negligence based on the fact alone. Let us therefore see whether talking, and what quality and quantity, are really integral with tonsorial manipulations. My reading of reference books upon the barber's antecedents reveals him as a gentleman extraordinary, a factotum of no mean attainments and a useful adjunct to civilization itself.

The barber's art is rooted in antiquity, and its field is rich in fascinating lore and history revolving about the art's versatility since early days and its reduction from a profession to a calling of more humble character. In biblical times he was shaving both the face and beard, presumably because there were no cosmetics or hair tonics in those days. The prophet Ezekiel, 5:1, commanded, apparently in keeping with the times: "And thou son of man, take thee a . . . barber's razor, and cause it to pass upon thine head and upon thy beard" (Holy Bible, King James Version, Oxford Ed.). Of course, the departure in modern times from the command to shave the head is indicative of a wisdom that has grown with the years.

The barber appears to have been introduced in Rome about the year 454 of that city,[1] antedating the Christian era. It was about that time that the barber first began to earn his reputation for versatility that was to attach to his calling down through the years. Indeed, he appears to have been the first medium for the dissemination of news of public or private interest. Historically, therefore, he is viewed as the original "newspaper," besides his other activities presently to be observed. Barbers are alluded to by Horace as "the most accurately informed in all the minute history both of families and of the state." The *Encyclopedia Americana* records that in Rome "as elsewhere, when once introduced, they became men of great notoriety, and their shops were the resort of all the loungers and newsmongers in the city."

The Italian lexicon published in 1865 advises that the index of publicity was whether a subject had been discussed in a barbershop. If it had, it was public enough, that it had then reached the dignity of public property. Indeed, the authors give what then appeared to be the classical definition of a "barber" as "the twin brother of the surgeon, the cousin of the physician, the vicar of the confessor and the substitute for the secretary," adding that whosoever desired to hear any news, all he had to do was to go to a barbershop. The book does

---

[1]{Ed. Note: 300 B.C.}

not tell us if any fee or honorarium was exacted for the service, but it seems that the events were narrated merely as an incident to the profession, the barber acting as the gatherer of information coming to him from patrons of all sorts.

That the news-gathering branch of the art was only a small part of the promiscuous duties imposed upon the barber by the community, and that the nature of his services may have aided the artist, with the passing of time, to become a loquacious and jesting fellow, is manifest upon further inquiry. The *Encyclopedia Americana* states that in bygone days the barber was also an elementary physician and surgeon. "The art of surgery and the art of shaving went hand in hand"; that the barbers dressed wounds; did blood-letting and other surgical operations. The title of "barber-surgeons" was generally applied to them and they were even incorporated as such by King Edward IV in 1461, being at the time the only persons who practiced surgery. The present barber's pole had its origin in those days, when the spiral bands or "fillets" around the pole were intended to indicate the bandage twisted around the arms previous to letting out blood. The basin which formerly hung from the pole designated the receptacle to receive blood, which (we learn otherwise) was drawn by making incisions or by applying leeches to the affected parts.

The new *International Encyclopedia* sustains the foregoing information, adding that the blood-letting barber-surgeon was honored as a professional man, and *Chambers' Encyclopedia* recites that the barber was also "celebrated for his garrulity, and general obliging qualities, such being required by those who place themselves in his hands"; that the barbershops of Athens and Rome were great meeting places for idlers and gossipers; and that in provincial towns they continue to serve such purposes up to the present time. The *Encyclopedia Britannica* supplements that "in addition to its attraction as a focus of news, a lute, viol or some such musical instrument was always kept for the entertainment of the waiting customers." We know that to be a fact in our own rural communities, and the custom would seem to be a salutary one, because the music no doubt serves to relieve the nervous tension of the intrepid patron or "patient" about to assume the attitude of the "customer in the chair" by placing himself in the physical control of the artist.

Common observation furnished proof that the barber is truly a philosophic person, of amiable and tractable disposition, ready to be accommodating, and always dispensing vocal wares with varying degrees of humor and intelligence, while the razor follows the facial contours and, maybe, the course of least resistance, depending upon when it was last sharpened. That barbers talk cannot be disputed. Some talk more, some less, some humorously, some not, but talk they do. It is traditional and hereditary with them. The subjects are varied and the train of thought develops in endless chain, tempered only by the customer's assertion of his right to be free from enforced restraint as soon as the operations are over.

The artist's sources of information are manifold, and with the next customer he puts to use what he has learned from the last one, thereby keeping in circulation all sorts of topics, although he may have a personal inclination for literature, art, music or the sciences; and it naturally follows that he becomes well-versed in the affairs of the world, past, present and the speculative future. From his ranks there have risen men who have infiltrated themselves in our social structure with commendable success. I sometimes suspect that great oratorical silver tongues of history may have begun their undying orating upon the willing or unwilling ears of the customer in the chair.

That the barber's qualifications are more or less generally understood as above stated appears to be reflected by that jovial character Figaro in Beaumarchais's comedy "The Barber of Seville," immortalized by Rossini. The opera is one of the wittiest of all dramas and the central hero, Figaro, the barber, is described as "a marvelous half autobiographic combination of gaiety and philosophy, disillusioned shrewdness, deep reflection and lambent wit; his dialogue, throughout, sparkles with overflowing wit, unexpected turns of phase, words of double intent, topsy-turvy application of proverbial wisdom and often quite superfluous jests" (*Ency. Amer.*). Figaro's many occupations, conjoined as they are with the principal one of shaving, appear to be typical of the barber's versatility of the times (1775), and of the requirements of the public.

That the barber's activities were multi-various indeed in medieval days and even in comparatively modern times is to be seen by a study of that famous character: (1) He gaily proclaims that he was the factotum of the whole city, and that as such everybody should make way for him to pass. (2) He announces that no profession compares with that of such a barber as he, for besides his services with scissors and razor, he is confidential adviser to all sorts of people, cavaliers and ladies alike. (3) He reveals himself as a perambulating matrimonial agency, by boasting that without him not a girl in Seville could find a husband. To him, he says, comes the little widow who would like to be married again, and it is all so easy, for what with his comb and razor by day, and his guitar at night, he is admitted everywhere. (4) Why, in the very house where Rosina, the old doctor's ward, lives is not he (Figaro) barber, coiffeur, surgeon, herbalist, druggist, vet and confidential man, in general? (5) He administers a purgative to a lawyer ill of indigestion. (6) He prepares wigs for ladies. (7) He shaves and cuts the hair of the officers of a whole regiment. (8) Acts as the go-between to the loving count and the gracious Rosina, and by his original stratagems, arranges for their meeting and marriage against the imprecations of her guardian, the old doctor, who himself was conspiring to marry the girl and her money. That Figaro acquits himself nobly in all his missions demonstrates that the recent barber's predecessor was a genial and astute fellow with courageous directness, witty lies, proverbial shrewdness and a somewhat charmed life.

Our own knowledge of the contemporary barber shows that he has lost none of the finesse of his ancestral prototype down through the ages. Indeed, he cannot escape from following in the footsteps of those that have gone before, for the very reason that his clients of yesteryear are the same today. There, in the barber's chair, the statesman, the executive, the professor, the tradesman, the peasant, the candlestick maker, the husband and the lover alike, each in turn trends his way to receive the benefits that nimble fingers may administer to his facial contours. That at the same time the artist pours upon his ears friendly words of general interest, humor or a philosophical discourse, is but an attribute incidental to the manipulations themselves. It goes without saying that fingering one all over the face is a strictly personal and privileged transaction. Therefore, being a student of human nature by force of his profession, the barber deals strictly with the customer in the chair, the individual whose fastidious or peculiar traits he must minister to.

His sources of information being varied and recurrent, he becomes a storehouse of human knowledge, and dispenses it by applying his strategy and his inborn philosophy to meet the exigencies of

112

the occasion. One cannot imagine a silent barber. Nor does he use his silver tongue without cause. While oftentimes prompted by the customers themselves, whose talkative disposition varies, it would seem that nature has predisposed the barber to overcome the difficulty of making a customer feel at ease, by so mixing the elements in him that his vocal chords and his mannerisms might be employed, softly but surely, to assuage the customer's inherent fears, and lull him into a sense of confidence that deprives his constricted situation of any of the terrors of the dentist's chair, or the awe which the witness chair inspires. Nor is the position of such a customer akin to that of the witness in the chair to whom a recent editorial referred as "the most miserable of all creatures," what with being the complacent friend of the side he espouses, the subjective instrument of the court's majesty, the football of the cross-examining attorney, the focus of the jury's inquisitorial powers, and the object of plaintiff's or defendant's fervent prayers.

Happily, to the customer in the barber's chair, such ordeals are spared. In that chair all traces of the man's condition in life are temporarily subjugated to the barber's physical control to which the customer readily submits unscathed by the experience, for the purpose of facial embellishment, common to all mankind. So situated, the customer in the chair furnished a vivid example of the truth of the great Lincoln's motto that "all men are created equal." It being his innate design to render his patient impervious to the risk attendant upon the use of the razor, the barber approaches the man before him tenderly but warily, and by the use of his faculties at once renders the personal encounter a friendly one, whether by propounding a question or by making a statement. A polite "good morning" from either side is enough incentive to start the ball rolling. From then on, with the customer's limited locomotion, there may ensue a conversation which, according to the given position of the razor, may assume the qualities of a suppressed duet in various forms, for the barber's chair is not a place where one may repose, in the words of Bryant, "like one who wraps the drapery of his couch about him and lies down to pleasant dreams." Courageous indeed is the man who ventures forth in a reclining position in the barber's chair, for well may he recall, before he engages in conversation, the words of Dante upon entering Inferno, "Abandon all hope all ye who enter here," since we all know

113

that the razor has a facile way of cutting flesh more so than the beard. And while the customer may appear to be resting, whether his eyes be open or shut, yet must he be on the qui vive,[1] although in docile mien, to answer the artist, if need be, by word of mouth, by grimace, by grunt, or by wiggling his toe, whichever he is permitted to do at the moment, having regard to the proximity of that ominous instrument to the throat and with an eye upon the barber's countenance, to see if he is still friendly.

And if you do not answer, you may ipso facto be treated as a cranky customer, which may so reflect upon the smooth cutting qualities of the razor as to produce a shave half pulled and half scraped, so that the face may smart for days. If you speak at an inopportune moment, you may flirt with injury, or at least with a mouthful of soap that will be far from appetizing. If you seek a compromise by winking, maybe intending thereby to tell the barber to shut up, the wink may have the opposite effect, for the barber may think that the customer is encouraging him in his discourse. If you move a foot, you may break a mirror and thus incur the proverbial seven years' hard luck; and if you shift your position, the barber reprimands you, humorously but firmly, because he loses his equipoise, or the razor may refuse to cut at all, if the hand that guides it is not attuned to the barber's thoughts, which find articulation through his silver tongue.

Grave problems may be pervading the customer's mind, and he may be meditating upon his next step the moment he is released from restraint, again to breathe in the free air; but those things do not coincide with the barber's thoughts, for he is a high-class salesman, not by forceful or high-pressure methods, but by a more subtle, persuasive process, which develops as the soapy nebula begins to accumulate around and about the facial orifices. It is then that the artist begins to approach the subject nearest to his heart and furthest from the average customer's mind, by trying to induce the customer to have his map or pate smeared with one or more of the dozens of familiar lotions of dubious value which daily seem to change in color and aroma, though not in substance or price, nor even in efficacy, as many of us perceive by a look in retrospective contemplation, to the

---

[1]{Ed. Note: In French, *Qui vive?* means "Who lives?" or "Who goes there?" To be "on the qui vive" means "to be on the alert."}

114

remains of a once luxuriant shock, that has either thinned and grayed or disappeared altogether.

Bearing upon the development of the art from remote days, I learn from the December issue of the *Reader's Digest* that in a barbershop in Rockefeller Center there is on display a collection of pictures showing various types and combinations of beards and moustaches in all ages and places, and ancient razors and tools, which may almost be regarded as a mirror of the progress of civilization itself.

In the light of the foregoing views, I hold to the opinion that the barber's business is fraught with a degree of inevitable risk, obvious and known to both the artist and the customer, and to which the patron is voluntarily exposed, as a necessary incident of the manipulations which must be performed to produce the ultimate result. The barber is traditionally a man's friend, and though adventurous within the sphere of his field, he may and usually is trusted to do his job with the least possible harm. More than that, from time immemorial he has accomplished his duty with dignity, tempered with humor and good fellowship. That is far from negligence. That injury sometimes results must be attributed, as here, to a fortuitous occurrence rather than to fault.

Prompted by the recognized fact that we do not know a good thing until we have to do without it, I venture to say that if the barber's courtesy, jocular ways, and pleasant disposition were suddenly to stop, there would be considerable hesitation to sit in his chair, which would not be unlike the sensation one must experience in facing the fatuous "life's darkest moment." The world need have no qualms about the barber's mission on earth, for he and his traits, recognized since biblical times, have successfully withstood the ravages of the centuries and fraught that appears will outlive many people and many customs in the far-flung corners of the world before his craft shall perish, if ever.

Basing my finding upon the barber's historical background, I am unable to discern any "unusual propensity for fooling around with customers," on the part of the defendant's employee. He appears to have proceeded about his work by talking while shaving, in a manner quite in keeping with the usages of the art in vogue since the dark days of ages past.

Plaintiff at most shows a pure accident. No extra precautions appear to be likely to have prevented it. The barber was engaged in the performance of a lawful act by lawful means. There is no evidence, nor in the nature of things was it probable that by the exercise of the utmost degree of care Jimmie could have foreseen that plaintiff would impulsively grab hold of the razor. . . .

Of course, the result here reached does not give Jimmie or his kindred artists a free rein in the discharge of their duties. They will undoubtedly be held to strict accountability in law if an accident is due to their negligence, whether it be founded upon a state of extreme or unreasonable garrulity or gesticulation, or both, or otherwise. This particular accident was regrettable enough, and in the nature of things a similar misfortune will not happen again in many a moon.

Therefore, since liability must be measured only in terms of law, I direct judgment for defendant on the merits.

It is sometimes said that a jury consists of twelve persons of average ignorance. Here, the jury was asked to decide a simple matter: whether or not the plaintiff should receive a judgment for the amount due under a promissory note.

SWINDLE v. MUNFORD
Supreme Court of Georgia
59 Ga. 337 (1877)

LOGAN E. BLECKLEY, JUDGE

The note sued upon was dated January 1, 1862, and due one day thereafter. It was for $154.75. The consideration, as proved at the trial, was merchandise purchased in 1860 and 1861—not payable in Confederate money nor rated at Confederate prices. Barber's table was put in evidence, according to which the difference between Confederate money and gold, at the date of the note, was twenty cents on the dollar. The jury returned a verdict in favor of the plaintiff for twenty dollars, and interest. . . .

{*Plaintiff, unhappy with recovering only $20 on his claim, moved for a new trial, which was granted. The defendant then asked the Georgia Supreme Court to intervene.*}

116

If a verdict can shock the moral sense, this does it. Twenty dollars on a note for $154.75, and not a cent ever paid! Doubtless the explanation is that the note was given during the war. The war destroyed many things, but justice was not killed out. It went through, and is still alive. Private debts are extinguished, not by arms, but by payment, or discharge in bankruptcy, or voluntary release. Debtors cannot fight out of their just obligations to creditors. . . .

Judgment affirmed.

The following early English decision may well be the "granddaddy" of all "landlord-tenant" cases. In a hard-nosed, iron-fisted display of upper-class British judicial fortitude, the court steadfastly refused to consider the "equitable" defenses raised by the tenant, upheld the sanctity of the contract, vindicated the proprietary rights of the "landed" gentry and resolutely enforced the strict terms of a commercial lease in favor of the landlord and against the tenant.

PARADINE v. JANE
Court of King's Bench, Michaelmas Term
[1558-1774] All E.R. Rep. 172; 82 E.R. 897;
Aleyn 26, Sty. 47 (1647)

LORD BACON AND HENRY ROLLE, J.J.

{The defendant, Mr. Jane, had leased a parcel of land from Paradine, but fell behind in the rent. By the time Paradine brought this suit for arrearages, Mr. Jane owed rent for three years ending Lady Day,[1] 1646. Mr. Jane defended the lawsuit on the grounds that during the interim, the German Prince Rupert had invaded the realm of England with an army of men, and had thrown Jane off the rented land, keeping him from occupying the property or receiving any benefit therefrom for nearly four years. Mr. Paradine nonetheless refused to release Mr. Jane from his rental obligations and filed a lawsuit against him.}

The plea {by Mr. Jane} was resolved insufficient on the following grounds: first, because the defendant had not answered to one quar-

---

[1]{Ed. Note: March 25.}

117

ter's rent; secondly, he had not averred that the army were all aliens, which shall not be intended, and then he has his remedy against them; and BACON J., cited Y.B. 33 Hen. 6 fo. 1, pl. 3, where the gaoler in bar of an escape pleaded that alien enemies broke {into} the prison, etc., and an exception was taken to it, for that he ought to show of what country they were, i.e., Scots.

Thirdly, it was resolved that the matter of the plea was insufficient, for although the whole army had been alien enemies, yet the defendant ought to pay the rent. This difference was taken, that where the law creates a duty or charge, and the party is disabled from performing it without any default in him, and has not remedy over, there the law will excuse him. As in the case of waste, if a house be destroyed by tempest or by enemies, the lessee is excused {citation omitted}. . . .

. . . But when the party by his own contract creates a duty or charge upon himself, he is bound to make it good, if he may, notwithstanding any accident by inevitable necessity because he might have provided against it by his contract. Therefore, if the lease covenants to repair a house, although it is burnt by lightning or thrown down by enemies {citation omitted} . . . yet he ought to repair it {citation omitted}.

The rent is a duty created by the parties upon the reservation, and had there been a covenant to pay it there would have been no question but the lessee must have made it good, notwithstanding the interruption by enemies, for the law would not protect him beyond his own agreement, no more than in the case of reparations.

This reservation, then, being a covenant in law and whereupon an action of the covenant has been maintained (as ROLLE, J., has said) it is all one as if there had been an actual covenant. Another reason was added, that as the lessee is to have the advantage of casual profits, so he must run the hazard of casual losses and not lay the whole burden of them upon his lessor. . . .

Judgment for plaintiff.

<hr />

The owners of a house adjacent to defendant's golf course filed a lawsuit to enjoin the operation of one of the holes in the nine-hole course and seeking damages for injuries to themselves and their property. The case was referred to a "master" (i.e., an assistant to the judge, appointed to inquire into specific matters) who filed a report of his findings with the court. The injunction was granted and plaintiffs were awarded damages. The defendant Country Club appealed.

FENTON v. QUABOAG COUNTRY CLUB, INC.

Supreme Judicial Court of Massachusetts
353 Mass. 534; 233 N.E.2d 216 (1968)

PAUL CASHMAN REARDON, JUSTICE

This appeal has to do with the game of golf and in particular with the abilities of certain golfers in the county of Hampden whose alleged transgressions gave rise to a suit. The plaintiffs, husband and wife, state in their bill that they are the owners of a home in Monson adjoining a golf course operated by the defendant, and after the recitation of a series of grievances seek an injunction designed to terminate the operation of one of the holes in the defendant's nine-hole course, together with damages for injuries to person and property.

The defendant's answer makes certain admissions and acknowledges the existence of a problem. It further states "that cooperation in the problem the * * * [plaintiffs] have been one way and although the * * * [plaintiffs] may have had no knowledge of the game of golf when they purchased the property, they have certainly, over the years, become somewhat familiar with the game, but rather than be cooperative and understanding of the interest of the Quaboag Country Club, Inc. * * * have maintained an inexorable position of antagonism toward the Club and its members, and when suggestions were made to them which were anything less than the complete surrender of the use of the ninth fairway to all intentions and purposes, the * * * [plaintiffs] continued to be dissatisfied."

A master to whom the case was referred filed a report which illuminates the deep antagonisms which spring to life when home and

119

family are threatened by devotees of the great outdoors. We refer to his findings.

In 1952 the plaintiffs, John F. and Miriam E. Fenton, "not familiar with the details of the game of golf," bought their house, garage and land from one Lussier and his wife. The east side of the premises fronted on the Monson-Palmer Road. Otherwise the property was bounded on all sides by land owned by the defendant. The Lussiers had purchased the land from the defendant in 1944 and had, as one may gather from the report, coexisted happily with the golf club, a state of affairs no doubt enhanced by the fact that during their tenure Lussier and his family had sold soft drinks and sandwiches to golfers on the course and thus found no fault when errant golf balls descended upon their property.

The club itself had a lengthy history. It opened in 1900 as a six-hole course, and in 1922 expanded to nine holes. "Adjoining the westerly boundary of the * * * [plaintiffs'] land is the * * * [defendant's] ninth fairway. It has occupied this location since before 1927, and even prior to that," as far back as 1900, "the east side of the now ninth fairway * * * [was] the east side of a fairway."

Into this picture, fraught with potential trouble which only a golfer could fully appreciate, came the plaintiffs "not familiar with the details of the game of golf." Any deficiency in their knowledge was soon remedied as they immediately came under the assault of balls "hit onto and over their property." "Except for a few isolated occasions, these balls were not intentionally directed" at the Fenton estate. However, the master has provided us with some chilling statistics which cast grave doubt on the proficiency of the golfers of Hampden County, at least those who were playing the defendant's course. From 1952 an annual average number of 250 balls "were left" on the land of the plaintiffs, save for the year 1960 when a grand total of 320 such deposits were made. Over the years sixteen panes of glass in the plaintiffs' house were broken, for six of which fractures the plaintiffs have received reimbursement. The cost of such replacements apparently defied inflation and remained constant throughout the years at $3.85 for each new pane.

Affairs worsened in 1961 when the defendant added a sand trap "to the northwest corner of the ninth green." Since golfers intent on achieving the green drove from the tee in a southerly direction, they

120

were faced with alternatives. They might aim somewhat to the west and face the sand trap, or they might veer more to the east and face the Fentons. The master inclined to the belief that they were prone to make the latter choice although, as he found, this was not without hazard, for the plaintiff John F. Fenton collected "all the balls he found on his land and sold them periodically."

Continued unbridled hooking and slicing caused further aggravation. Some years back the Fentons were possessed of a German Shepherd dog which developed apprehension at the approach of golfers to the point that they were forced to dispense with his companionship. In his place they acquired a Doberman evidently made of sterner stuff. The dog is still with them notwithstanding that he has been struck by a flying golf ball. On one occasion the male plaintiff himself stopped an airborne ball supposedly directed to the ninth green but winging its way off course. At another time a Fenton family steak cookout was interrupted by a misdirected ball which came to rest "just under the grill." There were additional serious evidences of mutual annoyance. In an episode "after dark, a ball was driven from the * * * [defendant's] fairway directly against the * * * [plaintiffs'] house." In another, a battered ball bearing the greeting "Hi, Johnnie" descended upon the plaintiffs' close. Hostile incidents occurred. One player venturing on the plaintiffs' property to retrieve a ball swung his club first at the Fentons' dog, then raised it at John Fenton, following which, according to the master's report, he "withdrew."

It need not be emphasized that from the year 1952 the plaintiffs were not silent in their suffering, and there was some talk about a fence. After the commencement of this suit the defendant constructed on its land a fence twenty-four feet high and three feet in from part of the boundary lines on the northern and western sides of the plaintiffs' land. The master states that while this fence has substantially, it has not entirely, abated the problem caused by the rain of golf balls. We are told that the erection of the fence in 1965 was followed by the flight of some eighty-one balls in that year onto the plaintiffs' territory. This somewhat minimized invasion the master terms "a continuing nuisance and trespass."

For all these depredations he assessed damages at $38.50 for those broken panes as yet unreimbursed, and $2,250 "for loss in the fair market value of * * * [the] property" because of the trespasses as well as because the fence "seriously diminishes the value of the property aesthetically." He also found damages at $2,600 for disturbance of the plaintiffs' "peace and comfort" for the thirteen years prior to the erection of the unaesthetic fence. He placed a value on the loss of the plaintiffs' peace and comfort since the fence went up at $50.

Following confirmation of the master's report, the court entered a final decree enjoining the defendant from so operating its course "as to damage the property of the Plaintiffs, or to cause golf balls to be cast upon or propelled upon or against the property of Plaintiffs." . . .

We have the case on appeals from the decrees.

1. We have no doubts about the propriety of the injunction. The plaintiffs are clearly entitled to an abatement of the trespasses (Stevens v. Rockport Granite Co. {citation omitted}). We paraphrase the apt expression of Chief Justice Rugg in the *Stevens* case: "The pertinent inquiry is whether the noise [the invasion of golf balls] materially interferes with the physical comfort of existence, not according to exceptionally refined, uncommon, or luxurious habits of living [e.g. golf addiction], but according to the simple tastes and unaffected notions generally prevailing among plain people [nongolfers]. The standard is what ordinary people [again those who eschew golf], acting reasonably, have a right to demand in the way of health and comfort under all the circumstances."

Were it not that this court cannot assume the function of a Robert Trent Jones, we should make a judicial suggestion that the defendant's burden under the injunction will be considerably eased by shifting the location of the trap to the northeasterly corner of the green on the assumption, and on this the record is silent, that none exists there now.

2. On the damages awarded, the plaintiffs are entitled to the sum of $38.50 for the cost of replacing the glass, and also for the sum of $2,650 awarded them for their distress and discomfort over fourteen years. . . .

3. There was error, however, in the award of damages based on the loss in the fair market value of the property due to what the master found to be a continuing trespass. . . .

122

The decrees are reversed. The case is remanded to the Superior Court for further proceedings consistent with this opinion.

So ordered.

In the following case, an enthusiastic debt collector sought to "garnish" (confiscate) the baggage of a debtor while it was in the custody of the railroad company. Although under applicable law the baggage itself may have been subject to the "garnishment" process, the contents of the baggage, consisting primarily of apparel and articles of personal necessity, were exempt.

THE WESTERN RAILROAD v. THORNTON & ACEE

Supreme Court of Georgia
60 Ga. 300 (1878)

LOGAN E. BLECKLEY, JUDGE

It may be doubted whether the personal baggage of a traveler can be reached or affected by garnishment. If the wearing apparel which his trunk contains is protected, the trunk containing it, and which is necessary for taking due care of it while his journey is in progress, and until his return to his abode, ought, it would seem, to be equally protected. The trunk is a part of his baggage proper, as well as its contents. For the time being, it is but an adjunct or incident, the apparel and other articles of necessity within it being the principal. Should not the rule apply, that the incident follows the principal? . . .

. . . The rind and pulp of an orange, or the envelope of a letter and the letter itself, are not much more closely connected than a passenger's trunk and its contents, when the trunk is in the care of the carrier and the key in the passenger's pocket. To delay or detain baggage by the use of the garnishment would, or might, work great inconvenience to the traveling public; which, in these times, is almost identical with the public at large. If a debtor's baggage could be stopped, that of his family being frequently mingled with it, all would be stopped together. The family, when at a distance from home, might thus be brought into perplexity and distress of a kind which all women and children, if not all men too, should be spared.

123

To catch up baggage for debt is the next thing to taking the person of the debtor. The traveler had almost as well be put in jail for an hour or two, as to have his trunk or valise locked up at the railroad station. Perhaps he would rather go to jail for a little while if he could have the company of his baggage, than be free on condition of parting with it. To separate him from that which is the object of his chief care and solicitude through the whole course of his wanderings, is hard upon him indeed. Between passenger and baggage there is a relation beyond that of mere ownership. When baggage is lost, it is not simple privation; it is bereavement. . . .

. . . Judgment reversed.

CHAPTER V

Passion, *Romance, Love, Lust,* Licentiousness, *Fornication,* Marriage, *Intrigue, Indifference,* Disenchantment, *Disgrace,* Dissolution and *Divorce*

I like to think that the work of a judge is an art. . . . After all, why isn't it in the nature of an art? It is a bit of craftsmanship, isn't it? It is what a poet does, it is what a sculptor does. He has some vague purposes and he has an indefinite number of what you might call frames of preference which among he must choose; for choose he has to, and he does.
—Learned Hand[1]

Law, say the gardeners, is the sun,
Law is the one
All gardeners obey
Tomorrow, yesterday, today.

Law is the wisdom of the old
The impotent grandfathers feebly scold;
The grandchildren put out a treble tongue,
Law is the senses of the young. . . .
—W. H. Auden[2]

---

[1]Remarks at Proceedings of a Special Session of the United States Court of Appeals for the Second Circuit in Commemoration of Judge Learned Hand's Completion of Fifty Years of Federal Service, quoted in H. Shanks, *The Art and Craft of Judging: The Decisions of Judge Learned Hand,* at flyleaf (1968).

[2]From "Law like Love," reprinted in *The Norton Anthology of Poetry,* pp. 532–533 (1970).

Marital bliss is a fragile and elusive condition, often not fully appreciated by the couple in question, especially when the court refuses to grant them a divorce. Historically, the courts had the right to deny feuding spouses a divorce altogether, presumably for the good of society and to promote and encourage "family values."

KMICZ v. KMICZ
County Court of Luzerne County, Pennsylvania
50 Pa. C.C. 588 (1920)

HENRY A. FULLER, P.J.

Libel in divorce by husband against wife.
Answer by wife.
Issue on cruel and barbarous treatment.
Trial by judge without jury.
She his second.
He her second.
Her dowry to him five ready-made children.
His contribution to her the same number.
None added since.
She without a vestige of feminine loveliness.
He without a mark of masculine attraction.
From start to finish a perfectly inexplicable and
   hopeless connubial absurdity.
One averred ground of divorce, her cruel and
   barbarous treatment.
Another, indignities to his person.
Only proved specific instance of former his nose
   broken by her use of a stove lifter.
Only proved specific instance of latter her unladylike
   behavior in the privacy of nuptial privilege.
Nose possibly broken in self-defense as testified.
Unladylike behavior possibly incited by his own lack
   of good manners.
No course of bad treatment on one side more than on the
   other.
Blame balanced as six and half a dozen.

126

Mutually mean.

He mean enough to seek divorce.

She mean enough to resist.

Parties too much alike ever to have been joined in marriage.

Also too much alike to be separated by divorce.

Having made their own bed must lie down in it.

Lying out of it, no standing in court.

Decree refused with allowance to respondent of $25
  for counsel fees to be paid by the libelant.

An "alienation of affections" lawsuit alleges that a third-party interloper has interfered with a marital relationship in some manner, thus depriving one spouse of the love, society, companionship and comfort of the other spouse. The following case involves a brazen tale of infidelity and marital intrigue set in rural Tennessee.

ARCHER v. ARCHER
Court of Appeals of Tennessee
31 Tenn. App. 657; 219 S.W.2d 919 (1947)

WINFIELD B. HALE, JUDGE

This is an alienation of affections suit which has shaken Raccoon Valley in Union County from center to circumference. It was brought by Lillie Archer, the former wife of Esker Archer, against Daisy Kiser (Archer), who, it is alleged, supplanted plaintiff in the affections of said Esker, and succeeded her as his wife some three weeks after Lillie and Esker were divorced. Upon a trial by a jury of the selection of the parties ... the plaintiff was awarded a judgment of $500 as the value of the affections so alienated, which apparently is not badly out of line in view of the matters hereinafter mentioned. This verdict was approved by the trial judge and the defendant appeals. ...

The evidence (in narrative form), when taken in the light most favorable to the verdict ... reveals that Esker and Lillie Archer were married in 1919, and remained on intermittently friendly terms for several years, or, at least, until seven children were born to them. In 1935 she filed a bill for divorce, charging cruel and inhuman treatment, and adultery with one Lucy Sturgeon. They became reconciled

127

and the divorce suit was withdrawn. Thereafter, on account of ill health, for a part of the time at least, Lillie refused to have marital relations with him and would "throw up" other women to him. This led to another separation in March 1942, when Esker and his sixteen-year-old son moved to another place and "batched" there for about three months. Again their difficulties were patched up, and they resumed cohabitation, living together until the final separation in the fall of 1944.

Apparently, this parting of the ways was due to the advent into Raccoon Valley of the defendant below, Mrs. Daisy Kiser. She was a widow, fifty-one years of age, and the mother of twelve children, the youngest of whom was eight years of age. She apparently was of some little property, being the owner of one of the few automobiles in Raccoon Valley, which she used liberally for the benefit of her neighbors, especially Esker, toward whom she pursued a good-neighbor policy which was extremely distasteful and obnoxious to his wife.

As to her personality and pulchritude there is no evidence except from a statement attributed to Esker soon after the Widow Kiser came to the Valley. Esker and Ben Shipley were working in a field near the highway when Mrs. Kiser came along in her car and called Esker to her. Then, to quote Shipley, "* * * the said Esker Archer did go down to the road where she was at. And on that occasion he {Esker} said . . . 'that Kiser woman would be plumb pretty if she had a new set of teeth.'" Soon afterward, when she was in Knoxville having dental work done, she accidentally ran into Esker and brought him back home.

Following this there developed a relationship which the jury found culminated in Esker's leaving home in October 1944, and instituting a divorce suit against Lillie. She filed an answer and cross bill, obtaining a divorce in February 1945. It is apparent that the relations of Esker and the Widow Kiser were contributing factors to the divorce suit. They were married some three weeks after the obtention of the divorce. This suit followed, with the result noted.

The record shows that Mrs. Kiser (now Archer) would go by Esker's home, honk her car horn, call him to her, and take him riding. On one trip she took him to Knoxville and left a note for him at a doctor's office. At other times he drove the car for her, once taking her to

128

a pie supper at the Raccoon school, after which they returned to her home, being joined there by some of the artists who had "made music" at the pie supper. Evidently a good time was had by all. On other occasions she would walk along a path by his home. She performed acts of neighborly kindness by taking him and his beans to market. He, in turn, would put brake fluid in her car, as well as act as chauffeur for her, and so on. She took him to dinner once because he loved fish. At another time she fed him and his son. At still another time, after Esker's separation from his wife, the plaintiff below, the Widow Kiser went to the house where he was staying, but said she did so to have him fix a flashlight. She would also park her car in front of his house, and Esker would, on occasion, ask her to go to the store for him. She contends these things were done innocently, but the jury found to the contrary. The evidence contained disputes as to material facts, and also as to the conclusions to be drawn from the whole evidence. We are concluded by the verdict, approved as it is by the trial judge. . . .

We think the evidence adopted by the jury authorized the inference that the defendant below did by feminine wiles and guile incite and welcome the attentions of this husband. The consistent and persistent manner in which she managed to get in his company, the trips they took, his visits to her home and their marriage within three weeks after his divorce all lead to the conclusion that she was the pursuer, although it was done with a degree of subtlety worthy of any daughter of Eve. This brings the case within the rule announced in Wilson v. Bryant {citation omitted}, to-wit:

> The weight of authority is that in alienation suits the plaintiff must establish that the defendant is the enticer—the active or aggressive party. If it develops that the plaintiff's spouse was merely bent on the gratification of lust, and was not particular in the choice of a guilty partner, plaintiff's case is not made out. Likewise we think plaintiff's case would fail if it should appear that for any other reason the plaintiff's spouse was the pursuer rather than the pursued. . . .

It is true that Esker Archer had in the past shown himself to have a roving eye and an errant disposition. He and his wife Lillie had many trials and vicissitudes. He had affection enough for her, and she for him, to bring about reconciliations, and they were living together when the defendant below appeared on the scene and, as the jury found, began her campaign for Esker's affections. Her actions, in part, were known to the plaintiff below, and the family jars then became a vicious circle of cause and effect, leading finally to the divorce court. Esker's affections, such as they were, were transferred from his wife to Mrs. Kiser.

The fact that the jury allowed only $500 indicates a rather low opinion as to the value of the husband's affections. They were worth but little, but such as they were belonged to the wife. The judgment below is affirmed with interest and costs.

Affirmed.

"May-December" relationships have always raised eyebrows in polite circles. In this case, Justice Musmanno analyzes the matrimonial wreckage in the aftermath of such a romance.

PAVLICIC v. VOGTSBERGER
Supreme Court of Pennsylvania
390 Pa. 502; 136 A.2d 127 (1957)

MICHAEL A. MUSMANNO, JUSTICE

George J. Pavlicic has sued Sara Jane Mills[1] for the recovery of gifts which he presented to her in anticipation of a marriage which never saw the bridal veil. At the time of the engagement George Pavlicic was thrice the age of Sara Jane. In the controversy which has followed, Pavlicic says that it was Sara Jane who asked him for his hand, whereas Sara Jane maintains that Pavlicic, following immemorial custom, offered marriage to her. We are satisfied from a study of the record that it was Sara Jane who took the initiative in proposing matrimony—and, as it will develop, the proposal was more consonant with an approach to the bargaining counter than to the wedding altar.

George Pavlicic testified that when Sara Jane broached the subject of holy wedlock, he demurred on the ground that he was too old for her. She replied that the difference in their ages was inconsequential

---

[1]The defendant was married twice and her name appears in various spellings in the record. For convenience in this discussion, she will be referred to as Sara Jane. For similar convenience the plaintiff George J. Pavlicic will be referred to as George.

so long as he was "good to her." Furthermore, she said that she no longer was interested in "young fellows"—she had already been married to a young man and their matrimonial bark had split on the rocks of divorce. Hence, she preferred an older man. George qualified. He was 75. Sara Jane was 26.

The May-December romance began on a very practical footing in April 1949, when Sara Jane borrowed from George the sum of $5,000 with which to buy a house, giving him a mortgage on the premises. In three and one-half years she had paid back only $449 on the mortgage. On the night of November 21, 1952, she visited George at his home and advanced the not illogical proposition that since they were to be married, there was no point in their having debts one against the other and that, therefore, he should wipe out the mortgage he held on her home. George said to her: "If you marry me, I will take the mortgage off." She said: "Yes," and so he promised to satisfy the mortgage the next day. To make certain that there would be no slip between the promise and the deed, Sara Jane remained at George's home that night; and on the following morning drove him in her automobile to the office of the attorney who was to make, and did make, arrangements for the satisfaction of the mortgage.

Being enriched to the extent of $4,551 by this transaction, Sara Jane expatiated on another rational thesis, namely, that since they were going to be married and they would be riding around together she should have a better car than the dilapidated Kaiser she was driving. She struck home with her argument by pointing out that in a new car he would not fall out, for it appears this was an actual possibility when he rode in her worn-out Kaiser. Thus, without any tarrying, she drove George from the Recorder of Deed's Office, where she and the mortgage had been satisfied, to several automobile marts and finally wound up at a Ford agency. Here she selected a 1953 Ford which she said would meet her needs and keep him inside the car. George made a down payment of $70 and on the following day he gave her $800 more, the latter taken from his safety deposit box. Still later he handed her a check for $1,350, obtained from a building and loan association—and Sara Jane had her new car.

Less than a year later, Sara Jane complained that her feet got wet in the Ford and she proposed the purchase of an Oldsmobile. She explained that by trading in the Ford, which she characterized as a "lemon," she would need only $1,700 to acquire the Oldsmobile. George was not averse to transportation which would keep his future wife's feet dry, but he said that since they were to be man and wife, and he apparently was paying for all the bills, it might be more businesslike if title to the car were placed in his name. This suggestion, according to George's testimony at the trial, made Sara Jane "mad" and he practically apologized for being so bold and inconsiderate as to ask title to an automobile which he was buying with his own money. Accordingly he withdrew his suggestion, said: "All right," and made out a check in Sara Jane's name for $1,700. And thus Sara Jane got her new Oldsmobile.

In January 1953, in the enthusiastic spirit of an anxious swain, George presented Sara Jane with a $140 wrist watch. Sara Jane selected the watch.

In February 1953, Sara Jane represented to George that they would both make a better appearance if she had an engagement and wedding ring. George took her to a jewelry store and she made a selection consistent with discretion. George paid $800.

Sara Jane then asked George to take care of the repairing of a ring she had received from her mother. It was a mere matter of adding a diamond. George paid the bill.

Even before George's bank book became Sara Jane's favorite literature she had prevailed upon him to advance substantial sums to her. In June 1952, she told George she needed $800 to cover her house with insulbrick. George gave her $800 to cover her house with insulbrick.

It is not to be said, however, that Sara Jane was completely lacking in affectionate ante-nuptial reciprocity. In June 1953, she bought George a wedding ring for him to wear. She conferred upon him at the same time a couple of woolen shirts. There is no way of learning how much the ring and shirts cost because she did not take George into her confidence or into the store where she purchased the items.

George testified that when he wore the wedding ring people laughed and asked him when he was to be married. He replied: "Pretty soon." He tried to live up to the prediction and asked Sara Jane for the wedding date. She said she could not name the month. In view of what was to develop, she could have added with truth that she could not name the year either.

In October 1953, Sara Jane expounded to George the economic wisdom of purchasing a business which would earn for them a livelihood in his old and her young age. She suggested the saloon business. George agreed it was a good idea. She contacted a saloon-selling agent and George accompanied her to various saloons which the agent wished to sell. George was impressed with one saloon called the "Melody Bar," but the price was above him. Sara Jane then said that if he would give her $5,000 she would buy a cheap saloon outside of Pittsburgh. George gave her $5,000. And Sara Jane disappeared—with the $5,000.

The next time she was heard from, she was in Greensburg operating Ruby's Bar—with George's $5,000. From Ruby's Bar she proceeded to the nuptial bower, where she married Edward Dale Mills. Although she had many times assured George she would marry him because she liked the idea of an old man, the man she then actually married was scarcely a contendor for Methuselah's record. He was only 26—two years younger than Sara Jane.

When George emerged from the mists and fogs of his disappointment and disillusionment he brought an action in equity praying that the satisfaction of the mortgage on Sara Jane's property be stricken from the record, that she be ordered to return the gifts which had not been consumed, and pay back the moneys which she had gotten from him under a false promise to marry. Sara Jane filed an Answer and the case came on for trial before Judge Marshall of the Allegheny County Court of Common Pleas. Judge Marshall granted all the plaintiff's prayers and entered a decree from which the defendant has appealed to this Court.

The defendant urges upon us the proposition that the Act of June 22, 1935, P.L. 450, 48 P.S. §171, popularly known as the "Heart Balm Act," outlaws the plaintiff's action. This is the first time that the Act of 1935 has come before this Court for interpretation and ruling. Although the Act contains several sections, the heart of it lies in the first sentence, namely "All causes of action for breach of contract to marry are hereby abolished."

There is nothing in that statement or in any of the provisions of the Act which touches contracts subsidiary to the actual marriage compact. The Act in no way discharges obligations based upon a fulfillment of the marriage contract. It in no way alters the law of condi-

133

tional gifts. A gift given by a man to a woman on condition that she embark on the sea of matrimony with him is no different from a gift based on the condition that the donee sail on any other sea. If, after receiving the provisional gift, the donee refuses to leave the harbor—if the anchor of contractual performance sticks in the sands of irresolution and procrastination—the gift must be restored to the donor. *A fortiori* would this be true when the donee not only refuses to sail with the donor, but, on the contrary, walks up the gangplank of another ship arm in arm with the donor's rival.

The title to the gifts which Sara Jane received, predicated on the assurance of marriage with George, never left George and could not leave him until the marital knot was tied. It would appear from all the evidence that the knot was fully formed and loosely awaiting the ultimate pull which would take title in the gifts from George to Sara Jane, but the final tug never occurred and the knot fell apart, with the gifts legally falling back into the domain of the brideless George.

The appellant in her argument before this Court would want to make of the Act of June 22, 1935, a device to perpetuate one of the very vices the Act was designed to prevent. The Act was passed to avert the perpetration of fraud by adventurers and adventuresses in the realm of heartland. To allow Sara Jane to retain the money and property which she got from George by dangling before him the grapes of matrimony which she never intended to let him pluck would be to place a premium on trickery, cunning, and duplicitous dealing. It would be to make a mockery of the law enacted by the Legislature in that very field of happy and unhappy hunting.

The Act of 1935 aimed at exaggerated and fictional claims of mortification and anguish purportedly attendant upon a breach of promise to marry. The legislation was made necessary because of the widespread abuse of the vehicle of a breach of promise suit to compel overly apprehensive and naive defendants into making settlements in order to avoid the embarrassing and lurid notoriety which accompanied litigation of that character. The legislation was intended to ward off injustices and incongruities which often occurred when by the mere filing of breach of promise suits innocent defendants became unregenerate scoundrels and tarnished plaintiffs became paragons of lofty sensibility and moral impeccability. It was not unusual in threatened breach of promise suits that the defendant preferred to buy his

134

peace through a monetary settlement rather than be vindicated by a trial which might leave his good name in shreds.

There is no doubt that in the history of romance a nation could be populated with the lovers and sweethearts (young and old) who have experienced genuine pain and agony because of the defection of their opposites who promised marriage and then absconded. Perhaps there should be a way to compensate these disillusioned souls, but it had been demonstrated that the action of breach of promise had been so misemployed, had given rise to such monumental deceptions, and had encouraged blackmail on such a scale, that the Legislature of Pennsylvania, acting in behalf of all the people, concluded that the evil of abuse exceeded to such an extent the occasional legitimate benefit conferred by a breach of promise suit that good government dictated its abolition.

Thus the law of 1935 prohibited, but prohibited only the suing for damages based on contused feelings, sentimental bruises, wounded pride, untoward embarrassment, social humiliation, and all types of mental and emotional suffering presumably arising from a broken marital promise. The Act did not in any way ban actions resulting from a tangible loss due to the breach of a legal contract. It could never be supposed that the Act of 1935 intended to throw a cloak of immunity over a 26-year-old woman who lays a snare for a 75-year-old man and continues to bait him for four or five years so that she can obtain valuable gifts and money from him under a false promise of marriage.

George Pavlicic is not asking for damages because of a broken heart or a mortified spirit. He is asking for the return of things which he bestowed with an attached condition precedent, a condition which was never met. In demanding the return of his gifts, George cannot be charged with Indian giving. Although he has reached the Indian summer of his life and now at 80 years of age might, in the usual course of human affairs, be regarded as beyond the marrying age, everyone has the inalienable right under his own constitution as well as that of the United States to marry when he pleases, if and when he finds the woman who will marry him. George Pavlicic believed that he had found that woman in Sara Jane. He testified that he asked her at least 30 times if she would marry him and on each occasion she answered in the affirmative. There is nothing in the law which required him to ask 31 times. But even so, he probably would have

135

continued asking her had she not taken his last $5,000 and decamped to another city. Moreover he had to accept 30 offers of marriage as the limit since she now had married someone else. Of course, mere multiplicity of proposals does not make for certainty of acceptance. The testimony, however, is to the effect that on the occasion of each proposal by George, Sara Jane accepted—accepted not only the proposal but the gift which invariably accompanied it.

The Act of 1935 in no way alters or modifies the law on antenuptial conditional gifts as expounded in 28 C.J. 651, and quoted by us with approval . . .

> A gift to a person to whom the donor is engaged to be married, made in contemplation of marriage, although absolute in form, is conditional; and upon breach of the marriage engagement by the donee the property may be recovered by the donor. . . .

As already stated, the Act of 1935 provides that "All causes of action for breach of contract to marry are hereby abolished." This language is as clear as the noonday sun. The appellant would darken it with the eclipse of artificial reasoning. The appellant would want us to read into the statute the provision that "All causes of action *for the recovery of property* based on breach of contract to marry are abolished." The appellant would want the statute to be read "All actions *resulting from* a breach of contract are abolished." But we cannot so read or so interpret the statute. The abolition is confined to actions *for* breach of contract to marry, that is, the actual fracture of the wedding contract.

It thus follows that a breach of any contract which is not the actual contract for marriage itself, no matter how closely associated with the proposed marriage, is actionable.

. . . we come to the conclusion that the final decree entered by Judge Marshall is eminently just and in accordance with established principles of law and equity. It is accordingly

Decree affirmed at appellant's costs.

"Caveat emptor" is not always the rule at the matrimonial bargain counter. As the following case demonstrates, courts will intervene to void a marriage when egregious fraud and misrepresentation is perpetrated upon an innocent young lady by a prevaricating rogue.

KEYES v. KEYES
Superior Court of New York City, Equity Term
6 Misc. 355; 26 N.Y.S. 910 (1893)

DAVID McADAM, J.

The defendant, by fraudulently misrepresenting himself as an honest, industrious man, induced the plaintiff, a confiding young woman, to become his wife. If the misrepresentation had been as to the defendant's social position, rank, fortune, manners, or the like, they would have furnished no ground for declaring the marriage void. Fabrications and exaggerations of this kind, while not commendable, are so common as to be tolerated by the law on grounds of public policy. Persons intending to act upon such representations must verify them at their peril, for though they enter into the inducements to marriage, they are not considered as going to the essentials of the relation, on the theory that the parties take each other for better or worse. Indeed, in some cases, marriage likens itself to the veritable mouse trap, which is "easier to get into than out of."

In this case the defendant represented himself as an honest, industrious man, and appearances favored him, when in truth he was a professional thief whose picture has a place in the rogues' gallery, and he is now "doing time" in the Clinton prison for crime. It was an unholy alliance, begotten in fraud, and the plaintiff is the victim. What fraud, in kind and amount, should be deemed sufficient to annul a marriage, has led to a fruitful amount of discussion and contrariety of opinion. The statue provides that a marriage may be annulled where the consent of one of the parties was obtained by force, duress, or fraud (Code, §1743, subd. 4), any one being sufficient. This provision was intended to protect the party imposed upon and to punish the one guilty of the wrong.

The difficulty in inducing courts to act upon this provision is the stupefying fear that dissolution may lead to carelessness and blind credulity on the part of those contemplating marriage. But "love is blind," always has been, and will be. Nothing born of the law will prevent indiscreet and unsuitable marriages. The average individual judges and acts on appearances, on his own likes and dislikes; and if he or she exercises his or her best judgment, and is deceived by the arts and wiles of an unscrupulous, designing person, there should be no unwillingness, in a proper case, to afford relief to the injured, when it can be done without injury to any one except the guilty. There can be no consent to a contract unless it be voluntary. If it be induced by misrepresentation, duress, or constraint, the guilty party will be allowed to obtain no benefit from it. . . .

In all these matters, much is left to the good sense and judgment of the court or jury, if there be one. . . .

In the present instance the plaintiff found, after marriage, that a professional thief had, by fraud, been substituted for the honest, industrious man she was led to believe she had married. While the cases are dissimilar, the result in either is substantially the same. Companionship, with its reciprocal duties, is the basis of marriage, and no respectable young woman should be obliged to divide the life companionship of a husband between herself and the penal institutions of the state. No conception of married life or reciprocal duties would tolerate such a thing. There could be nothing more degrading in its influence. Such a husband is not a fit subject for the household, nor one to be looked up to for advice and guidance. Men may have vices at the time of their marriage, and if these are dropped at or before the time of their vows, they should not be resurrected and made the basis of domestic strife, but where they are continued after marriage they may give rise to serious matrimonial difficulties. In Wier v. Still {citation omitted}, a widow induced to marry a "jail bird" by means of false representations as to his respectability was refused relief on the ground of her folly and credulity. Bigelow, in his work on fraud {citation omitted}, cites the above case "as especially applicable to a widow."

And in Moot v. Moot {citation omitted}, the court, in granting a decree of nullity, was influenced by the fact that the plaintiff was a "school girl"—distinctions obviously founded more on the judicial policy or discretion of the courts than upon strict legal principles. . . .

As the plaintiff's age is between that of the school girl and the widow, there would seem to be a discretionary choice of alternatives left for the court to determine which rule it will adopt to satisfy the requirements of this controversy. If the defendant had reformed after marriage and become exemplary in conduct, the court might have required the plaintiff to overlook the past and screen it from the world with the mantle of charity, but he had not chosen the pathway of the penitent and is, in consequence, again under state surveillance, in its penitentiary at Clinton. Consortium and conjugal society have scarcely risen to the dignity of memories. The consequence is not a temporary sorrow, which may be buried under the oblivion of recurring time, or forgotten in the solitude of despair, but an ever-present affront and reproach that "will not down."

The fraud perpetrated upon the plaintiff goes to the substance and essence of the contract, and while this may be regarded as an exceptional case, resting on its own peculiar merits, yet if the statute authorizing a decree of nullity for fraud does not reach such a case, it is difficult to imagine one it is capable of comprehending. There are, fortunately, no children to bear the obloquy of the marriage; and unless a premium is to be placed on fraud, and the guilty taken under the protecting aegis of the law, there is no reason founded on principle or policy why the plaintiff should not have that justice which the decree prayed for will afford. The application must be granted.

Historically, courts were extremely reluctant to grant divorces and struggled mightily to find reasons to keep the "family unit" together at all costs, regardless of the seemingly horrific circumstances.

MAIN v. MAIN
Supreme Court of Iowa
168 Iowa 353; 150 N.W. 590 (1915)

SILAS M. WEAVER, J.

The petition filed July 3, 1912, shows that the parties were married on November 16, 1911, and charges that defendant is a person of "very high and violent temper," which she does not try to control; that without cause she curses and swears at plaintiff, and applies to him vile names and epithets; that she possesses a revolver, and has repeatedly threatened to shoot and kill him, and that when, thus cast out, he took his team and started to find refuge at his farm in the country, defendant took another horse, pursued and overtook plaintiff, again threatening to kill him, and that, seeing her reach for her revolver, he submitted to her demand and drove back to the home "to avoid further trouble and to protect his person." On this showing he asks an absolute divorce.

... Answering the petition defendant denied all its allegations of abuse and ill treatment, and further alleged that in June 1912, the plaintiff willfully and without cause deserted her, and has ever since absented himself from her, refusing to live with her, though she has often requested him to return to the bosom of his family.

Defendant further alleges that plaintiff is the owner of much valuable property, and worth at least $100,000, while she herself is without means to defend the action or for her support. She therefore asks that the petition be dismissed, and that she have judgment against plaintiff for alimony and support so long as he continues to live apart from her, and that she have general relief.

Replying to the answer, plaintiff denies the same, and alleges that, while he has property to the amount of about $100,000, he is indebted to the extent of $30,000. The trial court denied the divorce, and {plaintiff appealed}. . . .

The court subsequently awarded defendant the use of the homestead, except a specified room or office therein set apart for the storage of plaintiff's personal effects, and requiring plaintiff to pay her $50 per month as alimony and support.

The appeal presents two questions for our consideration—the merits of the plaintiff's demand for a divorce, and the merits of the defendant's claim for support money and attorney's fees.

A reading of the testimony satisfies us that the trial court did not err in dismissing the petition. At the time of the trial plaintiff was 66, and the defendant 42, years of age. Defendant had been twice married, once widowed and once divorced. Plaintiff had been twice married and twice divorced—each time at the suit of his wife. He had subsequently been defendant in an action for breach of promise, and had sought the graces of other women with a fervor not altogether platonic.

The parties did not drift into love unconsciously, as sometimes happens with younger and less experienced couples. Both knew from the start exactly what they wanted. She wanted a husband with money—or money with a husband. He wanted a wife to adorn his house and insure that conjugal felicity of which fate and the divorce court had repeatedly deprived him. With an ardor, the warmth of which was in no manner diminished by the frosts of age, he pressed his suit for defendant's favor for a period of a year and a half, though it is but fair to say the speed of his wooing was held in check by the pendency of the damage suit above referred to which had been brought against him by another member of the sex which has been the bane of his strenuous life. He visited defendant frequently and had ample opportunity to ascertain her virtues, faults and peculiarities—so far at least as these things are ever visible to a suitor before marriage. In short, they had ample opportunity to become well acquainted with each other and form a fair judgment whether marriage was desirable. Considering their worldly experience and matrimonial trials, it is not credible that either believed the other an angel, and in this respect it is quite clear that neither was mistaken.

Counsel for plaintiff tell us that defendant is an adventuress who came to Colfax, where plaintiff resided, for the express purpose of "trapping him into a marriage in order that she might secure a portion of his money," and that their subsequent union was thus brought about with an ulterior view to her financial advantage. In support of this claim a woman testifying for plaintiff states that shortly before the marriage she said to defendant, "No woman of our age would marry an old man of 70 unless she married him for money," and that defendant responded, "You are darned right they don't. If there wasn't some money back of old John Main I wouldn't marry him," and that to this remark she added the further information that she came to Colfax at the suggestion of friends who told her she might there trap a rich old widower, and that she did come and "set her trap" for plaintiff and "caught him." Waiving the improbability that a wise trapper such as defendant is said to be would be bragging of her catch to another woman before the trap was sprung, and accepting the truth of her story, it is very far from affording ground for a divorce. It may show a lack of affection and lay bare the sordid motive which prompts marriages of the kind we have here to deal with, but it is otherwise irrelevant to the issue.

The desire for a home and the comforts of wealth has been the controlling influence of many marriages, especially of those who have passed the bloom of youth, and it is not at all inconsistent with a faithful observance of all the duties and proprieties of the married state. Strategy and management in securing an eligible matrimonial partner is not the exclusive privilege of the man, and the game law of the state provides no closed season against the kind of "trapping" of which appellant complains.

That this marriage has proven an unhappy one is perfectly clear, and that neither has treated the other with the consideration and kindness which ought to mark the conduct of husband and wife we have no doubt; but the charges of extreme cruelty endangering life are by no means sustained. We shall not take the time to embody in the opinion the testimony bearing upon that question. The squabbles and quarrels between the parties, as related by them upon the witness stand, are, as a rule, trivial to the verge of the ridiculous. The threat or assault which plaintiff seems to think most serious, and the only one which is specifically charged in the petition, dwindles in his testimony to the charge that when plaintiff took to his carriage and sought to escape to his farm he was pursued and overtaken by the defendant, who insisted in very ungentle terms that he return home, and that upon his refusal to do so she threatened to kill him, and began feeling under her skirt in a manner which convinced him she had a revolver in her stocking, whereupon he turned his horses toward town and drove back at top speed, closely pursued by defendant, breathing threatenings and slaughter.

Defendant's story of this episode is of a very different character, and, if she tells the truth, plaintiff was never in the slightest danger of bodily injury. We do not undertake to say which is the more credible. Assuming that the parties are of equal veracity or inveracity—which is the charitable view—there is a manifest lack of that preponderance of evidence for the plaintiff which justifies the court in dissolving the marriage contract. Certain it is that plaintiff has failed to make good the one material allegation of his petition that his life is or will be endangered at the hands of his wife.

The profane and abusive language which plaintiff claims was

142

heaped upon him by the defendant is quite generally denied by her, though enough perhaps is admitted to add an unsavory spice to their domestic discussions whenever these became animated. It must be said, however, that in vigorousness of diatribe plaintiff was himself at least a good second, and if we may judge from their own statements neither is made of that delicate moral fiber which characterizes those whom hard words can kill. While marriage is a civil contract, it is one against the obligation of which the common-law plea of failure of consideration is of no avail. The grounds of divorce are purely statutory, and of these, as we have already said, none has been established.

It is further objected that the allowance made is excessive. The amount to be granted in such cases is largely within the sound discretion of the trial court, and will not be disturbed in the absence of apparent abuse of such discretion. We see nothing unreasonable in the allowance made to the wife. The plaintiff has seen fit to withdraw from the home upon what we have found insufficient grounds, and he is in duty bound to contribute a reasonable amount for his wife's support. Fifty dollars per month is not an extravagant sum upon which to live and maintain a home. If he can do better by returning to his home, living peaceably with his wife, and supplying her reasonable needs, as married men and heads of families ordinarily do, there is no law to prevent him from pursuing that course, and when the family relations has been restored the court has undoubted power to set aside the order to which he now objects. . . .

We discover no grounds for disturbing the decree or order appealed from, and they are affirmed.

DEEMER, C.J., and EVANS, LADD, and GAYNOR, J.J., concurring.

The elements of youth, lust, drink, a ladder, dim lights, opportunity and misperception all conspired and merged in the following case, resulting in a conviction for rape against the accused and a dilemma for the English Appellate Justices.

REGINA v. COLLINS
Court of Appeals of England, Criminal Division
[1972] 3 W.L.R. 243, [1972] 2 All E.R. 1105,
56 Cr. App. R. 554 [1972]

EDMUND DAVIES, L.J.

This is about as extraordinary a case as my brethren and I have ever heard either on the Bench or while at the Bar. Stephen William George Collins was convicted on 29th October 1971 at Essex Assizes of burglary with intent to commit rape and he was sentenced to 21 months' imprisonment. He is a 19-year-old youth, and he appeals against that conviction by the certificate of the trial judge. The terms in which that certificate is expressed reveals that the judge was clearly troubled about the case and the conviction.

Let me relate the facts. Were they put into a novel or portrayed on the stage, they would be regarded as being so improbable as to be unworthy of serious consideration and as verging at times on farce. At about two o'clock in the early morning of Saturday, 24th July 1971, a young lady of 18 went to bed at her mother's home in Colchester. She had spent the evening with her boyfriend. She had taken a certain amount of drink, and it may be that this fact affords some explanation of her inability to answer satisfactorily certain crucial questions put to her. She had the habit of sleeping without wearing night apparel in a bed which is very near the lattice-type window of her room. At one stage of her evidence she seemed to be saying that the bed was close up against the window which, in accordance with her practice, was wide open. In the photographs which we have before us, however, there appears to be a gap of some sort between the two, but the bed was clearly quite near the window.

At about 3:30 or 4:00 A.M. she awoke and she then saw in the moonlight a vague form crouched in the open window. She was unable to remember, and this is important, whether the form was on the outside of the window sill or on that part of the sill which was inside the room,

144

and for reasons which will later become clear, that seemingly narrow point is of crucial importance. The young lady then realized several things: first of all that the form in the window was that of a male; secondly that he was a naked male; and thirdly that he was a naked male with an erect penis. She also saw in the moonlight that his hair was blond. She thereupon leapt to the conclusion that her boyfriend, with whom for some time she had been on terms of regular and frequent sexual intimacy, was paying her an ardent nocturnal visit.

She promptly sat up in bed, and the man descended from the sill and joined her in bed and they had full sexual intercourse. But there was something about him which made her think that things were not as they usually were between her and her boyfriend. The length of his hair, his voice as they had exchanged what was described as "love talk," and other features led her to the conclusion that somehow there was something different. So she turned on the bed-side light, saw that her companion was not her boyfriend and slapped the face of the intruder, who was none other than the appellant. He said to her, "Give me a good time tonight," and got hold of her arm, but she bit him and told him to go. She then went into the bathroom and he promptly vanished.

The complainant said that she would not have agreed to intercourse if she had known that the person entering her room was not her boyfriend. But there was no suggestion of any force having been used on her, and the intercourse which took place was undoubtedly effected with no resistance on her part.

The appellant was seen by the police at about 10:30 A.M. later that same morning. According to the police, the conversation which took place then elicited these points: He was very lustful the previous night. He had taken a lot of drink, and we may here note that drink (which to him is a very real problem) had brought this young man into trouble several times before, but never for an offense of this kind. He went on to say that he knew the complainant because he had worked around her house. On this occasion, desiring sexual intercourse—and according to the police evidence he had added that he was determined to have a girl, by force if necessary, although that part of the police evidence he challenged—he went on to say that he walked around the house, saw a light in an upstairs bedroom, and he knew that this was the girl's bedroom. He found a step ladder, leaned it against the wall and climbed up and looked into the bedroom. What

145

he could see inside through the wide open window was a girl who was naked and asleep. So he descended the ladder and stripped off all his clothes, with the exception of his socks, because apparently he took the view that if the girl's mother entered the bedroom it would be easier to effect a rapid escape if he had his socks on than if he was in his bare feet. This is a matter about which we are not called on to express any view, and would in any event find ourselves unable to express one. Having undressed, he then climbed the ladder and pulled himself up on to the window sill. His version of the matter is that he was pulling himself in when she awoke. She then got up and knelt on the bed, she put her arms around his neck and body, and she seemed to pull him into the bed. He went on:

* * * I was rather dazed, because I didn't think she would want to know me. We kissed and cuddled for about ten or fifteen minutes and then I had it away with her but found it hard because I had had so much to drink.

The police officer said to the appellant:

It appears that it was your intention to have intercourse with this girl by force if necessary and it was only pure coincidence that this girl was under the impression that you were her boyfriend, and apparently that is why she consented to allowing you to have sexual intercourse with her.

It was alleged that he then said:

Yes, I feel awful about this. It is the worst day of my life, but I know it could have been worse.

Thereupon the officer said to him—and the appellant challenges this—"What do you mean, you know it could have been worse?" to which he is alleged to have replied:

Well, my trouble is drink and I got very frustrated. As I've told you I only wanted to have it away with a girl and I'm only glad I haven't really hurt her.

Then he made a statement under caution, in the course of which he said:

When I stripped off and got up the ladder I made my mind up that I was

146

going to try and have it away with this girl. I feel terrible about this now, but I had too much to drink. I am sorry for what I have done.

In the course of his testimony, the appellant said that he would not have gone into the room if the girl had not knelt on the bed and beckoned him into the room. He said that if she had objected immediately to his being there or to his having intercourse he would not have persisted. While he was keen on having sexual intercourse that night, it was only if he could find someone who was willing. He strongly denied having told the police that he would, if necessary, have pushed over some girl for the purpose of having intercourse.

There was a submission of no case to answer on the ground that the evidence did not support the charge, particularly that ingredient of it which had reference to entry into the house "as a trespasser." But the submission was overruled, and, as we have already related, he gave evidence.

Now, one feature of the case which remained at the conclusion of the evidence in great obscurity is where exactly the appellant was at the moment when, according to him, the girl manifested that she was welcoming him. Was he kneeling on the sill outside the window or was he already inside the room, having climbed through the window frame, and kneeling on the inner sill? It was a crucial matter, for there were certainly three ingredients that it was incumbent on the Crown to establish. Under Section 9 of the Theft Act of 1968, which renders a person guilty of burglary if he enters any building or part of a building as a trespasser and with the intention of committing rape, the entry of the appellant into the building must first be proved. Well, there is no doubt about that, for it is common ground that he did enter this girl's bedroom. Secondly, it must be proved that he entered as a trespasser. We will develop this point a little later. Thirdly, it must be proved that he entered as a trespasser with intent at the time of entry to commit rape therein.

The second ingredient of the offence—the entry must be as a trespasser—is one which has not, to the best of our knowledge, been previously canvassed in the courts. Views as to its ambit have naturally been canvassed by the textbook writers, and it is perhaps not wholly irrelevant to recall that those who were advising the Home Secretary before the Theft Bill was presented to Parliament

147

had it in mind to get rid of some of the frequently absurd technical rules which had been built up in relation to the old requirement in burglary of a "breaking and entering." The cases are legion as to what this did or did not amount to, and happily it is not now necessary for us to consider them. But it was in order to get rid of those technical rules that a new test was introduced, namely that the entry must be "as a trespasser."

What does that involve? According to the learned editors of Archbold[1]:

> Any intentional, reckless or negligent entry into a building will, it would appear, constitute a trespass if the building is in the possession of another person who does not consent to the entry. Nor will it make any difference that the entry was the result of a reasonable mistake on the part of the defendant, so far as trespass is concerned.

If that be right, then it would be no defence for this man to say (and even were he believed in saying), "Well, I honestly thought that this girl was welcoming me into the room and I therefore entered, fully believing that I had her consent to go in." If Archbold is right, he would nevertheless be a trespasser, since the apparent consent of the girl was unreal, she being mistaken as to who was at her window. We disagree. We hold that, for the purpose of Section 9 of the Theft Act of 1968, a person entering a building is not guilty of trespass if he enters without knowledge that he is trespassing or at least without acting recklessly as to whether or not he is unlawfully entering. . . .

Having so held, the pivotal point of this appeal is whether the Crown established that the appellant at the moment that he entered the bedroom knew perfectly well that he was not welcome there or, being reckless whether he was welcome or not, was nevertheless determined to enter. That in turn involves consideration as to where he was at the time that the complainant indicated that she was welcoming him into her bedroom. If, to take an example that was put in the course of argument, her bed had not been near the window but was on the other side of the bedroom, and he (being determined to have her sexually even against her will) climbed through the window and crossed the bedroom to reach her bed, then the offence charged

---

[1]*Criminal Pleading, Evidence and Practice* (37th ed., 1969), p. 572, §1505.

would have been established. But in this case, as we have related, the layout of the room was different, and it became a point of nicety which had to be conclusively established by the Crown as to where he was when the girl made welcoming signs, as she unquestionably at some stage did.

How did the learned judge deal with this matter? We have to say regretfully that there was a flaw in his treatment of it. . . .

. . . Unfortunately the trial judge regarded the matter as though the second ingredient in the burglary charged was whether there had been an intentional or reckless entry, and when he came to develop this topic in his summing-up that error was unfortunately perpetuated. The trial judge told the jury:

> He had no right to be in that house, as you know, certainly from the point of view of [the girl's mother], but if you are satisfied about entry, did he enter intentionally or recklessly? What the Prosecution says about that is, you do not really have to consider recklessness because when you consider his own evidence he intended to enter that house, and if you accept the evidence I have just pointed out to you, he, in fact, did so. So, at least, you may think, it was intentional. At the least, you may think it was reckless because as he told you he did not know whether the girl would accept him.

We are compelled to say that we do not think the trial judge by these observations made it sufficiently clear to the jury the nature of the second test about which they had to be satisfied before the appellant could be convicted of the offence charged.

There was no doubt that his entry into the bedroom was "intentional." But what the appellant had said was, "She knelt on the bed, she put her arms around me and then I went in." If the jury thought he might be truthful in that assertion, they would need to consider whether or not, although entirely surprised by such a reception being accorded to him, this young man might not have been entitled reasonably to regard her action as amounting to an invitation to him to enter. If she in fact appeared to be welcoming him, the Crown do not suggest that he should have realized or even suspected that she was so behaving because, despite the moonlight, she thought he was someone else. Unless the jury were entirely satisfied that the appellant made an effective and substantial entry into the bedroom without the complainant doing or saying anything to cause him to believe that she was consenting to his entering it, he ought not to be convicted of the offence charged.

The point is a narrow one, as narrow maybe as the window sill which is crucial to this case. But this is a criminal charge of gravity and, even though one may suspect that his *intention* was to commit the offense charged, unless the facts show with clarity that he in fact committed it he ought not to remain convicted.

Some question arose whether or not the appellant can be regarded as a trespasser *ab initio* {from the beginning}. But we are entirely in agreement with the view expressed in Archbold that the common law doctrine of trespass ab initio has no application to burglary under the Theft Act of 1968. One further matter that was canvassed ought perhaps to be mentioned. The point was raised that, the complainant not being the tenant or occupier of the dwelling-house and her mother being apparently in occupation, this girl herself could not in any event have extended an effective invitation to enter, so that even if she had expressly and with full knowledge of all material facts invited the appellant in, he would nevertheless be a trespasser. Whatever be the position in the law of tort, to regard such a proposition as acceptable in the criminal law would be unthinkable.

We have to say that this appeal must be allowed on the basis that the jury were never invited to consider the vital question whether this young man did enter the premises as a trespasser, that is to say knowing perfectly well that he had no invitation to enter or reckless of whether or not his entry was with permission. . . .

Appeal allowed. Conviction quashed.

CHAPTER VI

Clever Schemes, *Bizarre Claims,* Ridiculous Contentions, *Novel Demands, Strange Lawsuits* and *Good Old-Fashioned* Fraud and Deceit

Judicial humor is a dreadful thing. In the first place, the jokes are usually bad; I have seldom heard a judge utter a good one. There seems to be something about the judicial ermine which puts its wearer in the same general class with the ordinary radio comedian. He just is not funny. In the second place, the bench is not an appropriate place for unseemly levity. The litigant has vital interests at stake. His entire future, or even his life, may be trembling in the balance, and the robed buffoon who makes merry at his expense should be choked with his own wig.

—William Prosser[1]

There is assuredly some differences of opinion among appellate judges about the basic problem whether humor can be proper in a judicial opinion. When we asked the presiding judges of sixty appellate courts for citations to judicial humor, about ten percent of the forty-odd who responded said that humor is never used in the courts. We cannot quarrel with that firm position, for that was our own view until we had worked for more than a year, off and on, in the preparation of this critique. In the event, humor is used occasionally by the great majority of our appellate courts. ... Laying aside the cases in which humor should never be used, we now share Cardozo's belief that an opinion may not be the worse for being lightened by a smile.

—Hon. George Rose Smith[2]

---

[1]William Prosser, *The Judicial Humorist,* p. viii (1952).
[2]Hon. George Rose Smith, "A Critique of Judicial Humor," 43 *Ark. Law Rev.* 1, 25–26 (1990).

Pundits and philosophers alike bemoan the fact that our society is unquestionably the most litigious in history. Whether this sad condition is the cause or the result of the unprecedented proliferation of lawyers across the land is left to the speculation of sociologists. So too is the question of whether our society has simply devolved into a collective pack of churlish cry-babies and greedy opportunists, ready and eager to race into court at the slightest provocation to self-righteously affix blame and (hopefully) establish financial liability against any convenient target defendant. In the following case, the plaintiff proceeded to file his action without an attorney, albeit with a style, creativity and zeal worthy of any member of the Bar, against a very well-known and formidable adversary.

UNITED STATES EX REL. MAYO
v. SATAN AND HIS STAFF
U.S. District Court, W. D. Pennsylvania
54 F.R.D. 282 (1971)

GERALD J. WEBER, DISTRICT JUDGE

{Plaintiff attempted to file a federal lawsuit alleging violation of his civil rights and petitioned the Court for permission to proceed "in forma pauperis," whereby the court waived the filing fees and other costs on account of the plaintiff's inability to pay. The theory is that one who is impoverished should not be deprived of the right to litigate. In reviewing the petition, however, the Court found several other practical problems with the plaintiff's lawsuit.}

Plaintiff ... alleges that Satan has on numerous occasions caused plaintiff misery and unwarranted threats, against the will of plaintiff, that Satan has placed deliberate obstacles in his path and has caused plaintiff's downfall. Plaintiff alleges that by reason of these acts Satan has deprived him of his constitutional rights.

We feel that the application to file and proceed in forma pauperis must be denied. Even if plaintiff's complaint reveals a prima facie recital of the infringement of the civil rights of a citizen of the United States, the Court has serious doubts that the complaint reveals a cause of action upon which relief can be granted by the Court.

We question whether plaintiff may obtain personal jurisdiction over the defendant in this judicial district. The complaint contains no allegation of residence in this district. While the official reports disclose no case where this defendant has appeared as defendant, there is an unofficial account of a trial in New Hampshire where this defendant filed an action of mortgage foreclosure as plaintiff.[1] The defendant in that action was represented by the preeminent advocate of that day, and raised the defense that the plaintiff was a foreign prince with no standing to sue in an American court. This defense was overcome by overwhelming evidence to the contrary. Whether or not this would raise an estoppel in the present case we are unable to determine at this time.

If such action were to be allowed we would also face the question of whether it may be maintained as a class action. It appears to meet the requirements of Fed.R. of Civ.P. 23 that the class is so numerous that joinder of all members is impracticable, there are questions of law and fact common to the class, and the claims of the representative party is typical of the claims of the class. We cannot now determine if the representative party will fairly protect the interests of the class.

We note that the plaintiff has failed to include with his complaint the required form of instructions for the U.S. Marshal for directions as to service of process.

For the foregoing reasons we must exercise our discretion to refuse the prayer of plaintiff to proceed in forma pauperis.

It is ordered that the complaint be given a miscellaneous docket number and leave to proceed in forma pauperis be denied.

----

[1]{Ed. Note: The judge makes reference to the short story "The Devil and Daniel Webster," by Stephen Vincent Benét.}

The publicity generated by lawsuits resulting in large cash settlements and lucrative jury awards for seemingly inconsequential or unmeritorious claims tends to stimulate and encourage the "creative legal thinking" of potential litigants. Such considerations may have been a factor in motivating the plaintiff to file the claim discussed in the following case.

SEARIGHT v. STATE OF NEW JERSEY
U.S. District Court, D. New Jersey
412 F. Supp. 413 (1976)

VINCENT P. BIUNNO, DISTRICT JUDGE

The complaint says that in October 1962, Searight was taken to the Eye, Ear and Speech Clinic in Newark, while in custody, and that the State of New Jersey there unlawfully injected him in the left eye with a radium electric beam. As a result, he claims that someone now talks to him on the inside of his brain. He asks money damages of $12 million.

The State has moved to dismiss for failure to state a claim, F.R.Civ.P. 12(b)(6), on the ground that it appears from the face of the complaint that the claim, if otherwise valid, is barred by the statute of limitations.

Ordinarily, that bar is a matter to be pleaded as a separate defense, but when the essential facts appear on the face of the pleading, it may be raised by motion as a matter of law as though by demurrer.

The incident is said to have happened in October 1962, and the complaint was filed in February 1976. Absent an Act of Congress (there is none), the lex loci {law of the place} governs. ... The applicable New Jersey statute allows 2 years after the cause of action accrues to file suit. N.J.S.A. 2A:14−2. Thus, suit was filed here more than 13 years after the statute had run out.

There is clear ground for dismissal. Yet, because Searight sues pro se {for himself; i.e., without an attorney}, the court ordinarily would direct that judgment of dismissal not be entered within a period of perhaps a month, during which he would be allowed leave to file an amended complaint that surmounts the bar, if he can.

But in this case, the court observes that for other considerations, equally obvious, it lacks jurisdiction to entertain the claim, and so may also dismiss for that reason, F.R.Civ.P. 12(h)(3). ...

The allegations, of course, are of facts which, if they exist, are not yet known to man. Just as Mr. Houdini has so far failed to establish communication from the spirit world (See E. L. Doctorow, 'Ragtime,' pp. 166–169, Random House, 1974), so the decades of scientific experiments and statistical analysis have failed to establish the existence of extrasensory perception (ESP). But, taking the facts as pleaded, and assuming them to be true, they show a case of presumably unlicensed radio communication, a matter which comes within the sole jurisdiction of the Federal Communications Commission, 47 U.S.C. §151, et seq.

And even aside from that, Searight could have blocked the broadcast to the antenna in his brain simply by grounding it. See, for example, Ghirardi, *Modern Radio Servicing,* first edition, p. 572, ff. (Radio & Technical Publishing Co., New York, 1935). Just as delivery trucks for oil and gasoline are "grounded" against the accumulation of charges of static electricity, so on the same principle Searight might have pinned to the back of a trouser leg a short chain of paper clips so that the end would touch the ground and prevent anyone from talking to him inside his brain.

But these interesting aspects need not be decided here. It is enough that the bar of the statute of limitations clearly appears from the face of the complaint and independently thereof, that the court lacks jurisdiction. The complaint will be dismissed with prejudice.

Courts uniformly disdain frivolous lawsuits. Although such cases are carefully scrutinized to ensure that no grain of genuine merit exists, attorneys who file frivolous actions or appeals risk incurring the considerable wrath and scathing wit of the judiciary which must expend its valuable time and resources in dealing with their handiwork. The following case stands as an eloquent beacon, warning litigants to refrain from pursuing unmeritorious claims.

McDONALD v. JOHN P. SCRIPPS NEWSPAPER

California Court of Appeals, Second Appellate District
210 Cal. App.3d 100; 257 Cal. Rptr. 473 (1989)

ARTHUR GILBERT, J.

Question—When should an attorney say "no" to a client? Answer—When asked to file a lawsuit like this one.

Master Gavin L. McDonald did not win the Ventura County Spelling Bee. Therefore, through his guardian ad litem,[1] he sued. Gavin alleges that contest officials improperly allowed the winner of the spelling bee to compete. Gavin claimed that had the officials not violated contest rules, the winner "would not have had the opportunity" to defeat him. The trial court wisely sustained a demurrer to the complaint without leave to amend.

We affirm because two things are missing here—causation and common sense. Gavin lost the spelling bee because he spelled a word wrong. Gavin contends that the winner of the spelling bee should not have been allowed to compete in the contest. Gavin, however, cannot show that but for the contest official's allowing the winner to compete, he would have won the spelling bee.

In our puzzlement as to how this case even found its way into court, we are reminded of the words of a romantic poet.

> *The [law] is too much with us; late and soon,*
> *Getting and spending, we lay waste our powers:*
> *Little we see in Nature that is ours;*
> *We have given our hearts away, a sordid boon!*

---

[1] We do not hold Gavin responsible.

156

(Wordsworth, "The World Is Too Much with Us" [1807], with apologies to William Wordsworth, who we feel, if he were here, would approve.)

FACTS

Gavin was a contestant in the 1987 Scripps Howard National Spelling Bee, sponsored in Ventura County by the newspaper, the *Ventura County Star—Free Press*. The contest is open to all students through the eighth grade who are under the age of 16. Gavin won competitions at the classroom and school-wide levels. This earned him the chance to compete against other skilled spellers in the county-wide spelling bee. The best speller in the county wins a trip to Washington, D.C., and a place in the national finals. The winner of the national finals is declared the national champion speller.

Gavin came in second in the county spelling bee. Being adjudged the second-best orthographer in Ventura County is an impressive accomplishment, but pique overcame self-esteem. The spelling contest became a legal contest.

We search in vain through the complaint to find a legal theory to support this metamorphosis. Gavin alleges that two other boys, Stephen Chen and Victor Wang, both of whom attended a different school, also competed in the spelling contest. Stephen had originally lost his school-wide competition to Victor. Stephen was asked to spell the word *horsy*. He spelled it "h-o-r-s-e-y." The spelling was ruled incorrect. Victor spelled the same word "h-o-r-s-y." He then spelled another word correctly, and was declared the winner.

Contest officials, who we trust were not copy editors for the newspaper sponsoring the contest, later discovered that there are two proper spellings of the word *horsy*, and that Stephen's spelling was correct after all.[2]

Contest officials asked Stephen and Victor to again compete between themselves in order to declare one winner. Victor, having everything to lose by agreeing to this plan, refused. Contest officials decided to allow both Victor and Stephen to advance to the county-wide spelling bee, where Gavin lost to Stephen.

---

[2]"**[H]orsey also horsy** 1: relating to, resembling, or suggestive of a horse 2: addicted to or having to do with horses or horse racing or characteristic of the manners, dress, or tastes of horsemen" (*Webster's Third New Internat. Dict.* [1961], p. 1093).

Taking Vince Lombardi's aphorism to heart, "Winning isn't everything, it's the only thing," Gavin filed suit against the *Ventura County Star–Free Press* and the Scripps Howard National Spelling Bee alleging breach of contract, breach of implied covenant of good faith and fair dealing, and intentional and negligent infliction of emotional distress.

In his complaint, Gavin asserts that contest officials violated spelling bee rules by allowing Stephen Chen to compete at the county level. He suggests that had Stephen not progressed to the county-wide competition, he, Gavin, would have won. For this leap of faith he seeks compensatory and punitive damages.

The trial court sustained Scripp's demurrer without leave to amend because the complaint fails to state a cause of action. The action was dismissed, and Gavin appeals.

DISCUSSION

Gavin asserts that he has set forth the necessary elements of a cause of action for breach of contract, and that these elements are: "(1) The contract; (2) Plaintiff's performance; (3) Defendant's breach; (4) Damage to plaintiff (4 Witkin, California Procedure, Pleading, §464 [3rd ed., 1985])."

Gavin's recitation of the law is correct, but his complaint wins no prize. He omitted a single word in the fourth element of an action for breach of contract, which should read "damage to plaintiff therefrom." (Witkin, Cal. Procedure [3rd ed., 1985], Pleading, §464, p. 504, italics added). Not surprisingly, the outcome of this case depends on that word. A fundamental rule of law is that "whether the action be in tort or contract compensatory damages cannot be recovered unless there is a causal connection between the act or omission complained of and the injury sustained." . . .

The erudite trial judge stated Gavin's shortcoming incisively. "I see a gigantic causation problem. . . ." Relying on the most important resource a judge has, he said, "Common sense tells me that this lawsuit is nonsense."

Even if Gavin and Scripps had formed a contract which Scripps breached by allowing Stephen Chen to compete at the county level in violation of contest rules, nothing would change. Gavin cannot show that he was injured by the breach. Gavin lost the spelling bee because he misspelled a word, and it is irrelevant that he was defeated by a contestant who "had no right to advance in the contest."

Gavin argues that had the officials "not violated the rules of the contest, Chen would not have advanced, and would not have had the opportunity to defeat" Gavin. Of course, it is impossible for Gavin to show that he would have spelled the word correctly if Stephen were not his competitor. Gavin concedes as much when he argues that he would not have been damaged if defeated by someone who had properly advanced in the contest. That is precisely the point.

Gavin cannot show that anything would have been different had Stephen not competed against him. Nor can he show that another competitor would have also misspelled that or another word, thus allowing Gavin another opportunity to win. "It is fundamental that damages which are speculative, remote, imaginary, contingent, or merely possible cannot serve as a legal basis for recovery." . . .

Gavin offers to amend the complaint by incorporating certain rules of the spelling bee which purportedly show that the decision to allow Stephen to advance in the competition was procedurally irregular. This offer to amend reflects a misunderstanding of the trial court's ruling. The fatal defect in the complaint is that Gavin cannot show that but for Stephen Chen's presence in the spelling bee, Gavin would have won.

"The general rule is that it is an abuse of discretion to sustain a demurrer without leave to amend unless the complaint shows that it is incapable of amendment {citation omitted}. But it is also true that where the nature of plaintiff's claim is clear, but under substantive law no liability exists, leave to amend should be denied, for no amendment could change the result." . . .

The third cause of action states that plaintiff has suffered humiliation, indignity, mortification, worry, grief, anxiety, fright, mental anguish and emotional distress, not to mention loss of respect and standing in the community. These terms more appropriately express how attorneys who draft complaints like this should feel.

A judge whose prescience is exceeded only by his eloquence said that ". . . Courts of Justice do not pretend to furnish cures for all the miseries of human life. They redress or punish gross violations of duty, but they go no farther; they cannot make men virtuous: and, as the happiness of the world depends upon its virtue, there may be much unhappiness in it which human laws cannot undertake to remove" (Evans v. Evans [1790], Consistory Court of London). Unfortunately, as evidenced by this lawsuit, this cogent insight, although as relevant today as it was nearly 200 years ago, does not always make an impression on today's practitioner.

In Shapiro v. Queens County Jockey Club {citation omitted} plaintiff's horse was the only horse to run the full six furlongs in the sixth race at Aqueduct Race Track after racing officials declared a false start. A half hour later the sixth race was run again, and plaintiff's horse came in fifth out of a total of six.

The Shapiro court held that plaintiff had no cause of action against the race track. Plaintiff could not support the theory that his horse would have won the second time around if all the other horses had also run the six furlongs after the false start. Plaintiff was not content to merely chalk up his loss to a bad break caused by the vicissitudes of life. The lesson to be learned is that all of us, like high-strung horses at the starting gate, are subject to life's false starts. The courts cannot erase the world's imperfections.

The Georgia Supreme Court, in Georgia High School Ass'n v. Waddell {citation omitted}, decided it was without authority to review the decision of a football referee regarding the outcome of the game. The court stated that the referee's decision did not present a justiciable controversy. Nor does the decision of the spelling bee officials present a justiciable controversy here.

Our decision at least keeps plaintiff's bucket of water from being added to the tidal wave of litigation that has engulfed our courts.[3]

SANCTIONS—A CLOSE CALL

Causation has been counsel's nemesis. Its absence makes Gavin's quest for "justice" an illusory one. The lack of causation in the complaint is the cause for dismissal of the complaint. Counsel could not show us or the trial court how an amendment could cure the complaint. The lesson should have been learned at the trial court. As the law disregards trifles (Civ. Code. §3533), so, too, one should not trifle with

---

[3]Judge Irving Kaufman of the Second Circuit Court of Appeals, in a speech, has spoken of the alarming tidal wave of litigation in this country that shows no signs of abatement (Cherna v. Cherna [Fla. Dist. Ct. App., 1983], 427 So.2d 395, 396, fn. 2).

the Court of Appeals. The filing of an appeal here, for a case so trivial, and so lacking in merit, makes it a likely candidate for sanctions.

To counsel's credit, we are convinced that he did not prosecute this appeal for an improper motive or to delay the effect of an adverse judgment. He, therefore, at least avoids two criteria set forth in In re Marriage of Flaherty {citation omitted}. This case, however, lacks merit, and we cannot conceive of a reasonable attorney who would disagree with this appraisal.

Falling within a criterion of *Flaherty*, however, does not in and of itself compel sanctions. The *Flaherty* court warned that "any definition must be read so as to avoid a serious chilling effect on the assertion of litigants' rights on appeal. . . . An appeal that is simply without merit is not by definition frivolous and should not incur sanctions. Counsel should not be deterred from filing such appeals out of a fear of reprisals." . . .

It is creative and energetic counsel who from time to time challenge existing law and question past policies. This insures that the law be a living and dynamic force. Although noble aims were not advanced here, we are mindful of the caution in *Flaherty* that the borderline between appeals that are frivolous and those that simply have no merit is vague, and that punishment should be used sparingly "to deter only the most egregious conduct." . . . We therefore decline to impose sanctions, but we hope this opinion will serve as a warning notice for counsel to be discerning when drawing the line between making new law or wasting everyone's time.

ADVICE TO GAVIN AND AN APHORISM OR TWO

Gavin has much to be proud of. He participated in a spelling bee that challenged the powers of memory and concentration. He met the challenge well but lost out to another contestant. Gavin took first in his school and can be justifiably proud of his performance.

It is this lawsuit that is trivial, not his achievement. Our courts try to give redress for real harms; they cannot offer palliatives for imagined injuries.

Vince Lombardi may have had a point, but so did Grantland Rice—It is "not that you won or lost—but how you played the game."

As for the judgment of the trial court, we'll spell it out. A-F-I-R-M-E-D. Appellant is to pay respondent's costs on appeal.

The unlucky judge in the following case was twice forced to consider an obtuse and convoluted claim filed by "Kent © Norman" (the plaintiff's actual name) against then-President Ronald Reagan. Fortunately for Mr. Reagan, the result in the second instance was the same as in the first.

KENT © NORMAN v. REAGAN
U.S. District Court, D. Oregon.
95 F.R.D. 476 (1982)

JAMES A. REDDEN, DISTRICT JUDGE

In this action, Kent © Norman[1] seeks redress of grievances. I previously dismissed the action as frivolous, see Bell v. Hood, 327 U.S. 678, 682–3, 66 S.Ct. 773, 776, 90 L.Ed. 939 (1946). A panel of the Ninth Circuit disagreed and reversed. A brief summary of the contents of this file may be helpful in understanding my present decision to dismiss this case for lack of prosecution.

There are numerous defendants and claims. The first defendant appears to be Ronald Reagan, who, in terms of the plaintiff's "amendment complaint," has caused the plaintiff great vexation:

> Plaintiff alleges that defendant Reagan has acted with deliberate, reckless, and nefarious disregard of his constitutional rights, in this, to wit:
> 1) Defendant caused "civil death" without legislation.
> 2) Defendant allowed plaintiff to suffer irrepairable [sic] harm and neglect.
> 3) Defendant has acted with redundance and malicious conduct in neglecting plaintiff.
> 4) Defendant allowed numerous abuses of plaintiff's person, property, and liberty while governor of California and president.
> 5) Defendant Reagan has deprived plaintiff of his right to vote and caused, either directly or indirectly, arrests upon false, incorrect, or misleading information.
> 6) Plaintiff has no adequate remedy at law to redress these wrongs without due course of process.

There are also a number of parking tickets in the file. The plaintiff apparently demands a jury trial in federal court for the parking fines assessed by Multnomah County. The plaintiff also seeks an order

---

[1] The plaintiff's name apparently includes the copyright sign.

requiring the Interstate Commerce Commission to investigate White Line Fevers From Mars, which is succinctly referred to elsewhere in the file as "W.L.F.F.M." This defendant is not, despite the name, of genuine extraterrestrial origin, but is apparently a fruit company which shipped marijuana and cocaine in "fruit boxes" for Mother's Day. The plaintiff's trucking license was suspended by the Interstate Commerce Commission as a result of some incident involving the plaintiff's transportation of White Line Fevers' fruit boxes. Plaintiff also seeks Supplemental Security Income (SSI) payments, apparently as a result of this incident, and punitive damages against Reagan and the Secretary of the Treasury for withholding of the SSI payments.

There are also certain other claims which the court is at a loss to characterize, and can only describe. There is included in the file a process receipt which bears the "Received" stamp of the Supreme Court of the United States. On this form are the notations, apparently written by the plaintiff, "Taxes due" and "D.C. Circuit was green" as well as "Rule 8 . . . Why did you return my appeal form? Why isn't the '1840' W. 7th mailbox still next to the 1830 one?" and "something suspicious about that mailbox." There are also other notations on the form.

There is also the following "claim":

> *The birds today*
> *Are singing loudly,*
> *The day is fresh*
> *With the sounds*
> *Upon the wind*
> *The crickets.*
> *The blackbirds*
> *The woodpeckers*
> *Beauty in every*
> *Spark of life*
> *Just So their sounds*
> *Are appreciated*
> *Their sounds are beauty*
> *The ants are silent*
> *But always searching*
> *The birds noise a song*
> *and the fade of the automobile tires*
> *Chirp. A shadow from*
> *a passing monarch butterfly*
> *Breathless in Colorado.*   *—Kent © Norman 1981*

It is possible, of course, that this is not intended as a claim at all, but as a literary artifact. However it may be that, liberally construed, the references to the birds, crickets, ants, and butterfly could constitute a Bivens claim. See Bivens v. Six Unknown-Named Agents, 403 U.S. 388, 91 S.Ct. 1999, 29 L.Ed.2d 619 (1971); U.S. ex rel. Mayo v. Satan and His Staff, 54 F.R.D. 282 (W.D. Penn. 1971).

At any rate, following the Ninth Circuit's remand the marshals attempted to serve the President and the other defendants. The plaintiff, however, seems to have lost touch with the court, or lost interest, or both. Since the receipt of the remand in the district court on March 1, 1982, he has taken no action on the case. Mail addressed to him is returned. The discovery deadline and Pre-trial Order deadline have passed, without any response to the court's notifications to the plaintiff. Perhaps the plaintiff has elected to pursue his remedies in some more convenient forum. I therefore DISMISS this action for want of prosecution.

The following is the shortest complete judicial opinion which we have yet been able to locate. As to what it means or to what subject matter it relates we have no clue. In legal terms, the opinion thus "stands on its own" and "speaks for itself."

HALL v. HALL
High Court of Chancery
21 E.R. 447; Dick. 710 (1788)

{EDWARD THURLOW, CHANCELLOR}.

Reprisal was said by Lord Thurlow, C., to be a common drawback.[1]

---

[1]{Ed. Note: This is the entire opinion.}

It had to happen sooner or later. Someone *had* to sue himself. Mr. Oreste Lodi was that someone; and *yes,* it occurred in California. To his credit, and in keeping with his schizophrenic tendencies, when the lower court ultimately dismissed his lawsuit, Mr. Lodi appealed and filed briefs, both as appellant *and* as respondent.

LODI v. LODI

Court of Appeals of California, Third Appellate District
173 Cal. App.3d 628; 219 Cal. Rptr. 117 (1985)

RICHARD M. SIMS III, ASSOCIATE JUSTICE

This case started when plaintiff Oreste Lodi sued himself in the Shasta County Superior Court.

In a complaint styled "Action to Quiet Title Equity," plaintiff named himself, under the title "Oreste Lodi, Beneficiary," as defendant. The pleading alleges that defendant Lodi is the beneficiary of a charitable trust, the estate of which would revert to plaintiff Lodi, as "Reversioner," upon notice. Plaintiff attached as Exhibit A to his complaint, a copy of his 1923 New York birth certificate, which he asserts is the "certificate of power of appointment and conveyance" transferring reversioner's estate to the charitable trust. Plaintiff Lodi goes on to allege that for 61 years (i.e., since plaintiff/defendant was born), defendant has controlled the estate, that plaintiff has notified defendant of the termination of the trust by a written "Revocation of all Power" (which apparently seeks to revoke his birth certificate), but that defendant "intentionally persist [sic] to control said estate...." Plaintiff requested an order that he is absolutely entitled to possession of the estate, and terminating all claims against the estate by any and all persons "claiming" under defendant.[1]

The complaint was duly served by plaintiff Lodi, as "Reversioner," upon himself as defendant/beneficiary. When defendant/beneficiary Lodi failed to answer, plaintiff/reversioner Lodi had a clerk's default entered and thereafter requested entry of a default judgment. At the

---

[1]The purpose of plaintiff's action is not entirely clear. However, we note plaintiff caused a complimentary copy of his complaint to be served upon the Internal Revenue Service. It may be that plaintiff hoped to obtain a state court judgment that, he thought, would be of advantage to him under the Internal Revenue Code.

hearing on the entry of a default judgment, the superior court denied the request to enter judgment and dismissed the complaint.[2]

In this court, appellant and respondent are the same person.[3] Each party has filed a brief.

The only question presented is whether the trial court properly dismissed the complaint even though no party sought dismissal or objected to entry of judgment as requested.

As is obvious, the complaint states no cognizable claim for relief. Plaintiff's birth certificate did not create a charitable trust; consequently, there was no trust which could be terminated by notice. In the arena of pleadings, the one at issue here is a slam-dunk frivolous complaint.

We conclude the trial court was empowered to strike or dismiss the complaint by section 436 of the Code of Civil Procedure which provides in pertinent part: "The court may, upon a motion . . . or at any time in its discretion, and upon terms it deems proper . . . [¶] (b) Strike out all or any part of any pleading not drawn or filed in conformity with the laws of the state, a court rule, or an order of the court."

Section 425.10 provides in pertinent part: "A complaint . . . shall contain . . . the following: [¶] A statement of the facts constituting the cause of action, in ordinary and concise language."

Discussing the notion of a "cause of action," Witkin writes: "California follows the 'primary right theory' of Pomeroy: 'Every judicial action must therefore involve the following elements: a primary right possessed by the plaintiff, and a corresponding primary duty devolving upon the defendant, a delict or wrong done by the defendant which consisted in a breach of such primary right and duty; a remedial right in favor of the plaintiff, and a remedial duty resting on the defendant springing from this delict, and finally the remedy or relief itself. . . . Of these elements, the primary right and duty and the delict or wrong combined constitute the cause of action. . . . [T]he existence of a legal right in an abstract form is never alleged by the plaintiff; but, instead

---

[2]The minute order indicates that the court also suggested to plaintiff/reversioner/defendant/ beneficiary that he seek the assistance of legal counsel.

[3]Plaintiff/reversioner filed a notice of appeal from the order of dismissal. No judgment was entered. However, in the interest of judicial economy, we treat the notice of appeal as one from the judgment (Cal. Rules of Court, rule 2[c]).

thereof, the facts from which that right arises are set forth, and the right itself is inferred therefrom. The cause of action, as it appears in the complaint when properly pleaded, will therefore always be the facts from which the plaintiff's primary right and the defendant's corresponding primary duty have arisen, together with the facts which constitute the defendant's delict or act of wrong'" (4 Witkin, Cal.Procedure [3d ed., 1985], Pleading, §23, pp. 66–67, quoting Pomeroy, Code Remedies [5th ed.] p. 528, emphasis in original).

Here, plaintiff's complaint fails to state facts showing a primary right by plaintiff or a primary duty devolving on defendant or a wrong done by defendant. The complaint therefore fails to state facts constituting a cause of action as required by section 425.10. Consequently, the complaint was not drawn in conformity with the laws of this state and was thus properly subject to the court's own motion to strike under section 436, subdivision (b).

We need not consider whether the court's power under this statute should be exercised where plaintiff seeks leave to amend. Here, so far as the record before us shows, plaintiff made no such request nor is any prospect of saving the pleading by amendment apparent. The trial court therefore properly struck and dismissed the complaint on its own motion (§436, subd. [b]).

In the circumstances, this result cannot be unfair to Mr. Lodi. Although it is true that, as plaintiff and appellant, he loses, it is equally true, as defendant and respondent, he wins! It is hard to imagine a more even-handed application of justice. Truly, it would appear that Oreste Lodi is that rare litigant who is assured of both victory and defeat regardless of which side triumphs.

We have considered whether respondent/defendant/beneficiary should be awarded costs of suit on appeal, which he could thereafter recover from himself. However, we believe the equities are better served by requiring each party to bear his own costs on appeal.

The appeal is dismissed. Each party shall bear his own costs.

167

The following opinion was authored by the legendary Judge John R. Brown, one of the truly great judicial humorists, whose fine wit and scrivening talents are self-evident.

CLEGG v. HARDWARE MUTUAL CASUALTY COMPANY

U.S. Court of Appeals, Fifth Circuit
264 F.2d 152 (1959)

JOHN R. BROWN, CIRCUIT JUDGE

{This case was tried before a jury and the plaintiff, Mr. Clegg, lost. In due course, Mr. Clegg filed an appeal, asserting a number of technical problems with the trial and the jury instructions. However, the defendant insurance company contended that the jury had simply "rejected plaintiff's thesis because it was patently unacceptable to thinking jurors."}

. . . The Insurer describes the claim as bizarre. If it is not that; it is an understatement to call it anything less than unique.

The Insurer's truck, southbound on Airline Highway near Norco, Louisiana, suddenly swerved onto its right shoulder to avoid hitting school children alighting from a northbound school bus. The truck hit and smashed several cars and ran into gasoline pumps of a roadside filling station, causing fire and widespread destruction. Clegg, of Baton Rouge, was standing nearby. He was not physically injured. He was not touched in any way by anything. What happened to him, he said, was that on seeing this holocaust and the need for someone to rush in to help rescue victims, he suddenly became overwhelmed by fear and realized for the first time in his life that he was not the omnipotent, fearless man his psyche had envisioned him to be. His post-accident awareness that this event had destroyed his self-deceptive image of himself precipitated great emotional and psychic tensions manifesting themselves as psychosomatic headaches, pain in legs and neck, a loss of general interest, a disposition to withdraw from social and family contacts, and the like.

As it might have appeared to the jury of lay persons, the medical theory was that the accident had made Clegg see himself as he really was, not as Clegg had thought himself to be. In short, the accident had destroyed the myth. No longer was he the brave invincible man. Now,

168

as any other, he was a mere human, with defects and limitations and a faint heart. It was, so the Insurer argued with plausibility to the jury, the strange case of a defendant being asked to pay for having helped Clegg by bringing him back to reality—helping him, as it were, to leave Mount Olympus to rejoin the other mortals in Baton Rouge.

To this elusive excursion into the id of Clegg, there were added many irrefutable earth-bound events that made it sound all the more strange. At the time of the accident, Clegg was a TV advertising salesman. Within a short space of time, he had changed employment. He became president of a company, in which he was apparently personally interested, at a salary over twice as high as he had previously earned. He bought and sold several pieces of real estate, had made $25,000 in one trade, and had purchased and moved into a new $40,000 home. Within nine months of the accident he had successfully undertaken a campaign to become elected a city Councilman of Baton Rouge. The psychiatrists, acknowledging these external facts, then reasoned that this was a part of his struggle by which to recapture his lost self-esteem, and that while these things were most assuredly being accomplished, it was being done at further damage to Clegg.

We have mentioned this briefly not to disparage the claim or intimate its insufficiency or sufficiency as a matter of law. The jury verdict has relieved us of the necessity of passing judgment on the inherent merits. The District Court submitted it as one under the Louisiana doctrine allowing recovery for emotional damages even though unaccompanied by physical injury. . . .

The medical thesis was advanced with great earnestness by two psychiatrists, both of whom were apparently well regarded in the medical community. So for our purposes here we may assume that on a proper showing of facts, or medical facts, or accepted medical theory as fact, the law may accommodate Blackstone and Freud to allow recovery for real psychic or psychosomatic harm. Rather, we have dwelt at some length on this phase of the case because it was, after all, a medical theory which we may assume arguendo the jury could have credited but was not compelled to. More important, it is against this background that the very narrow claim of error and harmful effect must be judged.

The Court gave a long and detailed general charge covering sixteen pages of the record. It covered the usual matters such as credibility, fact-finding function of the jury, principles of negligence law, due care, proximate cause, elements of damages, and was generally indistinguishable from the many general charges which Louisiana Federal Judges, on their common law oasis in the midst of a civil law system, have to give in these direct action cases. No exception was taken to any substantive instruction on the governing principles of law. . . .

. . . The real controversy raged over the question whether Clegg had really suffered any damage at all. The plaintiff said he was worse off and that this episode had triggered this psychic mechanism. The Insurer, just as stoutly, claimed that Clegg was better, not worse, off, and that it was simply absurd to say that a truck owner should be held responsible for any such farfetched consequences. This was the issue, then, of proximate cause.

Finally, there was the question of the money award to compensate for the damages if any were found. From Clegg's standpoint, this ranged from some $1,900 covering numerous small items of medical, psychiatric, hospital bills, and car rental to a demand for $75,000 to $250,000 for mental pain and anguish. To the Insurer the amount was zero.

These were the precise questions, in that very order, which counsel argued vehemently. These were the precise questions, in that very order, which the Court asked the jury to answer. Indeed, to read the arguments now, it is almost as though each had been advised specifically that these very questions would be put. Moreover, these are the very precise questions which the jury would have to answer under the same general principles stated to them had the verdict form been the traditional one. . . .

. . . To resolve this elusive and abstruse medico-psychic debate was, as plaintiffs counsel put it, "the function of the jury." To this the District Court responded, "Well, they functioned." And since no error is found and the verdict is binding on all, including this Court, we may conclude that the Court below had the prerogative to say that "They functioned right."

Affirmed.

One of the ancient "maxims" of jurisprudence states that "he who comes to equity" (i.e., applies to the court for relief) must come with "clean hands." In the following case, the fearsome, cantankerous and semi-literate "frontier" Judge, Richard C. Barry, was able to discern that plaintiff John Brown did *not* have "clean hands," and was not about to put up with it.

BROWN v. SCHEOPH

Justice Court of California, Tuolomne County
Case No. 39 (1850)

R. C. BARRY, JUSTICE PEACE

This was a case in which John Brown brought sute to recover from E. Scheoph one goold watch, and 2 goold wrings of the valee of about 250 dolars. After hearing the evidence in the caze I adjeudged that Brown was trying to swindle Mr. Scheoph. I therefore dismissed the case and found 50 dolars which not having I caused him to be taken to jail until he paid.

Costs of Court $40, 20 of which Mr. Scheoph pade.

May 31, 1850

U. H. Brown, acting Constable.

It is the duty and the province of our courts to attempt to make reasonable sense out of some of the most convoluted and byzantine fact patterns imaginable. In the following case, the court does an admirable job of describing and analyzing the facts, applying the relevant law and tossing in a peck of humor to boot.

THE PEOPLE OF CALIFORNIA
v. GLEGHORN

California Court of Appeals, Second Appellate District
193 Cal. App.3d 196; 238 Cal. Rptr. 82 (1987)

STEVEN J. STONE, PRESIDING JUDGE

May a person who enters the habitat of another at 3 o'clock in the morning for the announced purpose of killing him, and who commences to beat the startled sleeper's bed with a stick and set fires

171

under him be entitled to use deadly force in self-defense after the intended victim shoots him in the back with an arrow? Upon the basis of these bizarre facts, we hold that he may not, and instead, must suffer the slings and arrows of outrageous fortune (with apologies to William Shakespeare and *Hamlet*, Act III, sc. 1).

Kelsey Dru Gleghorn appeals his conviction by jury of one count of simple assault (Pen. Code, §240) and one count of battery with the infliction of serious bodily injury (Pen. Code, §243, subd. [d]). He contends the trial court erred in denying his motion for mistrial based on his allegation of inconsistent verdicts and insufficient evidence to support the conviction on count II and erred in instructing the jury pursuant to CALJIC 5.42. We find no error and affirm the judgment.

FACTS

This case is a parable of the dangers of weaponry in the hands of unreasonable powers who become unduly provoked over minor irritations. Melody Downes shared her house with several persons, including appellant. She rented her garage to Michael Fairall for $150 per month. She believed he was to give her a stereo as part of the rent. He believed her intent was only to borrow it. He asked for the return of the stereo; she said she sold it.

Fairall, a man of obvious sensitivity, smashed all the windows of her automobile, slashed the tires and dented the body. Not quite mollified, he kicked in her locked door, scattered her belongings in the bedroom and broke an aquarium, freeing her snake. (It was scotched, not killed. See *Macbeth*, W. Shakespeare.)

Ms. Downes advised appellant of Fairall's behavior, he apparently took umbrage. On the fateful night in question, Fairall, having quaffed a few, went to the garage he called home and then to bed, a mattress laid upon a lofty perch in the rafters. He was rudely awakened by a pounding on the garage door accompanied by appellant's request that he come out so that appellant might kill him. Fairall wisely advised him that they could exchange pleasantries in the morning.

Undeterred, appellant opened the garage door, entered with stick in hand and began beating on the rafters, yelling for Fairall to come

172

down. In the darkness, Fairall claimed he could see sparks where the board hit the rafters. Appellant said that if Fairall did not come down, he would burn him out. No sooner said than done, appellant set a small fire to some of Fairall's clothes.

Fairall, who happened to have secreted a bow and quiver of arrows in the rafters to prevent its theft, loosed one but did not see where it landed.[1] Fairall, abandoning his weapons, swung down from the rafters and was immediately hit from behind. He yelled for someone to bring a hose and attempted to extinguish the fire with his hands.

Meanwhile, appellant, in an ill humor from the gash in his back caused by the arrow, continued to beat him, causing a two-inch-wide vertical break in Fairall's lower jaw, tearing his lips, knocking out 6 to 10 teeth, mangling two fingers and lacerating his arm, stomach and back. Fairall also suffered burns on the palms of his hands.

Fairall testified under a grant of immunity given concerning the vandalism of the car.

DISCUSSION
1. Verdicts Not Inconsistent.

The jury returned verdicts of guilty of simple assault as a lesser included offense of assault by means of force likely to incur great bodily injury (Pen. Code, §245, subd. [a][1]) on count I and of battery with the infliction of serious bodily injury on count II. Appellant moved for a new trial. . . .

Generally, if one makes a felonious assault upon another, or has created appearances justifying the other to launch a deadly counter attack in self-defense, the original assailant cannot slay his adversary in self-defense unless he has first, in good faith, declined further combat, and has fairly notified him that he has abandoned the affray {citation omitted}. However, when the victim of simple assault responds in a sudden and deadly counter assault, the original aggressor need not

---

[1]"I shot an arrow into the air, it fell to earth, I knew not where" ("The Arrow and the Song," Henry Wadsworth Longfellow). In this case, appellant learned where it had landed—in his back.

attempt to withdraw and may use reasonably necessary force in self-defense {citation omitted}.

Appellant contends that, since he initially committed only a simple assault, he was legally justified as a matter of law in standing his ground even though he was the initial attacker, and in utilizing lethal force against Fairall. . . .

The right of self-defense is based upon the appearance of imminent peril to the person attacked {citation omitted}. The right to defend one's person or home with deadly force depends upon the circumstances as they reasonably appeared to that person {citation omitted}. That right cannot depend upon the appellant's supposedly non-felonious secret intent {citation omitted}. Similarly, justification does not depend upon the existence of actual danger but rather upon appearances, i.e., if a reasonable person would be placed in fear for his or her safety, and defendant acted out of that fear {citation omitted}.

Moreover, even though a person is mistaken in judgment as to the actual necessity for use of extreme measures, if he was misled through no fault of carelessness on his part and defends himself correctly according to what he supposed the facts to be, his act is justifiable. . . .

Here, the jury could reasonably infer from the evidence that: (1) Fairall acted reasonably upon the appearances that his life was in danger or (2) even if Fairall acted unreasonably in shooting appellant with the arrow and appellant was justified in responding with deadly force, appellant continued to beat his attacker long after the attacker was disabled. If a person attacked defends himself so successfully that his attacker is rendered incapable of inflicting injury, or for any other reason the danger no longer exists, there is no justification for further retaliation.

The evidence supports a finding that Fairall did not threaten or take any action against appellant after Fairall descended from the loft. On the other hand, if the jury found, as it could have, that Fairall was justified in reasonably fearing for his life on the appearances of appellant's actions, appellant never obtained the right of self-defense in the first place. We find no error. . . .

The judgment is affirmed.

The following case involves an energetic and creative effort
by a former "scholar" at Columbia University to avoid paying
the balance due on his student loan.

TRUSTEES OF COLUMBIA UNIVERSITY
v. JACOBSEN

Superior Court of New Jersey, Appellate Division
53 N.J. Super. 574; 148 A.2d 63 (1959)

SIDNEY GOLDMANN, S.J.A.D.

... Columbia brought suit in the district court against defendant
and his parents on two notes made by him and signed by them as
co-makers, representing the balance of tuition he owed the
University. The principal due amounted to $1,049.50, but plaintiff
sued for only $1,000, waiving any demand for judgment in excess of
the jurisdictional limit of the court.

Defendant then sought to file an answer and counterclaim
demanding, among other things, money damages in the sum of
$7,016. The counterclaim was in 50 counts which severally alleged
that plaintiff had represented that it would teach defendant wisdom,
truth, character, enlightenment, understanding, justice, liberty, honesty, courage, beauty and similar virtues and qualities; that it would
develop the whole man, maturity, well-roundedness, objective thinking and the like; and that because it had failed to do so it was guilty
of misrepresentation, to defendant's pecuniary damage. ...

Following oral argument the Law Division judge refused to disqualify himself and concluded that the statements attributed by
defendant to plaintiff did not constitute a false representation. The
judgment under appeal was then entered.

Following a successful freshman year at Dartmouth, defendant
entered Columbia in the fall of 1951. He continued there until the end
of his senior year in the spring of 1954, but was not graduated because
of poor scholastic standing. Plaintiff admits the many quotations from
college catalogues and brochures, inscriptions over University buildings and addresses by University officers cited in the schedules
annexed to the counterclaim. The sole question is whether these
statements constitute actionable misrepresentations. ...

The attempt of the counterclaim, inartistically drawn as it is, was

175

to state a cause of action in deceit. The necessary elements of that action are by now hornbook law; a false representation, knowledge or belief on the part of the person making the representation that it is false, an intention that the other party act thereon, reasonable reliance by such party in so doing, and resultant damage to him. . . .

We are in complete agreement with the trial court that the counterclaim fails to establish the very first element, false representation, basic to any action in deceit. Plaintiff stands by every quotation relied on by defendant. Only by reading into them the imagined meanings he attributes to them can one conclude—and the conclusion would be a most tenuous, insubstantial one—that Columbia University represented it could teach wisdom, truth, justice, beauty, spirituality and all other qualities set out in the 50 counts of the counterclaim.

A sampling from the quotations cited by defendant will suffice as illustration. Defendant quotes from a Columbia College brochure stating that

> . . . Columbia College provides a liberal arts education. . . . A liberal arts course . . . has extremely positive values of its own. Chief among these, perhaps, is something which has been a principal aim of Columbia College from the beginning: It develops the whole man. . . . [Columbia's] aim remains constant: to foster in its students a desire to learn, a habit of critical judgment, and a deep-rooted sense of personal and social responsibility. . . . [I]ts liberal arts course pursues this aim in five ways. (1) It brings you into firsthand contact with the major intellectual ideas that have helped to shape human thinking and the course of human events. (2) It gives you a broader acquaintance with the rest of the world. (3) It guides you toward an understanding of people and their motivations. (4) It leads you to a comprehending knowledge of the scientific world. (5) It helps you acquire facility in the art of communication. . . .

He then cites the motto of Columbia College and Columbia University: *"In lumine tuo videbimus lumen"* ("In your light we shall see light"), and the inscription over the college chapel: "Wisdom dwelleth in the heart of him that hath understanding." He also refers to an address of the president of Columbia University at its bicentennial convocation:

> There can never have been a time in the history of the world when men had greater need of wisdom. . . . I mean an understanding of man's rela-

tionship to his fellow men and to the universe. . . . To this task of educational leadership in a troubled time and in an uncertain world, Columbia, like other great centers of learning in free societies, unhesitatingly dedicates itself. . . .

We have thoroughly combed all the statements upon which defendant relies in his counterclaim, as well as the exhibits he handed up to the trial judge, including one of 59 pages setting out his account of the circumstances leading up to the present action. They add up to nothing more than a fairly complete exposition of Columbia's objectives, desires and hopes, together with factual statements as to the nature of some of the courses included in its curricula. As plaintiff correctly observes, what defendant is seeking to do is to assign to the quoted excerpts a construction and interpretation peculiarly subjective to him and completely unwarranted by the plain sense and meaning of the language used. To defendant a college is not "Mark Hopkins at one end of a log and the student at the other," but his dream of a universal scholar *cum* philosopher *cum* humanitarian at one end of the school bench and defendant at the other.

At the heart of defendant's counterclaim is a single complaint. He concedes that:

> I have really only one charge against Columbia: that it does not teach Wisdom as it claims to do. From this charge ensues an endless number of charges, of which I have selected fifty at random. I am prepared to show that each of these fifty claims in turn is false, though the central issue is that of Columbia's pretense of teaching Wisdom.

We agree with the trial judge that wisdom is not a subject which can be taught and that no rational person would accept such a claim made by any man or institution. We find nothing in the record to establish that Columbia represented, expressly or even by way of impression, that it could or would teach wisdom or the several qualities which defendant insists are "synonyms for or aspects of the same Quality." The matter is perhaps best summed up in the supporting affidavit of the Dean of Columbia College, where he said that "All any college can do through its teachers, libraries, laboratories and other facilities is to endeavor to teach the student the known facts, acquaint him with the nature of those matters which are unknown, and thereby assist him in developing mentally, morally and physically. Wisdom is

177

a hoped-for end product of education, experience and ability which many seek and many fail to attain."

Defendant's extended argument lacks the element of fraudulent representation indispensable to any action of deceit. We note, in passing, that he has cited no legal authority whatsoever for his position. Instead, he has submitted a dictionary definition of "wisdom" and quotations from such works as the Bhagavad-Gita, the Mundaka Upanishad, the Analects of Confucius and the Koran; excerpts from Euripides, Plato and Meander; and references to the Bible. Interesting though these may be, they do not support defendant's indictment of Columbia. If his pleadings, affidavit and exhibits demonstrate anything, it is indeed the validity of what Pope said in his Moral Essays:

> *A little learning is a dangerous thing;*
> *Drink deep, or taste not the Pierian spring. . . .*

The papers make clear that through the years defendant's interest has shifted from civil engineering to social work, then to physics, and finally to English and creative writing. In college he became increasingly critical of his professors and his courses; in his last year he attended classes only when he chose and rejected the regimen of examinations and term papers. When his non-attendance at classes and his poor work in the senior year were called to his attention by the Columbia Dean of Students, he replied in a lengthy letter that "I want to learn, but I must do it in my own way. I realize my behavior is non-conforming, but in these times when there are so many forces that demand conformity I hope I will find Columbia willing to grant some freedom to a student who wants to be a literary artist." In short, he chose to judge Columbia's educational system by the shifting standards of his own fancy, and now seeks to place his failure at Columbia's door on the theory that it had deliberately misrepresented that it taught wisdom.

III.

In light of our conclusion that the defendant has failed to state a cause of action in deceit based on fraudulent representation, we need not deal with plaintiff's further contentions. . . .

V.

In view of the entirely unjustified accusations made against the trial judge and the intemperate characterization (so admitted by defendant at the oral argument) of the proceedings below, defendant's appendix and brief will be suppressed and all copies withdrawn from the clerk's files.

The judgment is affirmed.

CHAPTER VII

Scoundrels, *C*rooks, *O*utlaws, *R*enegades, *R*ogues, *K*naves and Other *M*iscreants; *T*heir *C*rimes, Grand and *P*etty; and the *P*rocesses and *P*rocedures *R*elated *T*hereto

Despite history, general observation, and daily chronicles which record countless examples of evidence to the contrary, the fable persists that every person, including the worst villains of mankind, standing on the brink of eternity, allow only pearls of veracity to fall from their lips. ... Napoleon Bonaparte, with a fertility which surpassed Baron Munchausen's, invented memorabilia which still confuses historians, as he made ready for his last Waterloo. Nor is it recorded that Herod, Nero, Caligula, Tamburlaine, Attila, Genghis Khan, Alaric the Goth, Mithridates, Ivan the Terrible, Stalin or any of the other infamous scoundrels down through the ages regaled their entourages with stories on the moral verities as they were ferried across the river Styx. ... Godless ruffians, feudists, bandits, gangsters, all bent on their greedy, rapacious and vengeful deeds, have no scruples about dying as they lived— with hate, dishonesty, and deceit in their mouths. ...
—Michael A. Musmanno, J.[1]

In works of labour, or of skill,
I would be busy too;
For Satan finds some mischief still
For idle hands to do.
—Isaac Watts[2]

---

[1]From dissenting opinion criticizing the rule that a dying declaration may be given same probative value as sworn testimony. In Commonwealth of Pennsylvania v. Brown, 388 Pa. 613; 131 A.2d 367 (1957).

[2]From State of Missouri v. Knowles, 739 S.W.2d 753 (1987), (Anthony P. Nugent, Jr., P.J.).

Once in a great while . . . (ahem) . . . lawyers are accused of being petty, carping, niggling, slippery, self-serving, nit-picking, sneaky, loophole-mongering bug-wits. For example, in the next case, the attorney for the defendant noticed a technical flaw in the criminal charges filed by the county prosecutor against his client.

STATE OF MISSOURI v. KNOWLES

Court of Appeals of Missouri
739 S.W.2d 753 (1987)

ANTHONY P. NUGENT, JR., PRESIDING JUDGE

> *In works of labour, or of skill,*
> *I would be busy too;*
> *For Satan finds some mischief still*
> *For idle hands to do.*
> —Isaac Watts

As Mark Twain might have put it, this is a tale about what gets into folks when they don't have enough to do.

Old Dave Baird, the prosecuting attorney up in Nodaway County, thought he had a case against Les Knowles for receiving stolen property, to-wit, a chain saw, so he ups and files on Les.

Now Les was a bit impecunious, so the judge appointed him a lawyer, old Dan Radke, the public defender from down around St. Joe. Now Dan, he looks at that old information[1] and decides to pick a nit or two, so he tells the judge that the information old Dave filed against Les is no good, that under the law it doesn't even charge Les with a crime. Dan says Dave charged that Les "kept" the stolen chain saw and that's not against the law. You don't commit that crime by "keeping" the chain saw, says Dan; the law says you commit the crime of "receiving" if you "retain" the saw, and that's not what Dave charged Les with, and the judge should throw Dave out of court. And that's exactly what the judge did.

But old Dave was not having any of that. No, sir! That information is right out of the book. MACH-CR 24.10. Word for word! Yes, sir!

Bystanders could plainly see the fire in old Dave's eyes. He was not

---

[1]{Ed. Note: An "information" is a formal accusation of crime against a defendant, similar to an "indictment."}

backing down. Sure. Dave could simply refile and start over with a new information by changing only one word. Strike "kept"; insert "retained." But that is not the point. Dave knows he is right.

And so he is.

So we'll just send the case back to Judge Kennish and tell the boys to get on with the prosecution. And here's why:

The prosecuting attorney filed an information charging defendant Leslie Paul Kowles with receiving stolen property {a chain saw} and ... that the defendant ... had "kept" the property. ... knowing or believing that it had been stolen. . . .

The form of the information precisely follows the form for the offense of receiving stolen property set out in Missouri Approved Charges-Criminal (MACH-CR No. 24.10) promulgated by the Missouri Supreme Court. . . .

Rather than simply filing a new information in a slightly modified form, the prosecuting attorney chose to go to the mat with defendant. . . .

> The statute in question {provides that the crime of receiving stolen property is established where the defendant} "receives, retains or disposes of property of another knowing that it has been stolen, or believing that it has been stolen."

. . . An indictment or information must plainly, concisely and definitely state the essential facts constituting the offense charged. The rules do not require that the charge be brought only in the language of the statute.

The only question presented here is whether an information meant to charge a defendant under the receiving statute is sufficient if it charges that he "kept" the property rather than charging that he "retained" it. The answer is quite simply, "Yes." That is the end of the case.

Accordingly, we reverse the judgment and order that the prosecution proceed on the first amended information.

All concur.

At times, the subject matter of a particular case is of such dimension and girth that the judge's creative and whimsical inclination simply cannot be artificially restrained; but rather, bursts forth, spilling out onto the pages of the opinion itself.

IN THE MATTER OF CHARLOTTE K.
Family Court, Richmond County, New York
102 Misc.2d 848; 427 N.Y.S.2d 370 (1980)

DANIEL D. LEDDY, JR., JUDGE

Is a girdle a burglar's tool or is that stretching the plain meaning of Penal Law Sec. 140.35? This elastic issue of first impression arises out of a charge that the respondent shoplifted certain items from Macy's Department Store by dropping them into her girdle.

Basically, Corporation Counsel argues that respondent used her girdle as a kangaroo does her pouch, thus adapting it beyond its maiden form.

The Law Guardian snaps back charging that with this artificial expansion of Sec. 140.35's meaning, the foundation of Corporation Counsel's argument plainly sags. The Law Guardian admits that respondent's tight security was an attempt to evade the store's own tight security. And yet, it was not a tool, instrument or other article adapted, designed or commonly used for committing or facilitating offenses involving larceny by physical taking. It was instead an article of clothing, which, being worn under all, was after all a place to hide all. It was no more a burglar's tool than a pocket, or maybe even a kangaroo's pouch.

The tools, instruments or other articles envisioned by Penal Law Sec. 140.35 are those used in taking an item and not in hiding it thereafter. They are the handy gadgets used to break in and pick up, and not the bags for carrying out. Such is the legislative intent of this section, as is evident from the Commission Staff Comments on the Revised Penal Law of 1965 Title I, Article 140, N. Sec. 140.35, which reads in relevant part:

> The new section, by reference to instruments "involving larceny" ... expands the crime to include possession of numerous other *tools*, such as those used for breaking into motor vehicles, stealing from public telephone coin boxes, tampering with gas and electric meters, and the like. (Emphasis added.)

The Court has decided this issue mindful of the heavy burden that a contrary decision would place upon retail merchants. Thus is avoided the real bind of having customers check not only their packages, but their girdles too, at the department store's door.

The Court must also wonder whether such a contrary decision would not create a spate of unreasonable bulges that would let loose the floodgates of stop-and-frisk cases, with the result of putting the squeeze on court resources already overextended in this era of trim governmental budgets.

Accordingly, the instant allegation of possession of burglar's tools is dismissed.

———————

The following opinion stands as a monument to the intrepid judicial spirit, ready always to fearlessly venture into uncharted jurisprudential territory, even to the point of submitting an opinion in poetic form as a rejoinder to a colleague's challenge.

BROWN v. THE STATE OF GEORGIA
Court of Appeals of Georgia
134 Ga. App. 771; 216 S.E.2d 356 (1975)

RANDALL EVANS, JUDGE

The D. A. was ready
His case was red-hot.
Defendant was present,
His witness was not.

He prayed one day's delay
From His honor the judge.
But his plea was not granted
The Court would not budge.

So the jury was empaneled
All twelve good and true
But without his main witness
What could the twelve do?[1]

———

[1] This opinion is placed in rhyme because approximately one year ago, in Savannah at a very convivial celebration, the distinguished Judge Dunbar Harrison, Senior Judge of Chatham

185

The jury went out
To consider his case
And then they returned
The defendant to face.

"What verdict, Mr. Foreman?"
The learned judge inquired.
"Guilty, your honor."
On Brown's face—no smile.

"Stand up," said the judge,
Then quickly announced
"Seven years at hard labor"
Thus his sentence pronounced.

"This trial was not fair,"
The defendant then sobbed.
"With my main witness absent
I've simply been robbed.

"I want a new trial—
State has not fairly won."
"New trial denied,"
Said Judge Dunbar Harrison.

"If you still say I'm wrong,"
The able judge did then say,
"Why not appeal to Atlanta?
Let those Appeals Judges earn part of their pay."

"I will appeal, sir"—
Which he proceeded to do—
"They can't treat me worse
Than I've been treated by you."

So the case has reached us—
And now we must decide
Was the guilty verdict legal—
Or should we set it aside?

Superior Courts, arose and addressed those assembled, and demanded that if Judge Randall Evans, Jr., ever again was so presumptuous as to reverse one of his decisions, that the opinion be written in poetry. I readily admit I am unable to comply, because I am not a poet, and the language used, at best, is mere doggerel. I have done my best but my limited ability just did not permit the writing of a great poem. It was no easy task to write the opinion in rhyme.

186

Justice and fairness
Must prevail at all times;
This is ably discussed
In a case without rhyme.

The law of this State
Does guard every right
Of those charged with crime
Fairness always in sight.

To continue civil cases
The judge holds all aces.
But it's a different ball-game
In criminal cases.

Was one day's delay
Too much to expect?
Could the State refuse it
With all due respect?

Did Justice applaud
Or shed bitter tears
When this news from Savannah
First fell on her ears?

We've considered this case
Through the night—through the day.
As Judge Harrison said,
"We must earn our poor pay."

This case was once tried—
But should now be rehearsed
And tried one more time.
This case is reversed!

Judgment reversed.

———————————

187

Richard C. Barry, the notorious and nearly illiterate Justice of the Peace for Tuolomne County, California, during the gold-rush era of 1849–1851, regularly meted out his stern brand of "frontier" justice with scant regard for either "book-law" or the rules of grammar and spelling. The following "Coroner's Reports," filed by Judge Barry in his capacity as acting Coroner for Tuolomne County, provide a unique glimpse of the primitive and often violent nature of life during the gold-rush period.

IN RE WILLEM DOF
Justice Court of California, Tuolumne County
Coroner's Report No. 1 (1850)

R. C. BARRY, JUSTICE PEACE AND CORONER PRO TEM
No. 1—Willem Dof who was murthered with Buck October 20th 1850, (one mile from ofice,) after heering the evedense do find that he was barberously murthered, and that there was found $13 on the boddy of deseased, which ammount I handed over to the Publick Administrator, J. M. Huntingdon. Nothing more found to be his—no clue to his murtherers. Justice Fees $10.

IN RE MICHAL BURCK
Justice Court of California, Tuolumne County
Coroner's Report No. 2 (1850)

R. C. BARRY, JUSTICE PEACE AND ACTING CORONER
No. 2—Michal Burck, found murthered one mile from my ofice October 20 1850, after dilegent sarch I find no deffects upon diseased. I couldn't find any clu to who murthered him.
Justice Fees $10.

IN RE GEORGE WILLIAMS
Justice Court of California, Tuolumne County
Coroner's Report No. 3 (1850)

R. C. BARRY, JUSTICE PEACE AND ACTING CORONER
No. 3—George Williams who cutt his throt with a razor October 22 1850. Having heerd the evidense it is evident it is a case of Felo de see. Said Williams had no property that I could find out.
Justice fees, $10.

188

IN RE DR. JAMES SAY

Justice Court of California, Tuolumne County
Coroner's Report No. 4 (1850)

R. C. BARRY, JUSTICE PEACE AND ACTING CORONER

No. 4—October 28th 1850. It was roomered that Dr. James Say was poisoned but upon a "bost morteum" examination by Dr. Bradshaw found that he died of disease of the hart. I found no property excepting $50 which I used in burrying the boddy.

Justice fees, $10.

IN RE T. NEWLY

Justice Court of California, Tuolumne County
Coroner's Report No. 5 (1850)

R. C. BARRY, JUSTICE PEACE AND ACTING CORONER

No. 5—T. Newley killed by Fuller who shot him with a gunn January 30 1851. I found no property on the diseased. After trying Fuller and finding him guilty he was committed by me, and sentensed by the Court to two years confinement. He broke jale and run off.

Justice fees $10.

IN RE WM. A. BOWEN

Justice Court of California, Tuolumne County
Coroner's Report No. 10 (1850)

R. C. BARRY, JUSTICE PEACE AND ACTING CORONER

No. 10—Wm. A. Bowen was found murthered morning of April 2, 1851—back of Washington street, ner Holdens Garden, was cut to deth with a knife—No clue to the guilty party, or who perpredaded the murther.

Justice fees $10.

IN RE WILLIAM BROWN
Justice Court of California, Tuolumne County
Coroner's Report No. 11 (1850)

R. C. BARRY, JUSTICE PEACE AND ACTING CORONER
Wm. Brown found hanging to a tree May 1, 1851 ner Wood's Creek, supposed he suicided himself two miles from town, no testimony. No property found to belong to him.
Justice fees $10.

IN RE ANONYMOUS
Justice Court of California, Tuolumne County
Coroner's Report No. 14 (1850)

R. C. BARRY, JUSTICE PEACE AND ACTING CORONER
No. 14—Unknown man June 11 1851 found dead on the trale to Sullivan's creek, no wounds on the boddy. After hearing all the surcumstances I concluded he died a natural deth. No property found on the boddy but a roll of blankets, a knife and pistol.
Justice fees $10.

IN RE JAMES HILL
Justice Court of California, Tuolumne County
Coroner's Report No. 18 (1850)

R. C. BARRY, JUSTICE PEACE AND ACTING CORONER
No. 18—Inquest on the body of Jas. Hill hung by the mob back of Lecocks, June 29, 1851. No clue to the parties purpedrading the hanging.
Justice Fees $10.

IN RE WILLIAM CLARK
Justice Court of California, Tuolumne County
Coroner's Report No. 19 (1850)

R. C. BARRY, JUSTICE PEACE AND ACTING CORONER
No. 19—Inquest upon the boddy of William Clark, July 16, 1851, was found dead in his bead about a mile north of this office in a Tent under verry supposed suspicions surcomstances but was found on

examination to have died suddenly a natural death by diseese of the hart and lungs. No property but an old Tent, and a few little cooking, and keeping fixtures. Appropriaded them burrying the body.

Justice Fees $10.

IN RE HUNGRY TOM
Justice Court of California, Tuolumne County
Coroner's Report No. 20 (1850)

R. C. BARRY, JUSTICE PEACE AND ACTING CORONER

No. 20—Hungry Tom, or Tom Welsh found stabed to deth July 20, 1851, supposed to have been fighting. No property found on his boddy but a large knife.

Justice Fees $10.

IN RE JUAN MONTALDA
Justice Court of California, Tuolumne County
Coroner's Report No. 21 (1850)

R. C. BARRY, JUSTICE PEACE AND ACTING CORONER

No. 21—Juan Montalda July 20, 1851, found killed with his guts cut out, and stabbed to deth under same surcomstances and place. No evidence produced on his boddy was $51 which I appropriated to burrying the bodies.

Justice Fees $10.

IN RE WILLIAM FORD
Justice Court of California, Tuolumne County
Coroner's Report No. 22 (1850)

R. C. BARRY, JUSTICE PEACE AND ACTING CORONER

William Ford, deputy sheriff, July 28, was shot and killed by a young man called Stud Horse Bob. Was considered justifiable, no property found with him but had some means in the hands of Major Holden who administered arrested him and examined the case no falt found.

Justice Fees $10.

Apparently, the judges of Northumberland County in the "jolly old" realm of England in A.D. 1279 did not approve, endorse or condone the old adage "finders keepers, losers weepers," as the following case clearly demonstrates.

IN RE TWO POTS

Assize Court of Northumberland County
Northumberland Assize Roll, 7 Edward I (1279)

ANONYMOUS, JUDGE

The jurors report that two pots were found in a field outside of the village of Tholkestor, and many valuables were found in them, but they do not know what the valuables were nor whose treasure it was. And they say that Simon, son of Folentinus and Robert Brand were the finders of this same treasure 22 years ago. They say that after they found the treasure, their standard of living increased a great deal. The aforesaid Simon is present; accordingly, let him be kept under guard. Robert is not present; accordingly, let him be put under arrest.

It is said that swift and sure punishment is the best deterrent to crime. Should this concept be expanded to permit the local authorities to impose immediate capital punishment by decapitation whenever a criminal suspect confesses to an offense?

IN RE GILBERT OF NIDDESDALE

Assize Court of Northumberland County
Northumberland Assize Roll, 40 Henry III (1256)

ANONYMOUS, JUDGE

The jurors report that a certain Gilbert of Niddesdale, a stranger, struck up an acquaintance with a certain hermit, whose name is Semannus of Bottlesham, and they were walking together in a certain moor, when this same Gilbert laid hold of that hermit and beat him, wounded him, and left him for dead, and stole from him his clothes and one penny, and fled. As he was fleeing, he ran into Randolph of Beleford, a sergeant of our lord the King, who laid hold of him and charged him with being a criminal, and took him to Alnwick. The aforesaid hermit came to Alnwick, and said that that other had robbed him and beat him, as was stated above. This same Gilbert confessed to same in the presence of the aforesaid bailiff and the people of the village of Alnwick. So the aforesaid sergeant had the aforesaid hermit cut Gilbert's head off. When the sheriff and coroner are asked by what warrant they had had Gilbert decapitated, they say that such is the custom of the county, that as soon as anyone is caught red-handed he is to be decapitated forthwith, and the plaintiff will receive the property of the one who is to be decapitated in place of what had been stolen from him.

Under ancient English law, when a crime occurred anywhere in the realm, it had to be vindicated either by means of some punishment imposed upon the criminal or, if the criminal escaped, by means of a fine assessed against the inhabitants of the village where the crime occurred. The fine, of course, was payable directly to the Crown. This system undoubtedly encouraged the citizenry to remain vigilant and actively involved in crime prevention.

IN RE JOHN OF CRAUMFORD
Assize Court of Northumberland County
Northumberland Assize Roll, 40 Henry III (1256)

ANONYMOUS, JUDGE

John of Craumford fled to the church of Bamburgh and there confessed to highway robbery, and abjured the realm in the presence of William of Bamburgh, who was then coroner. He had no property. Witness has been borne that the entire town charged him with highway robbery and wanted to arrest him, but he escaped from their hands to the aforesaid church, as related above; accordingly the village is to be fined. The 12 jurors concealed this matter; accordingly they, too, are to be fined.

For generations, legal scholars and judges alike have debated the merits of the so-called "dying declaration" rule, which provides that certain accusatory statements made by a dying person as to who or what caused the fatal injuries may be introduced into evidence at the trial of a criminal defendant, with the presumption that such statements (which are otherwise considered hearsay) have the *same* evidentiary "value" as live testimony delivered under oath. The problem, of course, is determining whether or not a dying declaration is really truthful and accurate, since at the time of trial, the declarant is dead and thus not available for cross-examination.

COMMONWEALTH OF PENNSYLVANIA
v. BROWN
Supreme Court of Pennsylvania
388 Pa. 613; 131 A.2d 367 (1957)

JOHN C. BELL, JR., JUSTICE

A narrow but very important question is raised in this case: Was it reversible error to charge the jury that a dying declaration in a homicide case has the same effect as if it were made under oath?

Mary E. Brown was indicted for murder but was convicted of voluntary manslaughter. Defendant and Vivian Gay, apparently in a fit of jealousy, attacked Dorothy Francis, the decedent, on the street. Dorothy Francis was killed by a knife wound in the breast. Who stabbed her was the crucial factual question, Vivian Gay blaming Mary Brown and Mary Brown blaming Vivian Gay. Two eyewitnesses testified that defendant, Mary Brown, attacked Dorothy Francis with a knife, while Vivian Gay beat her with a golf club. . . . Dorothy Francis, just before her death and at a time when she knew she was about to die, made a dying declaration that Mary Brown, the defendant, stabbed her. . . .

A dying declaration should in our judgment be given the same value and weight as sworn testimony, and any statement to the contrary in prior cases will not be followed by us.

Judgment affirmed.

MICHAEL A. MUSMANNO, JUSTICE *(dissenting)*

The Majority Opinion in this case helps to perpetuate the myth that dying persons always tell the truth. Despite history, general observation and daily chronicles which record countless examples of evidence to the contrary, the fable persists that every person, including the worst villains of mankind, standing on the brink of eternity, allow only pearls of veracity to fall from their lips. Adolf Hitler told some of the most monumental falsehoods which ever disgraced the human race (even for that congenital prevaricator) as he prepared to kill himself in the subterranean bunker in Berlin in the closing days of his conscienceless life. Napoleon Bonaparte, with a fertility which surpassed Baron Munchausen's, invented memorabilia which still confuse historians, as he made ready for his last Waterloo. Nor is it recorded that Herod, Nero, Caligula, Tamburlaine, Attila, Genghis Khan, Alaric the Goth, Mithridates, Ivan the Terrible, Stalin or any of the other infamous scoundrels down through the ages regaled their entourages with stories on the moral verities as they were ferried across the river Styx.

The perpetrators of all the unsolved murders in the world are liars who go down to their grave wholly oblivious to the angels of truth crying for confession and revealment. Atheists who repudiate belief in a Supreme Being have no inhibitions against wagging their tongues in spurious tales as death rattles in their throats. Godless ruffians, feudists, bandits, gangsters, all bent on their greedy, rapacious and vengeful deeds, have no scruples about dying as they lived—with hate, dishonesty and deceit in their mouths.

In her recently published book on the life and times of Sir Edward Coke, Catherine Drinker Bowen relates how in Lord Cobham's accusation of treason against Sir Walter Raleigh it was generally accepted that, because Lord Cobham was himself soon to be executed, his charges could only represent truth: "Impossible that a man with death so close upon him would lie thus to the Lords. What had he to gain thereby?" Yet it developed later that Cobham had lied because he hoped thereby to receive sovereign clemency. He in fact later did escape the death penalty.

To say that the world can invariably depend on the truth-speaking accuracy of a dying person is to ignore the most fundamental, physiological facts. Putting aside for the moment the undependability of knaves in their last, gasping moments, it should be manifest on the slightest reflection that even the statements of the most honorable persons on their deathbeds are not necessarily reliable. A dying person is at the ebb of his physical and mental resources. With every corpuscle struggling for survival, with every brain cell ringing in alarm, with the lungs fighting for that extra breath of air which may prolong the buoyancy of the ship of life sinking rapidly in the dark waves of oblivion, the mind is not always capable of assembling the forces of memory, concentration and lingual control so as to guide speech into the channels of rational utterance. To juridically announce that a dying statement is the superlative demonstration of revealed fact is to glorify error, honor fallacy and place the seal of infallibility on the most fallible of human assertions.

Moreover, it is not always certain that a person in extremis is consciously aware that the candle is about to be extinguished or will admit to himself that his body is reverting to mortal dust. It is an assumption which has never been proved, nor can it be proved, that when a moribund speaks, he knows his minutes are numbered. He may declare that he is dying, but with the exception of those who are preparing for suicide or execution, it cannot be established that with the very acknowledgment of anticipated death, he is not hoping and expecting that an untapped reservoir of strength may prolong what no one surrenders voluntarily.

These observations are so obvious and so irrefutable that one cannot help but wonder why the phantasy has grown that the last words heard above the tumult of the last battle for survival should be the last word in precision, accuracy and trustworthiness. This illusion has come floating down the centuries, with each generation further inflating its ever-expanding balloon proportions, and the time had arrived to burst the age-ridden fallacy which almost amounts to superstition. I was hoping that, with the excellent opportunity before it to do so, this Court would with the lance of logic pierce the bag of this spurious dirigible and bring it down to the terra firma of realism from which it should never have ascended.

It is bad enough to assert that a dying declaration represents the highest expression of certitude, but to say, as the Majority of this Court says in the case before us for review, that dying words must be invested with all the solemnity and sanctity of a statement made under oath, approaches credulousness. More than that, such a ruling is unjust because it clamps about the neck of the accused a yoke which he cannot possible shake off. He is accused by a person he

196

cannot see, he is charged with words he cannot refute, he is attacked with an accusation he cannot counter-attack through cross-examination. Such a ruling requires juries in effect to accept fallible evidence as infallible proof; it calls upon juries to look upon dying speeches as if they were delivered at the altar of forthrightness when in fact they may have been concocted in the laboratory of cunning and deceit.

That there is something awesome about final pronouncements is not to be questioned, but the awesomeness does not assure that an incense lamp of integrity has been lighted at the bedside of the pronouncer. It could just as well be that the gasping speaker is projecting his voice through the smoke of dissimulation. An expiring murderer could have as much motive to falsify as he had to kill. If the Sixth Commandment did not deter him from slaughtering his fellow-man, the Ninth Commandment would present no barrier to his bearing false witness. One who has already smashed the temple of life would find no difficulty in upsetting the pedestal of truth. Hence, the absolute need in treating of dying declarations to present the facts as they are, unvarnished with preconceived notions of sanctity and dependability.

Let the jury know just what occurred and let them decide whether the declarant, in the calm, dispassionate atmosphere of a tribunal of law, would have testified in the same manner as he spoke amid all the passions, fears and pain which assailed him at the moment of his fatal utterance. Let the jury decide whether the declarant would be as categorical in his statements if he were in a courtroom, where he is subject to the laws of perjury as he was when he was beyond the reach of the law and the reprisal of refutation.

Of course, it could happen and it does happen, that at the very breaking of the thread of life one will speak gospel even if he never spoke it before. It can happen and does happen, that as one's soul departs on the flood tide of perpetuity he may wish to leave on the shores behind him only the chapel of haloed truth, but there is nothing in the chronicles of the human race which warrants the conclusion that this is a common experience of man. The probity or falsity of what is left on the shore can only be determined by probing the circumstances which surround the launching of the craft of infinity on the seas of everlastingness. . . .

197

The Majority Opinion fears that a jury could not distinguish between the weight of an unsworn dying declaration and the weight of sworn testimony in court. What is the difference between a statement given as part of the res gestae and sworn testimony in court? Judges do not charge that the jury must accept the spontaneous utterance of the victim of an automobile accident at the time of the accident as if it were spoken before a judge and jury. Why should they invest a dying declaration, which is also in the nature of a spontaneous utterance, with the solemnity of a jurat? A dying declaration would have no standing at all in court were it not that it is an exception to the hearsay rule. To now pile on that exception an additional exception by calling it a sworn statement when it is not a sworn statement at all comes, as I view it, close to depriving a defendant of due process of law. It is already too much that he is denied the constitutional right to confront an accusing witness without magnifying, beyond reality, the nature of that accusation.

The Majority Opinion says:

> Some authorities which limit the value and weight to be given to dying declarations, point out that the declarant may be influenced by hatred or revenge or similar unworthy motives, but this is equally applicable to any despicable character who takes the witness stand.

But there is this difference which the Majority overlooks. The "despicable character who takes the witness stand" must face the batteries of cross-examination. He may, it is true, be influenced by hatred or revenge as the dying person may be, but he cannot conceal his lies, if he is lying, under the impermeability of a shroud.

The Majority says that:

> When a person is faced with death which he knows is impending and he is about to see his Maker face to face, is he not more likely to tell the truth than is a witness in Court who knows that if he lies he will have a locus penitentiae, an opportunity to repent, confess and be absolved of his sin?

The answer to this is Yes. But not all persons are like the person the Majority here describes. If they were, iniquity, injustice, tyranny and inhumanity would disappear from the confines of the earth. It is because there are persons who defy goodness and honor and who accept the cut rates of Mr. Satan at his sulphuric supermarket rather than pay the just price which decency and justice demand, that evil still walks the earth.

In the case at bar it appears that two women, Vivian Gay and the defendant Mary Brown, armed with a golf stick and a knife, set upon one Dorothy Francis with the intention of doing her no good. Jealousy and criss-cross love affairs had fired the passions of this termagant trio and they fought desperately on the street. The arena of battle encompassed a street, a lawn, a flower garden and a truck, around which the shrewish combatants chased one another, as testified to by the husband of Vivian Gay, apparently one of the heart-interests in the quadrangle. This pivotal figure testified that on August 16, 1954, he was walking on the Old Lincoln Highway in Malvern with Dorothy Francis when Mary Brown and his wife Vivian came running toward them. At this point Vivian Gay announced: "The party is on." And it was. . . .

The testimony as to what actually happened during the fatal melee was contradictory, conflicting and generally confusing; one of the witnesses testified: "Three of them all tussling there." But at the hospital, in answer to questions put to her by a police officer, Francis replied that it was Mary Brown who stabbed her. In his charge the Trial Judge said to the jury that the statement made by Dorothy Francis was "to be received by you and considered by you just as though it were made under oath by Dorothy Francis." Later he also said: "If you so find [that Dorothy Francis believed she was dying] then you give that statement the same effect as though it were made under oath in your hearing."

There can be no doubt whatsoever that the Trial Judge's instruction—that the jury was to consider Dorothy Francis's statement as if made under oath in their hearing—considerably influenced the jury and probably dictated to them their verdict. The instruction relieved the jury of the worry and anguish of seeking to ascertain the actual culprit amid the tangle of testimony as to just what did occur in the gory struggle which raged and spent its fury over the suburban expanse mentioned. The jury could well have concluded that if Dorothy Francis's statement had to be accepted by them as sworn testimony, and she did say that Mary Brown killed her, who should know better than she who killed her? The Judge simplified the case for the jury, but the situation was not so simple as the Trial Judge made it. When one speaks of a dying declaration the average listener assumes that the declarant, in full possession of his faculties, coolly and clearly announces: "X shot me" or "Y stabbed me." But the picture is rarely so clearly etched, and it certainly was not so etched in this case. Mary Scott, a student nurse, who was present at the hospital when the police officer was questioning Dorothy Francis, testified that "She [Dorothy Francis] was *mumbling all the time*, but there were times when the mask was off when she was examined." (Emphasis supplied.)

While Dorothy Francis's life blood drained, and her lips mumbled as the officer questioned her, did her answers mirror the irrefutable realities of the battle and flight in which she sought to flee, hide, fight back and escape? Did the mortal wound come from the jagged metal end of the golf stick or from the blade of the knife? These were questions which the jury should have resolved, untrammeled by the command of the presiding Judge that the muttering answers of Dorothy Francis in the hospital were to be accepted as if spoken in court with all the solemnity, dignity and guarantees vouchsafed every accused.

Even so, the jury must have still had some grave doubts because they convicted Mary Brown only of voluntary manslaughter although she had been indicted for murder. Moreover, this was her second trial. The first jury was unable to agree on a unanimous verdict.

Apart from the injustice which may have happened to Mary Brown, I fear for the fate of other defendants who may be innocent but yet be convicted because this Court has placed its anticipated imprimatur of sworn testimony on what may be a mere matter of muttering, mumbling moribundity.

CHAPTER VIII

Wills, *Trusts*, *Probate* and *Religion*, and *Other Matters* *Concerning* the *Hereafter*

... Why may not that be the skull of a lawyer? Where be his
quiddities now, his quillities, his cases, his tenures, and his
tricks? Why does he suffer this mad knave now to knock him
about the sconce with a dirty shovel, and will not tell him of
his action of battery? Hum! This fellow might be in's time a
great buyer of land, with his statutes, his recognizances, his
fines, his double vouchers, his recoveries. [Is this the fine of his
fines, and the recovery of his recoveries], to have his fine pate
full of fine dirt? Will his vouchers vouch him no more of his
purchases, and double ones too, than the length and breadth of
a pair of indentures? The very conveyances of his lands will
scarcely lie in this box; and must th' inheritor himself have no
more, ha?
—Hamlet[1]

The lawyers, Bob, know too much.
They are chums of the books of old John Marshall.
They know it all, what a dead hand wrote,
A stiff dead hand and its knuckles crumbling,
The bones of the fingers a thin white ash.
The lawyers know a dead man's thoughts too well.

In the heels of the higgling lawyers, Bob,
Too many slippery ifs and buts and howevers,
Too much hereinbefore provided whereas,
Too many doors to go in and out of....
—Carl Sandburg[2]

---

[1]William Shakespeare, *Hamlet, Prince of Denmark,* Act V, Scene i.
[2]From 'The Lawyers Know Too Much," reprinted in *Masterpieces of American Poets,* by
Mark Van Doren, Garden City Publishing Co., p. 448 (1932).

The strange facts described in the following ancient English case raise a number of unique and tantalizing legal issues, including questions of burglary, assault, battery, self-defense, insanity, sanctuary, deodand, witchcraft and religion.

IN RE JOHN OF KERNESLAWE
Assize Court of Northumberland County
Northumberland Assize Rolls, 7 Edward I (1279)

ANONYMOUS, JUDGE

A certain unknown woman, a sorceress, entered the house of John of Kerneslawe at the hour of vespers, and assaulted John in such a way that John signed himself with the sign of the cross. This occurred during the evening when the "Benedicite"[1] was being recited. And this same John, in defending himself, as if from the Devil, struck the sorceress with a staff, so that she died. Afterwards, by decision of the entire clergy, her body was burned. John went insane following this incident. Later, when John regained his senses, he remembered the incident, and thinking he might be punished because of it, fled to the diocese of Durham. He is not suspected of any felony; hence, he may return if he wishes; but his property is confiscated on account of his flight. Value of his property: £4 5s.

At what point may a person's "idiosyncracies" be considered so bizarre and unusual as to justify a court in declaring the person "incompetent" to make a will? Such was the question addressed by the court in the following case.

POTTS v. HOUSE
Supreme Court of Georgia
6 Ga. 324 (1849)

JOSEPH H. LUMPKIN, J.

{James Pott died, leaving a will of questionable validity. Two lower courts ruled that the will was valid, and the matter was appealed to the Georgia Supreme Court. The sole remaining issue in

---

[1]{Ed. Note: The "Benedicite" is a canticle, a biblical song of praise.}

the case was the state of Mr. Potts's mind when he executed the document.}

The Jury returned a verdict affirming the judgment of the Court of Ordinary, and declaring that the paper propounded was the last will and testament of James Potts, senior, deceased. . . .

I have endeavored, in this analysis of the case, to condense and simplify it as much as possible. The real question to be decided in both Courts in this case was, whether {or not} there was a valid will. The executor and those who claim under it, hold the affirmative. They must prove, therefore, not only that the instrument purporting to be a testamentary paper was formally executed, but, also, that the testator was of sound and disposing mind and memory. . . .

We will now, in conclusion, examine some of the general doctrines involved in the charge respecting wills; and I must say His Honor, Judge Hill, discharged this portion of his arduous functions with equal skill and perspicuity, and we are not prepared to say that he underrated the degree of testamentary capacity necessary to make a will, in maintaining that imbecility of mind did not disqualify, provided it stopped short of idiocy or lunacy. Before investigating this case, I had supposed that more capacity was required to make a will than I now find warranted by the authorities; and in remanding this cause to the Circuit for a new trial, with instructions, I am inclined to think that we rather overrated the amount of mind which this exacts of the testator. At any rate, I have myself more clear and definite views respecting this subject than I have hitherto entertained.

Still, I find no acknowledged standard of "weights and measures" by which to regulate this as well as all similar investigations. We apprehend that this thing, from its very nature, is incapable of being fixed and determined. All attempts to draw the line between capacity and incapacity have ended where they began, namely: in nothing. All agree that there must be a sound and disposing mind and memory, but to define the precise quantum, *hoc opus, hic labor est* {This is a task, this is a deed requiring effort}[1].

One thing is certain—that eccentricity, however great, is not sufficient, of itself, to invalidate a will. . . . Mason Lee, the testator in this

---

[1]{Ed. Note: From Vergil's *Aeneid,* Book VI, line 129.}

case, supposed himself to be continually haunted by witches, devils and evil spirits, which he fancied were always worrying him. He believed that all women are witches. (In this, perhaps, he was not so singular!) He lived in the strangest manner—wore an extraordinary dress, and slept in a hollow log. He imagined that the Wiggin's relatives, whom he desired to disinherit, were in his teeth; and to dislodge them, he had fourteen sound teeth extracted, evincing no suffering from the operation.

He had the quarters of his shoes cut off, saying that if the devil got into his feet he could drive him out the easier. His constant dress was an osnaburg shirt, a negro cloth short coat, breeches and leggings. His wearing apparel, at his death, was appraised at one dollar. He always shaved his head close, as he said that in the contests with the witches, they might not get hold of his hair, and also, to make his wits glib. He had innumerable swords, of all sizes and shapes, to enable him to fight the devil and witches successfully; they were made by a neighboring blacksmith.

In the day-time, neglecting his business he dozed in a hollow gum-log, for a bed, in his miserable hovel; and at night, kept awake fighting with his imaginary unearthly foes. He fancied, at one time, that he had the devil nailed up in a fireplace, at one end of his house, and had a mark made across his room, over which he never would pass, nor suffer it to be swept. He would sometimes send for all his negroes to throw dirt upon the roof of his house, to drive off ghosts. He had no chair, or table, or plate in his house. He used a forked stick. His meat was boar and bull beef and dumplings, served up in the same pot in which it was boiled, and placed on a chest, which answered him for both table and chair. He made his own clothes; they had no buttons; his pantaloons were as wide as petticoats, without a waistband, and fastened around him with a rope. His saddle was a piece of hollow gum-log, covered with leather, and of his own make. His kennel, on which he ate, slept and dozed away his time, was three feet wide, five feet long, and four feet high. He suffered no bull or boar, on his plantation, to be castrated. He cut off all the tails of his hogs and cattle, close to the roots; he said the cows made themselves poor, by fighting the flies with their tails, but cut them off and they would get as fat as squabs. He once brought a horse from home, cut off its ears, and mounted it instantly while bleeding. He mutilated in the same manner, all his horses and mules. He hoed his corn after frost, saying it would come out green again.

His bargains were peculiar, and generally losing. He gave long credits, without interest. He sold one place for $7,000, to be paid in 17 years, without interest, and if the purchaser did not like the bargin at the end of that time, he was at liberty to give it up, without paying rent. He said that the land at the expiration of that time, would be worth ten times as much as when he sold it. He purchased a large body of poor flat pine land, without seeing it, and put his negroes there, without a hut to live in. They cleared and girdled the trees of 2,000 acres, for the purpose, he said, of planting it in pinders (ground nuts), by which, he said, he should make a fortune.

He never went to church, nor voted, nor was required to do patrol or militia duty. He had a sulky made; his directions were, to have the shafts exactly nine feet long, and the chair and seat to be square—the sticks of which were to be worked with a drawing knife—not turned—and the cross-bars were to be square.

But enough of these whimsicalities. The will was established; and upon the appeal, the supervisory tribunal, through its organ, Judge Nott, declared that "the evidence [a part of which only I have quoted] seems very well to have authorized the verdict which the Jury rendered."

If the maxim be sound, that what is against reason, cannot be law, one might, I think, well doubt the principle of this case, without being branded as a skeptic. I subscribe, however, to the doctrine, that it is not every man of a frantic appearance and behavior, who is to be considered *non compos mentis* {not of sound mind}, either as it regards contracts, obligations or crimes; and that one may be addicted occasionally or habitually to the strangest peculiarities and yet possess a testable capacity. . . .

. . . But old age does not deprive a man of the capacity of making a testament; for a man may make a will, how old soever he may be, since it is not the integrity of the body but of the mind, that is requisite in testaments, provided the understanding has not become destroyed, by surviving the period that Providence has assigned to the sanity and stability of the mind.

The want of recollection of names, is one of the earliest symptoms of the decay of memory, by reason of old age; but it is not sufficient to create incapacity, unless it is quite total, or extend to the immediate family and property of the deceased. I once walked more than a hundred yards with Luther Martin of Maryland, for the purpose of being introduced to his grand-son, whom he had brought to college, without his being able to recall to his mind the name of his son-in-law, the father of the young man. And yet, I have no idea that his faculties were so far gone and shattered, as to have lost their testamentary power. If the testator be capable of doing an act of thought or memory, it is enough.

Jacob Bennet, the testator, was between 90 and 100 years old, when he made his will, disposing of his negroes (New York!!), furniture and stock, on his farm. His will was executed—Chancellor Kent holding, that neither age, nor sickness, nor extreme distress, or debility of body, will affect the capacity to make a will, if sufficient understanding remains. He feelingly observes, that "it is one of the painful consequences of extreme old age, that it ceases to excite interest, and is apt to be left solitary and neglected. The control which the law still gives to a man, over the disposal of his property, is one of the most efficient means which he has, in protracted life, to command the attention due to his infirmities. The will of such an aged man ought to be regarded with great tenderness, when it appears not to have been procured by fraudulent acts, but contains those very dispositions which the circumstances of his situation, and the course of natural affections dictated" Van Alst v. Hunter {citation omitted}). . . .

{Justice Lumpkin believed that, on balance, there was some question as to Mr. Potts's testamentary capacity and sent the case back for a new trial.}

Adhering to the principle of "caveat emptor," real estate brokers are generally not eager to disclose *all* the known or suspected defects attributable to a property they are attempting to sell. As shown by the following case, such lack of candor may assume supernatural dimensions.

STAMBOVSKY v. ACKLEY
Supreme Court of New York, Appellate Division
572 N.Y.S.2d 672 (1991)

ISRAEL RUBIN, J.

Plaintiff, to his horror, discovered that the house he had recently contracted to purchase was widely reputed to be possessed by poltergeists, reportedly seen by defendant seller and members of her family on numerous occasions over the last nine years. Plaintiff promptly commenced this action seeking rescission of the contract of sale. Supreme Court reluctantly dismissed the complaint, holding that plaintiff has no remedy at law in this jurisdiction.

The unusual facts of this case, as disclosed by the record, clearly warrant a grant of equitable relief to the buyer who, as a resident of New York City, cannot be expected to have any familiarity with folklore of the Village of Nyack. Not being a "local," plaintiff could not readily learn that the home he had contracted to purchase is haunted. Whether the source of the spectral apparitions seen by defendant seller are parapsychic or psychogenic, having reported their presence in both a national publication (*Readers' Digest*) and the local press (in 1977 and 1982, respectively), defendant is estopped to deny their existence and, as a matter of law, the house is haunted.

More to the point, however, no divination is required to conclude that it is defendant's promotional efforts in publicizing her close encounters with these spirits which fostered the home's reputation in the community. In 1989, the house was included in a five-home walking tour of Nyack and described in a November 27th newspaper article as "a riverfront Victorian (with ghost)." The impact of the reputation thus created goes to the very essence of the bargain between the parties, greatly impairing both the value of the property and its potential for resale. . . .

. . . While I agree with the Supreme Court that the real estate broker, as agent for the seller, is under no duty to disclose to a potential buyer the phantasmal reputation of the premises and that, in his pursuit of a legal remedy for fraudulent misrepresentation against the seller, plaintiff hasn't a ghost of a chance, I am nevertheless moved by the spirit of equity to allow the buyer to seek rescission of the contract of sale and recovery of his down payment.

New York law fails to recognize any remedy for damages incurred as a result of the seller's mere silence, applying instead the strict rule of caveat emptor. Therefore, the theoretical basis for granting relief, even under the extraordinary facts of this case, is elusive if not ephemeral. "Pity me not but lend thy serious hearing to what I shall unfold" (William Shakespeare, *Hamlet*, Act I, Scene V [Ghost]).

From the perspective of a person in the position of plaintiff herein, a very practical problem arises with respect to the discovery of a paranormal phenomenon: "Who you gonna' call?" as the title song to the movie *Ghostbusters* asks. Applying the strict rule of caveat emptor to a contract involving a house possessed by poltergeists conjures up visions of a psychic or medium routinely accompanying the structural engineer and Terminix man on an inspection of every home subject to a contract of sale. It portends that the prudent attorney will establish an escrow account lest the subject of the transaction come back to haunt him and his client—or pray that his malpractice insurance coverage extends to supernatural disasters.

In the interest of avoiding such untenable consequences, the notion that a haunting is a condition which can and should be ascertained upon reasonable inspection of the premises is a hobgoblin which should be exorcised from the body of legal precedent and laid quietly to rest. . . .

. . . {W}ith respect to transactions in real estate, New York adheres to the doctrine of caveat emptor and imposes no duty upon the vendor to disclose any information concerning the premises . . . unless there is a confidential or fiduciary relationship between the parties . . . or some conduct on the part of the seller which constitutes "active concealment." . . . Normally, some affirmative misrepresentation . . . or partial disclosure . . . is required to impose upon the seller a duty to communicate undisclosed conditions affecting the premises. . . .

Common law is not moribund. *Ex facto jus oritur* {law arises out of facts}. Where fairness and common sense dictate that an exception should be created, the evolution of the law should not be stifled by rigid application of a legal maxim.

The doctrine of caveat emptor requires that a buyer act prudently to assess the fitness and value of his purchase and operates to bar the purchaser who fails to exercise due care from seeking the equitable remedy of rescission. . . . For the purposes of the instant motion to dismiss the action . . . plaintiff is entitled to every favorable inference which may reasonably be drawn from the pleadings . . . specifically, in this instance, that he met his obligation to conduct an inspection of the premises and a search of available public records with respect to title. It should be apparent, however, that the most meticulous inspection and search would not reveal the presence of poltergeists at the premises or unearth the property's ghoulish reputation in the community. Therefore, there is no sound policy reason to deny plaintiff relief for failing to discover a state of affairs which the most prudent purchaser of it would not be expected to even contemplate. . . .

Where a condition which has been created by the seller materially impairs the value of the contract and is peculiarly within the knowledge of the seller or unlikely to be discovered by a prudent purchaser exercising due care with respect to the subject transaction, nondisclosure constitutes a basis for rescission as a matter of equity. Any other outcome places upon the buyer not merely the obligation to exercise care in his purchase but rather to be omniscient with respect to any fact which may affect the bargain. No practical purpose is served by imposing such a burden upon a purchaser. To the contrary, it encourages predatory business practice and offends the principle that equity will suffer no wrong to be without a remedy.

Defendant's contention that the contract of sale, particularly the merger or "as is" clause, bars recovery of the buyer's deposit is unavailing. Even an express disclaimer will not be given effect where the facts are peculiarly within the knowledge of the party invoking it. . . . Moreover, a fair reading of the merger clause reveals that it expressly disclaims only representations made with respect to the physical condition of the premises and merely makes general reference to representations concerning "any other matter or things affecting or relating to the aforesaid premises." As broad as this language may be, a reasonable interpretation is that its effect is limited to tangible or physical matters and does not extend to paranormal phenomena. Finally, if the language of the contract is to be construed as broadly as defendant urges to encompass the presence of poltergeists in the house, it cannot be said that she has delivered the premises "vacant" in accordance with her obligation under the provisions of the contract rider. . . .

In the case at bar, defendant seller deliberately fostered the public belief that her home was possessed. Having undertaken to inform the public at large, to whom she has no legal relationship, about the supernatural occurrences on her property, she may be said to owe no less a duty to her contract vendee. It has been remarked that the occasional modern cases which permit a seller to take unfair advantage of buyer's ignorance so long as he is not actively misled are "singularly unappetizing." . . . Where, as here, the seller not only takes unfair advantage of the buyer's ignorance but has created and perpetuated a condition about which he is unlikely to even inquire, enforcement of the contract (in while or in part) is offensive to the court's sense of equity. Application of the remedy of rescission, within the bounds of the narrow exception to the doctrine of caveat emptor set forth herein, is entirely appropriate to relieve the unwitting purchase from the consequences of a most unnatural bargain. . . .

{The Court permitted the Plaintiff (Buyer) to proceed with the lawsuit seeking to cancel the contract to buy the house.}

It has been said that "no church can have any higher obligation resting upon it than being 'just'" (Lyons v. The Planters Loan & Savings Bank [1890], 86 Ga. 485). Does this obligation extend so far as to impose liability upon a church for the injuries suffered when a praying worshipper is flattened and trampled by another frenzied parishioner sprinting down the isle during an energetic revivalist ceremony?

BASS v. AETNA INSURANCE COMPANY
Supreme Court of Louisiana
370 So.2d 511 (1979)

JOHN A. DIXON, JR., JUSTICE

Mr. and Mrs. Loyd Bass sued Aetna Insurance Company, insurer of Mr. Kenneth Fussell under a homeowner's policy, and Southern Farm Bureau Casualty Insurance Company, insurer of Shepard's Fold

Church of God, seeking damages for personal injuries suffered by Mrs. Bass when Mr. Fussell, a member of the Shepard's Fold Church, ran down the church aisle and collided with Mrs. Bass, also a member of the church, who was in the aisle praying.

The defendants denied all allegations of negligence of the part of their insureds, and, alternatively, pleaded the affirmative defenses of assumption of the risk and contributory negligence. After trial on the merits, the Twenty-Second Judicial District Court for the Parish of St. Tammany dismissed plaintiffs' suit and on appeal the dismissal in an unpublished opinion. Upon plaintiffs' application we granted writs.

On the evening of February 12, 1974, during a revival service, the Shepard's Fold Church of God was very crowded with not enough seats to accommodate all the parishioners. Consequently, Mrs. Bass and other parishioners who could not find seats were standing in the aisles of the church. Reverend Rodney Jeffers, in the course of preaching to the congregation, stated that the doors of the church should be opened and referred to the possibility of "running." Immediately afterward, Mr. Fussell began running up the aisle and ran into Mrs. Bass, who was in the aisle praying with her head bowed. As a result, Mrs. Bass fell and was injured.

The issues are whether Mr. Fussell was negligent, whether the Shepard's Fold Church of God was negligent, and, if so, whether the plaintiffs' action is barred by either the defenses of assumption of the risk or contributory negligence.[1] Although Mr. Fussell testified that he was "trotting" under the Spirit of the Lord and does not remember actually running into Mrs. Bass, another witness testified that she saw Mr. Fussell run into Mrs. Bass and knock her down.

If Fussell's defense is that he was not in control of his actions, it can be compared with voluntary intoxication, which will not exonerate one from delictual responsibility. A worshiper in church has no more right to run over a fellow worshiper in the aisle than a passerby on the sidewalk. Mr. Fussell breached his duty and was negligent when he trotted or ran down the aisle of the church without regard for the safety of other parishioners in the aisles.

Actionable negligence also results from the creation or mainte-

---

[1]The "Act of God" defense cannot be seriously considered. An "Act of God" means "force majeure." See Stone, "Tort Doctrine," §45 in 12 *Louisiana Civil Law Treatises* (1977).

nance of an unreasonable risk of injury to others. In determining whether the risk is unreasonable, not only the seriousness of the harm that may be caused is relevant, but also the likelihood that harm may be caused {citation omitted}. In the instant case, according to both Mrs. Bass and Reverend Jeffers, there were approximately three hundred seventy-five parishioners in the church on the night of the accident, and many of the parishioners were standing in the aisles.

Reverend Jeffers recognized the likelihood that harm might be caused by this crowded condition because he testified that he asked that the aisles be cleared, that he encouraged "open response to the Spirit," and that running or moving "in the Spirit" were common forms of religious expression in Shepard's Fold Church. Another defense witness testified that Reverend Jeffers, recognizing the crowded aisles, asked if somebody would run for him[2] (which apparently is what Mr. Fussell did). Reverend Jeffers did not stop the service to clear the aisles, but continued to maintain an unreasonable risk of injury to the parishioners. The Shepard's Fold Church is responsible for the negligence of its pastor, Reverend Jeffers, under these circumstances {citation omitted}.

Concluding that both Mr. Fussell and the church were negligent, we next consider the defenses of assumption of the risk and contributory negligence. The Court of Appeals, in affirming the trial court, concluded that Mrs. Bass assumed the risk by remaining in the aisle with her eyes closed, and that she was contributorily negligent by remaining after having been alerted that running might occur.

Assumption of the risk and contributory negligence are affirmative defenses {citation omitted} and as we stated in Langlois v. Allied Chemical Corp. {citation omitted}:

> The determination of whether a plaintiff has assumed a risk is made by subjective inquiry, whereas contributory negligence is determined objectively under the reasonable man standard. . . .

> . . . Assumption of the risk therefore is properly applicable to those

---

[2]In response to defense counselor, Mr. Cassidy's questions, Mr. Fitzgerald testified on direct examination:

Q. Did you hear Reverend Jeffers make any statement about opening the doors?
A. Yes, he said to open the doors.
Q. Tell the Court what he said, as best you recall.
A. The best I recall he said to open the doors, he felt like running and he didn't have room because of the crowd and would somebody please run for him.

situations where plaintiff, with knowledge of the peril, voluntarily enters into a relationship with defendant involving danger to himself because of defendant's contemplated conduct.

We cannot agree with the Court of Appeals' conclusion that Mrs. Bass assumed the risk. Although Mrs. Bass had belonged to the Church of God faith for approximately fifty-five years and the Shepard's Fold Church for approximately twenty-five years, neither she nor any other witness had seen or heard of any injury or collision in any Church of God church. Before the accident, no one, including Mrs. Bass, felt endangered by worshiping in this church. Mrs. Bass unequivocally testified that she had never seen anyone run in the church. The evidence fails to persuade us that Mrs. Bass actually, subjectively[3] comprehended that by praying in the aisle she was incurring a risk of being run over {citation omitted} or that she could or should have known or understood that she was incurring such a risk as, for example, in Schofield v. The Continental Insurance Co. {citation omitted} where the spectator at a Zulu parade at Mardi Gras was hit by a coconut thrown from a float.

The defense failed to prove that Mrs. Bass voluntarily assumed or exposed herself to this risk. Movement in the aisles was not an extraordinary condition in this church because worshipers frequently went to the altar, "the very central focal point in the church," for prayer. Heedless running in the aisle was an unusual and extraordinary hazard, to which plaintiff did not knowingly expose herself {citation omitted}.

Contributory negligence is also an affirmative defense; the defendants bear the burden of proving contributory negligence by a preponderance of the evidence. Contributory negligence is objectively determined under the "reasonable man" standard {citation omitted}. It is not contributory negligence to bow one's head when praying in church, whether in the pew or in the aisle. . . .

For the reasons assigned, the judgments of the district court and of the Court of Appeals are reversed; the case is remanded. . . .

---

[3]Although there is testimony that Reverend Jeffers asked the people to clear the aisles, Mrs. Bass and at least one other parishioner, a defense witness, testified that they did not hear this request. Mrs. Bass and several witnesses did hear Reverend Jeffers ask that the doors be opened and mention running, but almost immediately afterward, according to Mr. Fussell's own testimony, Mr. Fussell began running down the aisle and into Mrs. Bass.

"It costs a fortune to raise kids these days" is an oft-repeated cliché which undoubtedly contains at least some basis in fact, especially when compared to the cost of supporting a bastard male child in rural Tennessee in 1900, as discussed in the following case.

HARPER v. LOVELL
Supreme Court of Tennessee
105 Tenn. 614; 59 S.W. 337 (1900)

JOHN S. WILKES, J.

{When young John F. Harper died, his mother brought this action to recover sums that should have been part of his estate. The lower court held in her favor, rendering a $737.96 judgment against Mr. Lovell, the boy's guardian. Mr. Lovell appealed and won, so she took the case to the Tennessee Supreme Court.}

... The ward, John F. Harper, was the bastard son of A. Ramsey, who died after making his will, never having been married. In his will he gave to John F. Harper $2,500 upon certain terms, and with certain limitations, as follows: "The interest on the share of John F. Harper shall be paid to him only when he becomes 21 years of age ... the interest to be paid annually for his benefit." ... Lovell qualified as guardian of John F. Harper in 1892, and received from the {estate} of Ramsey {John F. Harper's deceased father} $666.86 in March 1894....

It appears that the ward {Harper} was a reckless, dissolute character, who would not work, and was killed before he reached 21 years of age. It also appears that the guardian {Lovell} had a store, and furnished to the ward articles out of it until he consumed in amount more than the guardian ever received; that the ward was due him in some amount before he ever received any fund.

The court of chancery appeals reports that many of the articles furnished were or could be considered necessaries, and some should not, but upon an examination of the entire list that court was satisfied that the legitimate expenses of the ward, together with a reasonable compensation for his services, more than cover the amount received from Ramsey's estate, and, this being apparent from an inspection of the account and list of expenses, a reference was not necessary. It appears that the guardian sent the boy to school so far as he could prevail on him to go, and paid some school bills, and for books and clothes.

A petition to rehear was filed in the court of chancery appeals, in which that court was requested to make part of its report an itemized account of the articles furnished to Harper from Lovell's store. The court of chancery appeals declined to do so, stating that there were over 200 items in it, and that it covered seven legal record pages, and it did not consider it proper to set out in so much detail the evidential facts upon which it based its conclusions, but only the result of its finding.

That court gives however, a sort of summary of the articles furnished, as follows: Tobacco was furnished 86 times, smoking tobacco 9 times, pipes 3 times, candy 48 times, sardines 24 times, knives 9 times, neckties 9 times, canned peaches 11 times, cheroots 10 times, oysters 46 times, apples 5 times.

That court reports also that it is impracticable to get the exact charge for separate items, as several would be grouped in one entry. For instance, oysters and sardines, 20 cents. How much was for oysters and how much for sardines that court cannot tell. Fifteen cents for sugar and snuff. How much for each could not be stated. Sugar and crackers, 10 cents; candy and tobacco, 15 cents; candy and oysters, 15 cents. They find, however, that $9.15 is charged for tobacco, $5.65 for oysters, $3.75 for sardines, $4.50 for candy, $2.90 for canned peaches, $3.37 for cigars and cheroots, $3.35 for neckties, $3.35 for pocket-knives, $2.10 for a double-barrelled gun, $3.66 for shot, powder and shells, 20 cents for cologne, 30 cents for hair dye, $1.25 for fish hooks, $1.00 for kid gloves, $1.50 for a pair of slippers for his sister, bay rum 30 cents, water melons 43 cents, hair oil 15 cents.

The court reports that the boy was about 18 years old; that he had no home, and no business, and would not work, and could not be controlled, and was generally worthless and reckless. The court of chancery appeals reports that among the necessaries might be classed oysters, sardines, crackers, canned peaches and a moderate supply of candy, as they were food, though not of the most wholesome kind. Also the gun, ammunition and handkerchiefs, and a small amount of cash, schooling, clothes, etc., and other items were classed as necessaries, as to which no serious question is made.

That court protests against the following articles as not articles of necessity: Cigars and cheroots, hair dye, hair oil, bay rum and breast-pins; that neckties, pocketknives and candy were furnished too lavishly. Kid gloves and slippers were placed under the ban, as were also tobacco, two quarts of chestnuts, cinnamon oil, onions, and honey. On this last item that court says that separately they might be allowed, but in combination they cannot. Chewing gum, cologne, rat poison, two watermelons in one day. The court was of opinion one might be allowed, but two were not necessaries, but extravagancies.

The court of chancery appeals was divided or in doubt as to the following items: Fish hooks, a trot line, tobacco in even moderate quantities, one box corn salve, and some other items of less importance. That court, however, repeats its former holding that, eliminating all improper charges, and allowing a reasonable compensation for services, there were legitimate credits for enough to cover all the funds received by the guardian.

Under the view that we take of the case it is not necessary that we pass upon the correctness of the classification made by the court of chancery appeals as to what are or are not necessaries. The language of the will of Ramsey, under which the legacy was raised, is quite crude and inconsistent, and not altogether intelligible; but we think that, under a proper construction of the item giving this legacy, neither the principal sum of $2,500 nor any part of it was to become the absolute property of John F. Harper until and unless he reached his majority of 21 years, and in the event of his death prior to that time the principal of the legacy was to revert to the estate of Ramsey, the testator. This being so, the guardian could consume no more than the interest upon the legacy for the benefit of the ward, and the principal would revert to the estate of Ramsey. . . .

. . . It follows that we reach the same result as to complainant's rights as did the court of chancery appeals, but upon different grounds, and the complainant's bill must be dismissed, at her costs.

It is sometimes noted, both critically and supportively, that judges wield "godlike" powers as they issue decrees and rulings from high atop their lofty stations. For the most part, judges have no quarrel with this view, and occasionally may even be inclined to exaggerate their role as "supreme (judicial) being."

ZIM v. WESTERN PUBLISHING COMPANY
U.S. Court of Appeals, Fifth Circuit
573 F.2d 1318 (1978)

IRVING L. GOLDBERG, CIRCUIT JUDGE

I

In the beginning, Zim[1] created the concept of the Golden Guides.[2] For the earth was dark and ignorance filled the void. And Zim said, let there be enlightenment and there was enlightenment. In the Golden Guides, Zim created the heavens (*Stars*) (*Sky Observer's Guide*) and the earth (*Minerals*) (*Geology*).[3]

And together with his publisher, Western, he brought forth in the Golden Guides knowledge of all manner of living things that spring from the earth, grass, herbs yielding seed, fruit-trees yielding fruits after their kind (*Plant Kingdom*) (*Non-flowered Plants*) (*Flowers*) (*Orchids*) (*Trees*), and Zim saw that it was good. And they brought forth in the Golden Guides knowledge of all the living moving creatures that dwell in the waters (*Fishes*) (*Marine Mollusks*) (*Pond Life*), and fowl that may fly above the earth (*Birds*) (*Birds of North*

---

[1]Dr. Zim is a noted science educator with a Ph. D. in science education from Columbia University. His special expertise is in the presentation of scientific subjects to popular audiences. The major focus of his efforts has been the development of a multivolume series of books on scientific subjects, the Golden Guides. Dr. Zim, the plaintiff in this suit, is a citizen of the state of Florida. Since the amount in controversy is in excess of $10,000, diversity jurisdiction exists under 28 U.S.C. §1332.

[2]The listing of titles in the following account is neither exhaustive nor chronologically accurate.

[3]Zim's actual role in the preparation of the books in the Golden Guide series varied from book to book. Zim was the principal author of some of the books; other books were prepared jointly by Zim and an expert in the particular field. The expert supplied the technical knowledge which Zim assembled and presented in a form suitable for lay readers.

America) (*Gamebirds*). And Zim saw that it was good. And they brought forth knowledge in the Golden Guides of the creatures that dwell on dry land, cattle, and creeping things (*Insects*) (*Insect Pests*) (*Spiders*), and beasts of the earth after their kind (*Animal Kingdom*). And Zim saw that it was very good.[4]

II

Then there rose up in Western a new Vice-President who knew not Zim. And there was strife and discord, anger and frustration, between them for the Golden Guides were not being published or revised in their appointed seasons. And it came to pass that Zim and Western covenanted a new covenant, calling it a Settlement Agreement. But there was no peace in the land. Verily, they came with their counselors of law into the district court for judgment and sued there upon their covenants.

And they put upon the district judge hard tasks. And the district judge listened to long testimony and received hundreds of exhibits. So Zim did cry unto the district judge that he might remember the promises of the Settlement Agreement. And the district judge heard Zim's cry, but gave judgment for Western. Yea, the district judge gave judgment to Western on a counterclaim as well. Therefore, Zim went up out of the court of the district judge.

III

And Zim spake unto the Court of Appeals saying, make a sacrifice of the judgment below. And the judges, three in number, convened in orderly fashion to recount the story of the covenants and to discuss and answer the four questions which Zim brought before them.[5] . . .

---

[4]According to Zim's brief before this court, well over 100 million of the Golden Guide books have been printed under Zim's name, earning him "millions of dollars" in royalties.

[5]The trial below was long and involved a host of exceedingly complex issues. The district judge's rulings on most of the difficult questions presented for resolution below have not been appealed. We restrict ourselves to discussion of those rulings challenged on appeal and note that we have been materially aided in our consideration of these issues by the district

IV

A. Parol Evidence

And the parties came before the district judge for an accounting of the royalties of Zim. Under Sections 3 and 4 of the 1970 Settlement Agreement, Zim was entitled to payments of royalties and bonuses for books in the Golden Guide Series. . . . The parties agree that Zim is to earn royalties and bonuses only on those books "published or to be published or distributed by Western. . . . "They disagree sharply, however, on the correct construction of "Western." Zim offered parol evidence, the testimony of the attorney who represented him during the contract negotiations, to support his view that "Western" means not only Western Publishing Co., the defendant here, but its affiliates and subsidiaries as well.

The district judge excluded the testimony on the grounds that "Western" was unambiguous as a matter of law in view of the first recital in the contract. There the parties to the contract were stated to be Zim and "Western Publishing Co., Inc. (a Wisconsin Corporation), its successors and assigns, herein referred to as 'Western.' . . ." In the district court's view, the contract provided its own definition of "Western" and that definition was not itself subject to ambiguity, i.e., "Western Publishing Co., Inc. (a Wisconsin Corporation), its successors and assigns," meant that jural entity and none other. Zim contends that this ruling denies him his "day in court" and is inconsistent with the Wisconsin parol evidence rule. . . .

. . . The law in Wisconsin appears to be that parol evidence is not admissible to contradict or vary the terms of an agreement, but may be considered in interpreting an ambiguous term. . . .

. . . In the case at bar, the parties made an effort in the written instrument to define the term whose meaning they now contest. They defined "Golden Guides" by reference to another term, "Western," the meaning of which the agreement also provides explicitly. "Western," the recitals tell us, is to stand for "Western Publishing Co., Inc. (A

---

been appealed. We restrict ourselves to discussion of those rulings challenged on appeal and note that we have been materially aided in our consideration of these issues by the district court's careful memorandum opinion and his skill, displayed at many points in the trial, in encouraging counsel to focus questions on specific issues before the court.

Wisconsin Corporation), its successors and assigns." Western Publishing Co., Inc. (a Wisconsin Corporation), is a definite entity, created by the law and legally distinct from separately incorporated affiliates or subsidiaries.

Here, then, counseled parties made a deliberate effort to define a crucial term in the agreement. They defined that term in words with a quite definite legal significance. When they wished to give that term some special meaning different from its definition in the agreement, they so provided in unmistakable terms. We think the district court was correct in its conclusion that the intent of the parties was unambiguously evidenced by the writing itself. Under Wisconsin law, the parol evidence was properly excluded.

B. The Contract Claims

Zim next contends that Western breached the 1970 Settlement Agreement by publishing revised versions of two of the Golden Guides, *Stars* and *Sky Observer's Guide*, without his approval. Zim bases his claim on Subsection 6.5—Zim releases to Western all Zim's right, interest and claim under all programs heretofore agreed upon or now under way for the revision of books published prior to the date hereof. It is agreed, however, that Western will not publish any revision, change, correction, alteration or updating of any book published prior to October 1, 1970, on which Zim is entitled to a royalty or bonus, without Zim's prior approval.

It is undisputed that both *Stars* and *Sky Observer's Guide* had been published prior to October 1, 1970. It is also undisputed that projects for the revision of both books were "under way" when the contract was executed. It is also undisputed that Western failed to obtain Zim's approval of the revisions prior to publication of the revised versions of the books. Zim vigorously contends that these facts establish a breach of contract by Western and that he was entitled to damages and an injunction against further publication without his approval.

Western counters by pointing out that the district judge found that Western had submitted all proposed changes to Zim for his approval, but that Zim "unreasonably withheld" his approval of the

220

response to the proposed changes excuses Western's publication of the revisions.

Zim's power of approval under subsection 6.5 cannot, however, be construed to be an unlimited power to prevent publication of revised versions of the Guides covered by 6.5. Zim bargained for the retention of his power to exercise his judgment as a science educator with enormous experience in the presentation of material in the Golden Guides format. That judgment, once exercised, was to be decisive; Western could not publish revisions of which Zim disapproved.

Nonetheless, justice and fairness considered in the light of the parties' interests here require that Zim's power not extend to holding Western hostage to dilatoriness, obstructionism or greed. . . . Zim's retained power to disapprove changes, therefore, has to be exercised within a reasonable time and in a reasonable manner, i.e., in a manner which makes it possible for Western to rework the manuscript in order to obtain his approval. Necessarily, this requires reasonable specificity in the statement of Zim's objections to any proposed changes. . . .

. . . Under these circumstances, we have no hesitation in concluding that Zim failed to exercise his power of disapproval within the time and in the manner required, and in so doing effectively waived his right to reject the proposed revisions. Zim's approval conditioned on execution of a new contract was an abusive use of his power and an attempt to reform the Settlement Agreement.

This is not to say that Zim was not honestly motivated by a desire to maintain and improve the quality of *Sky Observer's Guide*. It is to say, however, that conditioning his approval in this manner was beyond the scope of his contractual power. Zim's failure to exercise his power properly operated to authorize Western's publication of the revised work. The district court's holding as to *Sky Observer's Guide* must be affirmed.

The situation with *Stars* is quite different. Although proposed revisions were sent to Zim in 1972, a final set of revisions was first sent to Zim in September 1974. Western at that time demanded that Zim examine the revisions and report within sixty days his approval or disapproval together with suggested changes. Western stated that it would consider his suggestions and advise him whether the changes would be made. Western stated it would then ask Zim whether he would be made. Western stated it would then ask Zim whether he wished to be shown as co-author, original project editor, or have his name removed entirely from the book. Western proceeded to publish the book notwithstanding Zim's express disapproval communicated within the sixty-day period.

It is apparent that Western breached the agreement here. Western's 1974 letter confused Zim's rights under subsections 6.4 and 6.5 of the agreement. Zim's prior approval of the revised version of *Stars* was a prerequisite to lawful publication by Western, absent waiver by Zim. Since there had been no waiver as to *Stars*, Western's publication of the book without Zim's approval constituted a breach of contract. . . .

C. The Tort Claims

. . . The third count of Dr. Zim's complaint alleged an unauthorized and wrongful appropriation of Zim's name, a claim sounding in tort under Florida law. Zim's claim again grows out of the publication of revised revisions of *Stars* and *Sky Observer's Guide*. Zim's name appeared on the spine of both books even though he never approved the revisions. Moreover, Zim's initials appeared beneath a foreword added to *Stars* which expressed his gratitude to the authors hired by Western to revise the book. Zim never approved this foreword either. . . .

Thus, Zim's complaint alleged a cause of action with respect to the use of his name in *Sky Observer's Guide* and *Stars*. We have already concluded, however, that Western was entitled under the contract to publish *Sky Observer's Guide* without Zim's actual approval in view of Zim's default. Western's right under the contract to publish the book in these circumstances operates as an authorization sufficient to privilege Western's use of Zim's name as a matter of tort law as well. . . .

. . . Just the opposite result obtains with respect to *Stars*. Paradoxically, if repeatedly in this case, he who observes the skies does not see the *Stars*. Western's use of Zim's name in *Stars* was unauthorized by the contract and was, therefore, tortious. Although Zim failed to prove any actual damages from the publication of the revised

222

version of *Stars*, under Florida law, nominal damages at least are recoverable; the plaintiff need not plead or prove actual damages. . . .

V

And when the judges of the Court of Appeals had passed through the wilderness of Zim, they recapitulated the history of their journey.

The ruling of the district judge regarding parol evidence on the meaning of "Western" is AFFIRMED. The court's conclusion that Western did not breach the Settlement Agreement or commit a tort by publishing the revised version of *Sky Observer's Guide* is also AFFIRMED. We REVERSE, however, the court's conclusion that Western committed no breach of the contract by publishing the revised version of *Stars*. We REMAND for a determination and award of nominal damages for the breach of contract. . . . We REVERSE the judgment for Western on its counterclaim. And it therefore shall come to pass that the district judge shall write another chapter in the chronicle of Zim.

AFFIRMED IN PART, REVERSED IN PART AND REMANDED.

CHAPTER IX

Accidents, *S*lips, *F*alls, *C*rashes, *C*runches, *W*recks, *B*umps, *T*humps and *L*umps

"Law is law" wrote the satirist who decided not to adopt it as a profession. "Law is like a country dance; people are led up and down in it till they are tired. Law is like a book of surgery— there are a great many terrible cases in it. It is also like physic—they who take least of it are best off. Law is like a homely gentlewoman—very well to follow. Law is like a scolding wife—very bad when it follows us. Law is like a new fashion—people are bewitched to get into it. It is also like bad weather—most people are glad when they get out of it."[1]

---

[1]From George A. Morton and D. MacLeod Mulloch, *Law and Laughter,* p. 1 (1913).

In the following case, the judge exercised true poetic license and no restraint in denying the plaintiff's claim that his prized oak tree was damaged when the defendant's automobile crashed into it. The opinion is reproduced here exactly as it appeared in the official reports, i.e., the text in poetic form with the legal discussion, rationale and citations appearing in the footnote.

FISHER v. LOWE
Court of Appeals of Michigan
122 Mich. App. 418; 333 N.W.2d 67 (1983)

JOHN H. GILLIS, JUDGE

We thought that we would never see
A suit to compensate a tree.
A suit whose claim in tort is prest
Upon a mangled tree's behest;

A tree whose battered trunk was prest
Against a Chevy's crumpled crest;
A tree that faces each new day
With bark and limb in disarray;

A tree that may forever bear
A lasting need for tender care.
Flora lovers though we three,
We must uphold the court's decree.

Affirmed.[1]

---

[1]Plaintiff commenced this action in tort against defendants Lowe and Moffet for damage to his "beautiful oak tree" caused when defendant Lowe struck it while operating defendant Moffet's automobile. The trial court granted summary judgment in favor of defendants pursuant to GCR 1963, 117.2(1). In addition, the trial court denied plaintiff's request to enter a default judgment against the insurer of the automobile defendant, State Farm Mutual Automobile Insurance Company. Plaintiff appeals as of right.

The trial court did not err in granting summary judgment in favor of defendants Lowe and Moffet. Defendants were immune from tort liability for damage to the tree pursuant to §3135 of the no-fault insurance act (M.C.I. §500.3135, M.S.A. §24.13135).

The trial court did not err in refusing to enter a default judgment against State Farm. Since it is undisputed that plaintiff did not serve process upon State Farm in accordance with the court rules, the court did not obtain personal jurisdiction over the insurer (GCR 1963, 105.4).

The following case is a venerable and oft-quoted "classic," containing one of the most famous lines in all of jurisprudence. The opinion is also one of the first to deal directly with the topic of insobriety.

ROBINSON v. PIOCHE, BAYERQUE & CO.
Supreme Court of California
5 Cal. 460 (1855)

SOLOMON HEYDENFELDT, J.

The Court below erred in giving the third, fourth and fifth instructions. If the defendants were at fault in leaving an uncovered hole in the sidewalk of a public street, the intoxication of the plaintiff cannot excuse such gross negligence. A drunken man is as much entitled to a safe street as a sober one, and much more in need of it.

The judgment is reversed and the cause remanded.

In the following case, an otherwise ordinary "slip and fall" accident at a wedding feast provided sufficient inspiration for Justice Musmanno to exercise his unique brand of legal wit and humor.

SCHWARTZ v. WARWICK-PHILADELPHIA CORPORATION
Supreme Court of Pennsylvania
424 Pa. 185; 226 A.2d 484 (1967)

MICHAEL A. MUSMANNO, JUSTICE

It was a wedding banquet and the guests were enjoying themselves in the traditional custom of nuptial celebrations. There was dining and dancing and then dancing and dining. Fork work interspersed with footwork. The banquetters would enjoy a spell of eating and then amble out to the dance floor to dance. When the music suspended, the dancers returned to their tables and became diners again. The mythical playwright who prepares the script for the strange and sometimes quixotic episodes which eventually end up in court, mixed his stage properties and characters in this presentation because he placed in the center of the dance floor a quantity of freshly cooked

asparagus and ladled over it a generous quantity of oleaginous asparagus sauce. In this setting it was inevitable that something untoward
would happen, and it did. One of the performers in the unrehearsed
play described what occurred.

Joseph Rosenberg, tall, weighing 185 pounds and wearing a tuxedo suit, was dancing with his sister-in-law, Mrs. Ruth Schwartz, who
was wearing a gold lamé dress made of a metallic brocade material,
when, as he described it, "I went up in the air and flipped on my back,
my buttocks, and I pushed her down, and as I pushed her down, I let
go, and she hit the floor, and my feet went up in the air."

Were is not for what he testified later, the casual reader could assume
Joseph Rosenberg was merely describing one of the modern dances
which, in acrobatic manipulations and grotesque gyrations, sound no
less exotic than the wild movements narrated above. Rosenberg
explained, however, that the terpsichorean maneuver he executed was
involuntary. He said he was a veteran of the ball room with some 35
years of successful dancing behind him and he had never previously
done such a flip as he described. He said that his excursion into space
rose from an asparagus pad in the middle of the floor, and that after
got up he noted his pants were "green and white, like sauce."

His dancing partner, Mrs. Schwartz, confirmed Rosenberg's testimony and stated that as a result of the squashed asparagus flounder-
ing, her dress was covered with "strings of like green asparagus," and
that the stain was 8 inches wide and 15 inches down from the side.
In addition, the floor was wet for a distance of 3 feet with asparagus
and sauce. Mr. Schwartz, the husband of Mrs. Schwartz, testified that
immediately after the tumble occurred, "I rushed over and there they
are sitting in a spill of green substance and sauces, and it was spread
over quite an area * * * the area seemed to be full of liquid and asparagus." He saw that Rosenberg's shoe was full of the "green substance,"
that the sole of the shoe was green and "there seemed to be something
sticking to it near the heel."

Twenty minutes after the dine-and-dance debacle, Mr. Rosenberg
and Mrs. Schwartz left the hotel, bruised, sore and asparagus-laden,
and in due time brought an action in trespass against Warwick-
Philadelphia Corporation, the caterers of the wedding feast.

At the end of the ensuing trial, the judge entered a compulsory
non-suit, asserting that the plaintiffs had not established a prima facie

case of negligence or proximate cause. There was evidence that the waiters carrying food to the tables not only walked over the dance floor, but did so while the dance was in progress. Since the dancing space was not large, it happened that the dancers and waiters sometimes competed for passage and, while no one testified to actually seeing asparagus slide from an uplifted tray, the jury could easily have found that in the gridiron clashes between dancers and waiters the asparagus fumbled out of the trays and onto the floor. How else did it get there?

The trial judge, an ex-veteran congressman and thus a habitué of formal parties and accordingly an expert in proper wearing apparel at such functions, all of which he announced from the bench, allowed testimony as to the raiment worn by the banquetters. All the men were attired in tuxedos, the pants of which were not mounted with cuffs which could transport asparagus and sauce to the dance floor, unwittingly to lubricate its polished surface. Ruling out the cuffs of the tuxedo pants as transporters of the asparagus, the judge suggested the asparagus, with its accompanying sauce, could have been conveyed to the dance floor by "women's apparel, on men's coats or sleeves, or by a guest as he table hopped." The Judge's conclusions are as far-fetched as going to Holland for hollandaise sauce. There was no evidence in the case that anybody table hopped; it is absurd to assume that a man's coat or sleeve could scoop up enough asparagus and sauce to inundate a dance floor to the extent of a three-foot circumference; and it is bizarre to conjecture that a woman's dress without pockets and without excessive material could latch on to such a quantity of asparagus, carry it 20 feet (the distance from the tables to the dance floor) and still have enough dangling to her habiliments to cover the floor to such a depth as to fell a 185-pound gentleman with 35 years' dancing experience who had never before been tackled or grounded while shuffling the light fantastic.

A non-suit must be based on fact and not on supposition, on testimony and not conjecture, on realities and not guesses. Since no one questioned the presence of asparagus and sauce on the dance floor where assuredly it should not have been, since there is no evidence it was carried there by guests because the Trial Judge's hypothesis that it could have gotten there hanging on to the men's coattails or women's dresses must be dismissed as visionary, since there was direct evidence that waiters transported asparagus across the floor aloft on trays and there was evidence that waiters physically jostled dancers and, since it is not difficult to conclude that in a clash between a hurrying waiter and a dancer writhing in the throes of a watusi, frug, twist, jerk or buzzard, the resulting jolt would tilt the tray, cascading asparagus and sauce to the floor to throw the terpsichorean gymnasts off balance, it is reasonably proper, and fair to conclude that this concatenation of circumstances made out a prima facie case of negligence against the establishment running the wedding feast. It requires no citation of authority to demonstrate that a waiter with a tray balanced on an uplifted arm is out of place on a ballroom floor during a late twentieth century dance which would make the Apache war dance seem tame in comparison.

It can be stated as an incontrovertible legal proposition that anyone attending a dinner dance has the inalienable right to expect that, if asparagus is to be served, it will be served on the dinner table and not on the dance floor.

Nor are the plaintiffs in this case required to rule out every possible hypothesis for the happening of the accident, including the coathanging asparagus flight of fancy of the Trial Judge, except the thesis on which they base their cause. This Court said in Smith v. Bell Telephone Co. {citation omitted}:

> It is not necessary, under Pennsylvania law, that every fact or circumstance point unerringly to liability; it is enough that there be sufficient facts for the jury to say reasonably that the preponderance favors liability * * * The facts are for the jury in any case whether based upon direct or circumstantial evidence where a reasonable conclusion can be arrived at which would place liability on the defendant * * * The right of a litigant to have the jury pass upon the facts is not to be foreclosed just because the judge believes that a reasonable man might properly find either way.

In Liguori v. City of Philadelphia {citation omitted}, we said:

> * * * since proof to a degree of absolute certainty is rarely attainable in any litigated factual controversy, the law requires only that the evidence as to the operative cause of the accident be enough to satisfy reasonable and well-balanced minds that it was the one on which the plaintiff relies.

The law applicable to a case of this kind was expounded as recently as 1961 in a case where the facts were somewhat similar to the ones at bar (Lederhandler v. Bolotini {citation omitted}). The plaintiff there was injured when she fell on an apple strudel which had fallen to the floor also used for dancing. The defendant maintained he could not be held liable for the appearance of the strudel on the floor because it could not be linked to any of his waiters, arguing specifically:

> To find as a fact that the strudel got there as a result of defendant's negligence one must resort to the use of an inference viz., strudel was served at the dinner, hence one of the waiters must have dropped a piece.

We affirmed a judgment in favor of the plaintiff, stating:

> A caterer who serves meals and has charge of the premises in which they are consumed has the responsibility to clear the premises of food which he or his staff allows to escape to the damage of others; or, if it gets to the floor through the intervention of someone else, the caterer is liable for any resulting damage if it remains on the floor a sufficient period of time for him to be aware of its presence, actually or by constructive notice. * * * We have held that the time of constructive notice depends on the particular circumstances of the case. . . . We said that there could conceivably be a situation where 5 minutes would be adequate notice and where 5 hours would be inadequate notice.

Moreover, if it is established that the alleged tortious act was the result of the defendant's active negligence, constructive notice need not be proved. The waiters here were admittedly employed by the defendant and if they negligently dropped asparagus to the floor, their acts, under the principle of respondeat superior, were the acts of the employer. . . .

The evidence presented at the trial in the instant case made out, if accepted by the jury, a prima facie case of negligence, and the plaintiffs were entitled to have the jury pass on the issues involved.

Judgment reversed with a procedendo.[1]

---

[1]{Ed. Note: A "procedendo" is a writ by which a cause which has been removed from an inferior court to a superior court is sent down again *to be proceeded* in there (*Black's Law Dictionary*, 4th ed. [1968]).}

DISSENTING OPINION

JOHN C. BELL, CHIEF JUSTICE

One cannot help wondering if plaintiffs had, in the alleged 35 years of dancing, ever been to any dance, let alone a wedding banquet dance. There was no evidence of constructive notice; moreover, plaintiffs undoubtedly voluntarily assumed the risk of this banquet dance floor which was obviously periled with asparagus sauce, winding waiters and grotesque exotic tribal dancing under modern names. A dancer cannot, with legal sanction, look only into the captivating eyes of his lovely partner.

I certainly dissent.

In the usual course of events, a person seated in a chair inside a public building, quietly conversing with friends, would not anticipate being struck suddenly from above by a 600-pound falling steer.

GUTHRIE v. POWELL
Supreme Court of Kansas
178 Kan. 587; 290 P.2d 834 (1955)

WILLIAM W. HARVEY, CHIEF JUSTICE

At all times mentioned herein defendants were partners in and the proprietors of a business known as the Winfield Sales Company located at the Cowley County Fair Grounds in or near the west edge of the city limits of Winfield, Kansas, and engaged in and operating what is generally known as a community sale business, buying and selling for their own account and the account of various patrons and customers diverse kinds of livestock and used and new merchandise, and holding forth said premises as a place of public resort to all interested persons.

On April 15, 1953, plaintiff and her husband, S. R. Guthrie, came to and attended the premises of said Winfield Sales Company for the purpose of being customers and patrons at the sale held there on that day. . . .

The premises used and occupied by said defendants as a place of

232

business consists of several frame buildings and livestock pens and runways, of which the principal building where most of said sales activities are conducted consists of a large room at the south end of said building in which patrons interested in buying and selling merchandise and inanimate personal property were congregated on said day, the business office of said defendants, a lunch stand, and a livestock pavilion located on the second story and reached by way of a ramp leading up from the first floor of said principal building. Said livestock sale pavilion is a recessed semi-circle of board seats surrounding a pit or sales arena approximately 30 feet long and 15 feet wide in which livestock is exhibited for sale. . . .

At about 1:00 P.M. of said day plaintiff was seated in a chair at the north end of the south main floor room engaged in visiting and conversing with women friends and acquaintances, most of whom were the wives of patrons attending said sale. Suddenly, there was a loud commotion and noise overhead and simultaneously bits of plaster and debris began to fall from the ceiling onto plaintiff and others standing or sitting near her which was followed instantaneously—as plaintiff later learned—by a six-hundred-pound steer falling through the ceiling immediately over and approximately twelve feet above her position, said beast falling and landing upon plaintiff as she sat in said chair, knocking her unconscious, flattening the chair and plaintiff to the floor and under said steer and causing painful, serious and permanent injuries to her as hereinafter set forth. . . .

. . . The plaintiff states and alleges that the fact that the steer fell through the ceiling onto the plaintiff causing the resulting injuries to plaintiff, was an occurrence which would not have taken place except for some act or acts of negligence of the defendants, their agents, servants or employees in the proper and safe operation, maintenance, conduct and handling of said premises and livestock being exhibited therein. . . .

Plaintiff is entitled to a trial in this case. . . . Affirmed.

How deep does a hole in a city street have to be in order to justify a jury's award of money damages to a citizen who claims to have fallen into it?

TEAGLE v. CITY OF PHILADELPHIA
Supreme Court of Pennsylvania
430 Pa. 395; 243 A.2d 342 (1968)

MICHAEL A. MUSMANNO, JUSTICE

A few minutes before midnight on July 2, 1961, Mrs. Beatrice Teagle, plaintiff here, while crossing Leland Street in Philadelphia, stepped into a hole in the street and sustained injuries. At the trial of the lawsuit instituted against the City of Philadelphia by the plaintiff, she testified that the hole into which she fell was 36 inches long, 2 feet wide, from 4 to 5 inches deep and was filled with black water. She explained that she could tell the depth of the hole by the wet mark on her stocking.

A Mrs. Dorothy Gross testified that on the night in question she was in her home; she heard a scream and ran out to the street where she saw two persons helping Mrs. Teagle out of the hole in which her foot was immersed. Mrs. Gross knew this defect in the pavement since she had reported it to the City authorities a year before.

The jury returned a verdict for the plaintiff and the defendant asks for judgment n.o.v. or a new trial "at least." Reason? A photograph of the offending hole introduced at the trial inexplicably showed a ruler stuck into it, its measure indicating the surface of the fortuitous pond to be 1½ inches above the supposed bottom. No one explained who inserted the ruler, no one testified as to whether the measuring rod was punched into the deepest part of the crater, its shallowest part, or somewhere in between. The photographer who took the picture was not called as a witness.

The defendant claims that the City should not be liable for a trivial depression in its public thoroughfares. The Courts have not declared what absolute minimum depth is required in a fissure in the street to establish negligence on the part of the municipality for allowing it to remain unrepaired. Nor can there be a judicial pronouncement on the subject because obviously negligence invariably depends on a number of concatenating circumstances.

The defendant argues that the measure appearing on the ruler in the photograph "must be accepted as conclusive evidence of the true depth." This is an argument of less depth than that measured on the ruler. As already stated, the ruler does not specify that the depth of the concavity was uniform throughout its length of 36 inches and its breadth of 2 feet, nor that it was at the precise point where the ruler stood guard that Mrs. Teagle's foot disappeared into the murky hollow.

In addition, photographs cannot be said always to be an undeviatingly accurate reproduction of the scenes they presumably depict. It is said that figures do not lie, but that liars can figure. It can also be said that while photographs do not lie, there can be pictorial legerdemain which transforms a ramshackle house into a mansion, a city dump into a panoramic vista, and an ugly duckling into a swan. Everyone has experienced the surprise of seeing for the first time a person whose photograph he had previously witnessed and noting how different the real person looks from the photographed individual. It is indeed the boast of some photographers that they can do more for a person with the camera than can be done for him or her in a barber shop, beauty shop and/or a tailor shop. . . .

Sometimes a photograph may be admitted for the limited purpose of showing "physical aspects" of a location rather than for the purpose of demonstrating that what is in the picture represents the situation at the time of the happening of the controverted episode. . . .

The plaintiff here was not present when the photographs were taken, she never saw the photographer, and, at the trial, did not vouch for the measurements supposedly indicated by the ruler. We repeat that there is not a syllable in the record to indicate that the plaintiff fell at that point in the photograph where the ruler lifted its measured head.

Nor did anyone come forward to say that the bottom of the ruler rested on terra firma. In fact, the photograph shows that it was held in position by a transverse beam, the latter extending from the curb to the adjoining pavement.

The Trial Judge presented both sides of the controversy to the jury in a charge luminous with clarity. He said, inter alia:

You have to consider all the surrounding circumstances in regard to this hole. This is an alleged defect, and before liability attaches to the City, you should consider the depth of the hole, the size of an obstruction constituting the impediment, and consider whether all the particular facts of this case are sufficient to indicate that an unsafe condition was existing here, and that this was due to the negligence of the City of Philadelphia.

Nothing could be fairer. The jury took the photographs with them into the jury room, they studied them and concluded there was more credibility in the sworn testimony of the plaintiff and Mrs. Gross than in the unaccounted-for, unexplained, phantom ruler dipping its lower extremity into the dark depths of the haphazard puddle.

This is the hole case, and we see nothing in the appellant's argument of such depth that it submerges the jury's verdict into such a cavern of unreliability that it compels this Court to send the parties back for a retrial, when it is very clear that justice, wisely measured by the ruler of common sense, has been fairly done.

Judgment affirmed.

Unlike their timid, modern-day counterparts who must cater to a coddled, squeamish and lawsuit-crazy public, the operators of carnival rides at Coney Island, New York, in 1929 were generally unfettered by legalistic regulatory niceties or wimpish concerns for the public safety. Their mission was to provide *genuine* "thrills and spills." And, for the most part, they accomplished this mission, with the help of a "friendly" court system and attractions such as the ominous and appropriately named "Flopper."

MURPHY v. STEEPLECHASE AMUSEMENT CO., INC.
Court of Appeals of New York
250 N.Y. 479; 166 N.E. 173 (1929)

BENJAMIN N. CARDOZO, C. J.

The defendant, Steeplechase Amusement Company, maintains an amusement park at Coney Island, N.Y. One of the supposed attractions is known as "the Flopper." It is a moving belt, running upward on an inclined plane, on which passengers sit or stand. Many of them are unable to keep their feet because of the movement of the belt, and are thrown backward or aside. The belt runs in a groove, with padded

236

walls on either side to a height of four feet, and with padded flooring beyond the walls at the same angle as the belt. An electric motor, driven by current furnished by the Brooklyn Edison Company, supplies the needed power.

Plaintiff, a vigorous young man, visited the park with friends. One of them, a young woman, now his wife, stepped upon the moving belt. Plaintiff followed and stepped behind her. As he did so, he felt what he describes as a sudden jerk, and was thrown to the floor. His wife in front and also friends behind him were thrown at the same time.

Something more was here, as everyone understood, than the slowly moving escalator that is common in shops and public places. A fall was foreseen as one of the risks of the adventure. There would have been no point to the whole thing, no adventure about it, if the risk had not been there. The very name, above the gate, "the Flopper," was warning to the timid. If the name was not enough, there was warning more distinct in the experience of others. We are told by the plaintiff's wife that the members of her party stood looking at the sport before joining in it themselves. Some aboard the belt were able, as she viewed them, to sit down with decorum or even to stand up and keep their footing; others jumped or fell. The tumbling bodies and the screams and laughter supplied the merriment and fun. "I took a chance," she said when asked whether she thought that a fall might be expected.

Plaintiff took the chance with her, but, less lucky than his companions, suffered a fracture of a knee cap. He states in his complaint that the belt was dangerous to life and limb, in that it stopped and started violently and suddenly and was not properly equipped to prevent injuries to persons who were using it without knowledge of its dangers, and in a bill of particulars he adds that it was operated at a fast and dangerous rate of speed and was not supplied with a proper railing, guard, or other device to prevent a fall therefrom. No other negligence is charged.

We see no adequate basis for a finding that the belt was out of order. It was already in motion when the plaintiff put his foot on it. He cannot help himself to a verdict in such circumstances by the addition of the facile comment that it threw him with a jerk. One who steps upon a moving belt and finds his heels above his head is in no position to discriminate with nicety between the successive stages of the shock, between the jerk which is a cause and the jerk, accompanying the fall, as an instantaneous effect.

There is evidence for the defendant that power was transmitted smoothly, and could not be transmitted otherwise. If the movement was spasmodic, it was an unexplained and, it seems, an inexplicable departure from the normal workings of the mechanism. An aberration so extraordinary, it is to lay the basis for a verdict, should rest on something firmer than a mere descriptive epithet, a summary of the sensations of a tense and crowded moment. . . . But the jerk, if it were established, would add little to the case. Whether the movement of the belt was uniform or irregular, the risk at greatest was a fall. This was the very hazard that was invited and foreseen.

Volenti non fit injuria {an injury is not done to a consenting person}. One who takes part in such a sport accepts the dangers that inhere in it so far as they are obvious and necessary, just as a fencer accepts the risk of a thrust by his antagonist or a spectator at a ball game the chance of contact with the ball. . . . The antics of the clown are not the paces of the cloistered cleric. The rough and boisterous joke, the horseplay of the clown, evokes its own guffaws, but they are not the pleasures of tranquillity. The plaintiff was not seeking a retreat for meditation. Visitors were tumbling about the belt to the merriment of onlookers when he made his choice to join them. He took the chance of a like fate, with whatever damage to his body might ensue from such a fall. The timorous may stay at home.

A different case would be here if the dangers inherent in the sport were obscure or unobserved {citation omitted} or so serious as to justify the belief that precautions of some kind must have been taken to avert them {citation omitted}. Nothing happened to the plaintiff except what common experience tells us may happen at any time as the consequence of a sudden fall. Many a skater or a horseman can rehearse a tale of equal woe.

A different case there would also be if the accidents had been so many as to show that the game in its inherent nature was too dangerous to be continued without change. The president of the amusement company says that there had never been such an accident before. A nurse employed at an emergency hospital maintained in connection with the park contradicts him to some extent. She says that on other occasions she had attended patrons of the park who had been injured at the Flopper, how many she could not say. None, however, had been badly injured or had suffered broken bones. Such testimony is not enough to show that the game was a trap for the unwary, too perilous to be endured. According to the defendant's estimate, 250,000 visitors were at the Flopper in a year. Some quota of accidents was to be looked for in so great a mass. One might as well say that a skating rink should be abandoned because skaters sometimes fall.

There is testimony by the plaintiff that he fell upon wood, and not upon a canvas padding. He is strongly contradicted by the photographs and by the witnesses for the defendant, and is without corroboration in the testimony of his companions who were witnesses in his behalf. If his observation was correct, there was a defect in the equipment, and one not obvious or known. The padding should have been kept in repair to break the force of any fall. The case did not go to the jury, however, upon any such theory of the defendant's liability, nor is the defect fairly suggested by the plaintiff's bill of particulars, which limits his complaint. The case went to the jury upon the theory that negligence was dependent upon a sharp and sudden jerk.

The judgment of the Appellate Division and that of the Trial Term should be reversed, and a new trial granted, with costs to abide the event.

The following case provides an articulate and informative journey through the mouth of the plaintiff, Harry B. Freer, discussing issues both dental and legal, and touching, in turn, on the mysteries of proper civil pleading and bicuspid mobility.

FREER v. PARKER
Supreme Court of Pennsylvania
411 Pa. 346; 192 A.2d 348 (1963)

MICHAEL A. MUSMANNO, JUSTICE

... The plaintiff, Harry B. Freer, averred in his Complaint that, as a result of the automobile collision, for which the defendant was responsible, he sustained various hurts, injuries and disablements, one of them being "loosening of teeth." At the trial the plaintiff's dentist testified that prior to the accident the plaintiff suffered from some loosening of teeth but that the violence of the collision, of which he was a victim, had further loosened his teeth, that they were "mobile," that "you could shake them with your fingers," and that he "splinted the teeth together to try to allow the bone to regenerate and tighten the teeth."

The defendant argues that there was thus demonstrated a variance between allegata and probata and that this variance entitled him to a new trial. The reason why the probata is required by law to concur with the allegata is that otherwise the defendant in a lawsuit would not know what he might be confronted with at the trial and he thus could not properly prepare for it. If, for instance, a plaintiff avers that his left arm was severed as a result of the litigated event and then stamps into court on a wooden leg, his arms intact, the defendant can well object because he has been caught by surprise. But if the plaintiff, as is the fact in this case, states in his Complaint that as a result of the legal bone of contention his teeth were loosened and the lay as well as medical evidence addresses itself to teeth loosening, it is difficult to see how the defendant can reasonably argue that he was left in the dark as to what to expect at the trial of the cause.

The defendant maintains that the plaintiff should have averred in his Complaint that the condition of his loose teeth was aggravated by the accident. But even if the plaintiff had so averred, the defendant would have known no more than what he was advised of in the Complaint as filed, namely, that the plaintiff's teeth were loosened by the vehicular violence of which the defendant reputedly was the author. Even if the plaintiff already chewed on loose teeth prior to the accident but the teeth were made looser by the accident, what still happened was that his teeth were loosened. A loose tooth can always become looser. In fact, that is more or less the melancholy story of teeth.

A tooth first manifests the slightest variation from perpendicularity; then it leans a little more, but, like the Leaning Tower of Pisa, it is still firmly imbedded in the terra firma of the jaw bone. One day, however, the tooth bearer will note, as he masticates a tough steak or bites into a bit of gravel in his oyster sandwich, that the tooth under surveillance wobbles a little more, but it is still useful and still resolute for further masticatory assaults on foods of a stronger constituency than mush. A person may have a number of teeth in that state; they may even resemble a slightly pushed-over picket fence but they are still good teeth, still serviceable tusks. If, because of violence applied to the mandibles, the whole dental battery is jostled and the individual molars, bicuspids, grinders and incisors are shaken in their sockets, it is certainly proper to say that there has been a loosening of teeth. A further loosening, it is true, but still a loosening.

In whatever stage of looseness a man's dental pearls may be, he is entitled to keep them in that state, and if they are tortiously subjected to jostling, jarring and jouncing, the tortfeasor may not be excused from responsibility for the further chewing dilapidation of his victim on the basis that he had bad teeth anyway.

If a Complaint avers that the plaintiff suffered a shortening of his left leg and it develops at the trial that the injured left leg was already, prior to the accident, 2 inches shorter than his normal right leg, he may not be denied compensation for the increased shortening from let us say, 2 inches to 4 inches because he did not specify in the Complaint what was the length of his leg prior to the accident. Once leg shortening is mentioned in the Complaint, the defendant is put on notice what to expect in the way of evidence at the trial and it is expected that he will come to the trial at least armed with a tape measure.

The defendant here suffered no surprise, and was in no way deceived by the phraseology in the Complaint. If he felt himself uninformed as to what the plaintiff intended to prove under the rather obvious heading of "loosening of teeth," he could have asked for a more specific Complaint. If he still remained perplexed, there was available to him a pre-trial discovery which would have permitted him to count and examine every tooth in the plaintiff's head and ascertain its stability, mobility and state of general welfare.

The appellant cites Littman v. Bell Telephone Co. {citation omitted}, as authority for new trial on the basis of the allegata-probata clash. The situation in that case was wholly different. There, the Court charged the jury that the plaintiff could recover for the aggravation of a pre-existing arthritis, of which there was not the slightest intimation in the Statement of Claim. There the defendant could not prepare for claims of arthritis because he had no way of knowing that the plaintiff ever had or had acquired arthritic decrepitude. Here, the defendant

241

could not possibly plead ignorance to knowledge of the plaintiff's "loosening of teeth." If a man's teeth are 10 percent loose before an accident and 60 percent loose after an accident, "loosening of teeth" accurately describes the deplorable dental deterioration, and adequately acquaints the defendant with what he must face at the trial in the way of claimed damages. . . .

That standard was certainly met in the case at bar. It was "loosening of teeth" all the way through.

Judgment affirmed.

In modern society, the underlying crime depicted in the following opinion would be known as a "car-jacking" (or more accurately, a "cab-jacking") from which the "cabbie" escaped. Bizarre by 1941 standards, the events inspired Judge Carlin to draft an opinion containing a classic and erudite discussion of the legal and theoretical underpinnings of the tort of "negligence."

CORDAS v. PEERLESS TRANSPORTATION CO.

City Court of New York, New York County
27 N.Y.S.2d 198 (1941)

FRANK A. CARLIN, JUSTICE

This case presents the ordinary man—that problem child of the law—in a most bizarre setting. As a lowly chauffeur in defendant's employ he became in a trice the protagonist in a breath-bating drama with a denouement almost tragic. It appears that a man, whose identity it would be indelicate to divulge, was feloniously relieved of his portable goods by two nondescript highwaymen in an alley near 26th Street and Third Avenue, Manhattan; they induced him to relinquish his possessions by a strong argument ad hominem couched in the convincing cant of the criminal and pressed at the point of a most persuasive pistol. Laden with their loot, but not thereby impeded, they took an abrupt departure and he, shuffling off the coil of that discretion which enmeshed him in the alley, quickly gave chase through 26th Street toward Second Avenue, whither they were resorting "with expedition swift as thought" for most obvious reasons.

Somewhere on that thoroughfare of escape they indulged in the stratagem of separation ostensibly to disconcert their pursuer and allay the ardor of his pursuit. He then centered on for capture the man with the pistol whom he saw board defendant's taxicab, which quickly veered south toward 25th Street on Second Avenue, where he saw the chauffeur jump out while the cab, still in motion, continued toward 24th Street; after the chauffeur relieved himself of the cumbersome burden of his fare, the latter also is said to have similarly departed from the cab before it reached 24th Street.

The chauffeur's story is substantially the same except that he states that his uninvited guest boarded the cab at 25th Street while it was at a standstill waiting for a less colorful fare; that his "passenger" immediately advised him "to stand not upon the order of his going but to go at once" and added finality to his command by an appropriate gesture with a pistol addressed to his sacroiliac. The chauffeur in reluctant acquiescence proceeded about fifteen feet, when his hair, like unto the quills of the fretful porcupine, was made to stand on end by the hue and cry of the man despoiled accompanied by a clamorous concourse of the law-abiding which paced him as he ran; the concatenation of "stop thief," to which the patter of persistent feet did maddingly beat time, rang in his ears as the pursuing posse all the while gained on the receding cab with its quarry therein contained.

The hold-up man sensing his insecurity suggested to the chauffeur that in the event there was the slightest lapse in obedience to his curt command that he, the chauffeur, would suffer the loss of his brains, a prospect as horrible to an humble chauffeur as it undoubtedly would be to one of the intelligentsia. The chauffeur apprehensive of certain dissolution from either Scylla, the pursuers, or Charybdis, the pursued, quickly threw his car out of first speed in which he was proceeding, pulled on the emergency, jammed on his brakes and, although he thinks the motor was still running, swung open the door to his left and jumped out of the car. He confesses that the only act that smacked of intelligence was that by which he jammed the brakes in order to throw off balance the hold-up man who was half-standing and half-sitting with his pistol menacingly poised.

Thus abandoning his car and passenger, the chauffeur sped toward 26th Street and then turned to look; he saw the cab proceeding south toward 24th Street where it mounted the sidewalk. The plaintiff-mother and her two infant children were there injured by the cab, which, at the time, appeared to be also minus its passenger who, it appears, was apprehended in the cellar of a local hospital where he was pointed out to a police officer by a remnant of the posse, herein-before mentioned.

He did not appear at the trial. The three aforesaid plaintiffs and the husband-father sue the defendant for damages predicating their respective causes of action upon the contention that the chauffeur was negligent in abandoning the cab under the aforesaid circumstances. Fortunately the injuries sustained were comparatively slight.

Negligence has been variously defined but the common legal acceptation is the failure to exercise that care and caution which a reasonable and prudent person ordinarily would exercise under like conditions or circumstances. It has been most authoritatively held that "negligence held in the abstract, apart from things related, is surely not a tort, if indeed it is understandable at all" (Cardozo, C.J., in Palsgraf v. Long Island Railroad Co. {citation omitted}). In Steinbrenner v. M. W. Forney Co. {citation omitted} it is said, "The test of actionable negligence is what reasonably prudent men would have done under the same circumstances"; Connell v. New York Central & Hudson River Railroad Co. {citation omitted} holds that actionable negligence must be predicated upon "a breach of duty to the plaintiff. Negligence is 'not absolute or intrinsic,' but 'is always relevant to some circumstances of time, place or person.'"

In slight paraphrase of the world's first bard it may be truly observed that the expedition of the chauffeur's violent love of his own security outran the pauser, reason, when he was suddenly confronted with an unusual emergency which "took his reason prisoner." The learned attorney for the plaintiffs concedes that the chauffeur acted in an emergency but claims a right to recovery upon the following proposition taken verbatim from his brief: "It is respectfully submitted that the value of the interests of the public at large to be immune from being injured by a dangerous instrumentality such as a car unattended while in motion is very superior to the right of a driver of a motor vehicle to abandon same while it is in motion even when acting under the belief that his life is in danger and by abandoning same he will save his life."

To hold thus under the facts adduced herein, would be tantamount to a repeal by implication of the primal law of nature written in indelible characters upon the fleshy tablets of a sentient creation by the Almighty Law-giver, "the supernal Judge who sits on high." There are those who stem the turbulent current for bubble fame, or who bridge the yawning chasm with a leap for the leap's sake or who "outstare the sternest eyes that look, outbrave the heart most daring on the earth, pluck the young suckling cubs from the she-bear, yea, mock the lion when he roars for prey"[1] to win a fair lady and these are the admiration of the generality of men; but they are made of sterner stuff than the ordinary man upon whom the law places no duty of emulation.

The law would indeed be fond if it imposed upon the ordinary man the obligation to so demean himself when suddenly confronted with danger, not of his creation, disregarding the likelihood that such a contingency may darken the intellect and palsy the will of the common legion of the earth, the fraternity of ordinary men, whose acts or omissions under certain conditions or circumstances make the yardstick by which the law measures culpability or innocence, negligence or care. If a person is placed in a sudden peril from which death might ensue, the law does not impel another to the rescue of the person endangered nor does it condemn him for his unmoral failure to rescue when he can; this is in recognition of the immutable law written in frail flesh.

Returning to our chauffeur. If the philosophic Horatio and the martial companions of his watch were "distilled almost to jelly with the act of fear" when they beheld "in the dead vast and middle of the night" the disembodied spirit of Hamlet's father stalk majestically by "with a countenance more in sorrow than in anger" was not the chauffeur, though unacquainted with the example of these eminent men-at-arms, more amply justified in his fearsome reactions when he was more palpably confronted by a thing of flesh and blood bearing in its hand an engine of destruction which depended for its lethal purpose upon the quiver of a hair? When Macbeth was cross-examined by Macduff as to any reason he could advance for his sudden despatch of Duncan's grooms, he said in

---

[1]{Ed. Note: From Shakespeare's *The Merchant of Venice.*}

plausible answer, "Who can be wise, amazed, temperate and furious, loyal, and neutral, in a moment? No man." Macbeth did not by a "tricksy word" thereby stand justified as he criminally created the emergency from which he sought escape by indulgence in added felonies to divert suspicion to the innocent. However, his words may be wrested to the advantage of the defendant's chauffeur whose acts cannot be legally construed as the proximate cause of plaintiff's injuries, however regrettable, unless nature's first law is arbitrarily disregarded.

Plaintiff's attorney in his brief cites the cases of Grunfelder v. Brooklyn Heights Railroad Co. {citation omitted} and Savage v. Joseph H. Bauland Co. {citation omitted} as authorities for a contrary holding. Neither case is apposite in fact or principle. In the classic case of Laidlaw v. Sage {citation omitted} is found a statement of the law peculiarly apropos:

> That the duties and responsibilities of a person confronted with such a danger are different and unlike those which follow his actions in performing the ordinary duties of life under other conditions is a well-established principle of law. * * * "The law presumes that *an act or omission done or neglected under the influence of pressing danger was done or neglected involuntarily.*" It is there said that this rule seems to be founded upon the maxim that self-preservation is the first law of nature, and that, where it is a question whether one of two men shall suffer, each is justified in doing the best he can for himself. (Italics ours {Carlin's}).

Kolanka v. Erie Railroad Co. {citation omitted} says: "The law in this state does not hold one in an emergency to the exercise of that mature judgment required of him under circumstances where he has an opportunity for deliberate action. He is not required to exercise unerring judgment, which would be expected of him, were he not confronted with an emergency requiring prompt action." The circumstances provide the foil by which the act is brought into relief to determine whether it is or is not negligent. If under normal circumstances an act is done which might be considered negligent, it does not follow as a corollary that a similar act is negligent if performed by a person acting under an emergency, not of his own making, in which he suddenly is faced with a patent danger with a moment left to adopt a means of extrication.

246

The chauffeur—the ordinary man in this case—acted in a split second in a most harrowing experience. To call him negligent would be to brand him a coward; the court does not do so in spite of what those swaggering heroes, "whose valor plucks dead lions by the beard," may bluster to the contrary. The court is loathe to see the plaintiffs go without recovery even though their damages were slight, but cannot hold the defendant liable upon the facts adduced at the trial. Motions, upon which decision was reserved, to dismiss the complaint are granted with exceptions to plaintiffs. Judgment for defendant against plaintiffs dismissing their complaint upon the merits. Ten days' stay and thirty days to make a case.

Those who dare to be seated in the front row at a circus performance may occasionally receive an unexpected and unwanted reward for so doing, much to their surprise, grief, shame, horror, humiliation, embarrassment and mortification.

CHRISTY BROS. CIRCUS
v. TURNAGE
Court of Appeals of Georgia
38 Ga. App. 581; 144 S.E. 680 (1928)

ALEXANDER W. STEPHENS, J.

There may be a recovery of damages for mental suffering, humiliation or embarrassment resulting from a physical injury of which they are inseparable components. . . . Any unlawful touching of a person's body, although no actual physical hurt may ensue therefrom, yet, since it violates a personal right, constitutes a physical injury to that person. . . . The unlawful touching need not be direct, but may be indirect, as by the precipitation upon the body of a person of any material substance. . . .

Where a petition alleged that the plaintiff was an unmarried white lady, and that while in attendance as a guest of the defendant at a circus performance given by the defendant, and while seated in one of the seats provided by the defendant for the defendant's guests at the circus, a horse, which was going through a dancing performance immediately in front of where the plaintiff was sitting, was by the defendant's servant, who was riding upon the horse, caused to back towards the plaintiff, and while in this situation the horse evacuated his bowels into her lap, that this occurred in full view of many people, some of whom were the defendant's employees, and all of whom laughed at the occurrence, that as a result thereof the plaintiff was caused much embarrassment, mortification, and mental pain and suffering, to her damage in a certain amount, that the damage alleged was due entirely to the defendant's negligence and without any fault on the part of the plaintiff, the petition set out a cause of action and was good as against a general demurrer. . . .

The court, fairly to the defendant, submitted all the issues presented. The evidence authorized the inference that the plaintiff was damaged, by reason of humiliation and embarrassment, in the sum of $500, and the verdict found for her in that amount was authorized.

CHAPTER X

Scurrilous, *Scandalous, Arbitrary, Capricious, Willful, Deliberate, Intentional, Malicious, Oppressive, Obstinate, Despicable, Outrageous, Loathsome, Egregious* and *Reprehensible Tortious* Acts and *Conduct*

... May not a judicial wayfarer, traveling in the dry and dusty highways of the law, at spells lighten his labor without lowering the dignity of his case by gathering a nosegay for use as do other wayfarers, so long as he does not loiter afield and miss the main traveled road to ultimate justice? ...
—Henry Lamm, J.[1]

---

[1]From Stumpe v. Kopp, 201 Mo. 419; 99 S.W. 1073 (1907).

The law is replete with distinctions, both subtle and obvious. The judge's task, of course, is to articulate the particular distinctions which lead to the resolution of the case. In the following instance, whether an item was to be characterized as real property (i.e., land) or personal property (i.e., chattel) had a direct influence on the outcome.

CARVER v. PIERCE
King's Bench, Michaelmas Term, 23 Charles I
82 E.R. 534; Sty. 66 (1648)

ANONYMOUS, JUDGE

Carver brings an action upon the case against Pierce for speaking these words of him, "Thou art a thief, for thou hast stollen my dung," and hath a verdict. The defendant moved in arrest of judgment, that the words were not actionable; for it is not certain whether the dung be a chattel, or part of the free-hold, and if so, it cannot be theft to take it, but a trespass, and then the action will not lye. Bacon Justice, Dung is a chattel, and may be stollen. But Roll Justice answered, Dung may be a chattel, and it may not be a chattel; for a heap of dung is a chattel, but if it be spread upon the land it is not, and said, the word thief here is actionable alone, and there are not subsequent words to mitigate the former words: for the stealing of dung is felony if it be a chattel. Bacon Justice said, It doth not appear in this case of what value the dung was, and how shall it then be known, whether it be felony or pety larceny? To this Roll answered, The words are scandalous notwithstanding and actionable, though the stealing of the dung be not felony. . . .

Attorneys have long been the object of contempt and scorn. In the following case, the attorney (Mr. Bestney) was unwilling to passively absorb a verbal assault inflicted upon his professional dignity by the perpetrator (Mr. Dison), and instead, sued him and won.

DISON AND BESTNEY'S CASE
King's Bench, Easter Term, 8 James I
77 E.R. 1480; 13 Co. Rep. 71 (1611)

ANONYMOUS, JUDGE

Humphry Dison said of Nicholas Bestney, Utter Barrister and Counsellor of Gray's-Inn, "Thou a Barrister? Thou art no Barrister, thou art a Barretor;[1] thou wert put from the bar, and thou darest not shew thyself there. Thou study law? Thou hast as much wit as a daw."[2] Upon not guilty pleaded, the jury found for the plaintiff, and assessed damages to £23 upon which judgment was given; and in a writ of error in the Exchequer-chamber, the judgment was affirmed.

Judges, though occupying noble and venerated positions, are not immune from ridicule by their constituencies. However horrific and vehement the criticism may be, when it amounts to less than slander, it is not considered a crime.

ANONYMOUS
King's Bench, Michaelmas Term, 15 Charles II
82 E.R. 1152; 1 KEB. 629 (1663)

ANONYMOUS, JUDGE

Of a justice of peace, that he is a logger-headed and a sloutch-headed bursen-bellied hound, is no cause of indictment before justices of peace in their sessions, partly for want of jurisdiction, partly because the words are not actionable:and after judgment, this was by Jones assigned for error. *Adjornatur* {it is adjourned}.

---

[1]{Ed. Note: "Barretor:" a disturber of the peace who spreads false rumors, and promotes discord and disquiet among neighbors.}

[2]{Ed. Note: "Daw" is short for "jackdaw," a bird resembling a crow; *daw* is itself a common word meaning "fool."}

251

Judges often aspire to be writers, and if given the chance, will sometimes venture beyond the bland, prosaic style customarily exhibited in judicial opinions and, on rare occasion, may even explore the upper reaches of lofty, pompous and grandiose linguistic legerdemain.

IN RE KIRK

Supreme Court of New Jersey
101 N.J.L. 450; 130 A. 569 (1925)

JAMES F. MINTURN, J.

The observant traveler, leaving the dizzy cliffs of Manhattan, in his progress up the Rhine of America, will inevitably have obtruded upon his expectant vision the bold outlines of a precipitous cliff of basaltic rock of glacial origin, which Gibraltar-like projects its giant outlines into the rolling waters of the majestic Hudson, guarding as it were the erstwhile fancied entrance of the visionary pioneer to the fabulous wealth of the Indies. Inquiry will elicit the information that this projection was intended by a natural prehistoric cataclysm to mark the gateway to the famous Palisades, and that stretched at its feet in bucolic simplicity are the remnants of the beautiful emerald slopes, termed by the primeval natives "awiehawk," and by the modern residents "Weehawken." Of these scenes the poet Fitz-Greene Halleck in ravishing transport wrote:

> *When life is old, and many a scene forgot,*
> *The heart will hold its memory of this.*

Upon these arboreal slopes, the traveler will be told, was enacted one of the greatest tragedies in American history, for there the scintillating Burr, in the days of the duel, took from human existence the erudite and heroic Hamilton, and to that extent sadly impoverished American public life.

Although a century of national existence has passed, no stately monument graces the site of that national tragedy, but, hidden away out of the vision of public observation, there has been erected by some public-spirited hand an attenuated inclosure that might be visualized as an adequate conception of Ibsen's *Doll House*, which contains a miniature carving of what we are

252

informed, in apologetic tones, is intended to serve as a bust of the lamented Hamilton. But, like all modern self-concentrated townships, this municipality shares the unique distinction, peculiar to the dress of modern modish femininity, that it possesses neither distinctive bodily lines, nor perceptible corporeal boundaries; so that the anxious traveler, intent upon seeking its historic landmarks, is unable without expert assistance to determine its terminus a quo or its terminus ad quem.

However, like all townships worthy of the name, it prides itself upon the possession of a town hall, which, like the Acropolis at Athens or the Forum at Rome, is the *Deus ex machina* {God from a machine} for all municipal lucubration, the fount of all public inspiration and the Mecca of all political ambition. It also enjoys the spiritual distinction of the early church, in that it is built upon a rock, from which adamantine tenure neither the iconoclastic hand of time nor the progressive evolutionary arguments of municipal ambition have been able to dislodge it, but, enshrouded in an atmosphere of modern mysticism, retirement and modesty, it stands, like the rock of ages, unmoved and immovable.

Upon stated evenings, amid the quietude of an environment which makes for serious reflection and dignified procedure, the business of the township was transacted without ostentation, and yet with becoming dignity, decorum and dispatch, until the memorable night of June 3, 1925, when in the quietude of their homes the confiding inhabitants were startled, astounded, humiliated and shocked to learn that one of their honored representatives, in the solemn conclave of a public session, had been called a "bootlegger" and a "souphead."

Such a flagrant contempt of the dignity of the town and its representatives was properly met by a proceeding under section 3 of the Disorderly Act (2 Comp. St. 1910, p. 1927) against this defendant, and in due time he was found guilty before the recorder, and sentenced to imprisonment, which, however, like the sword of Damocles, is hanging over him while he behaves himself within the unobservable and indistinguishable limits of the township.

The defendant, upon this review, insists that, if there be such an offense as is charged against him, it was not committed in a public place. This contention is certainly unique, for, if any place be public, the hall erected by the public for the transaction of public business,

253

like a public park, is peculiarly within that designation State v. Lynch {citation omitted}.

But his strenuous contention is, and this connotes serious pause and no little bewilderment, that his utterances were terms of compliment and distinction, rather than offensive epithets, so as to be comprehended within the term "disorderly conduct." Thus it is argued that, while the bootlegger, like some of the early saints, may have had an unholy beginning, he has risen like the Phoenix, and stands today as the chivalric Bayard, *sans peur et sans réproche* {without fear and without reproach}, the cynosure of every eye and the hope of every heart, wherever liberty unrestrained possesses an admirer, and license unchallenged commands a champion. In various social circles, where bibulousness is ever the dominant thought, and the proverbial hip pocket is seldom a vacuity, is he not recognized like Robespierre as the saviour of popular liberty?

In financial and business circles, does he not command extensive credit, when the ordinary purveyor of dry goods receives scant accommodation? Does he not boast of his estates and acquisitions, when the ordinary laborer in the vineyard struggles like Sisyphus to maintain his never-decreasing burden? Does not the government, in recognition of his potentiality and prowess, spend princely sums to padlock him on land and suppress his activities upon the raging main? Like the publican, does he not often occupy a prominent pew in our temples of worship; and are not the faithful publicly exhorted to pray for his deliverance from the bondage and prosecutions of the merciless minions of the law? Surely, to quote Holy Writ, "By their fruits shall ye know them." But, with all its plausibility and force, this alluring picture of modern success and godliness presents another side. Reared above it all, like the condemning hand which consigned the Babylonian to disaster and oblivion,[1] is the handwriting of the Constitution and the law, which condemns this unique malefactor as a criminal, and consigns him to the same moral and legal category as the pirate and the outlaw.

No financial, social or religious recognition can remove the brand of Cain from the brow, or place a heroic halo upon the head of one who stands as a common felon before the law. When, therefore, this

---

[1] {Ed. Note: See Daniel 5:5ff.}

254

defendant publicly charged a member of the council in a public place with being a bootlegger, he charged him in legal effect with being a criminal, and thereby subjected himself to the charge leveled against him in this compliant.

The mystical term "souphead," however, stands in another category, and awakens delectable memories of the early well-kept home, fast disappearing, like many other cherished American institutions, before the tinsel invasion of that birdlike roost, appropriately termed a flat. This euphonious appellation seems to have had a local application peculiar to the days when that attractive dish was made and consumed with relish and avidity, by the habitués of that ancient comfort station known as a barroom.

The libraries and lexicons of neighboring municipalities furnish no clue to its origin, doubtless due to the fact that, in those less-favored localities, the canned variety fulfilled the local needs. Nor are we in any wise assisted in this research by the erudite researches of learned counsel, possessed as they are with a large and varied experience in the sociological conditions of the past. The difficulty of classification and etymology is therefore quite manifest, and as in all such researches, when modern learning fails, recourse must be had to the ancient founts of inspiration. The antique genus "souphead" was doubtless the proud possessor of a mentality surcharged, among other things, with the diluted essence of succulent garden products, not radically indistinguishable from the modern vegetarian, whose dietary code has its genesis in soup as a fundamental substratum.

{The} *Magnum caput* {big head} of the luxurious Roman was possessed by a character *sui generis* {of his own kind, unique}, a product of the rich Etruscan vineyards, not unlike the overstimulated graduate of the embossed barroom of later times, and subjected its possessor alternately to pity, ribaldry and ridicule, but in no proper sense could this proud product of inebriety be classed as a "souphead."

When souphouses existed as a social safety valve, assuming the status in modern life occupied by the Toman *panem et circenses*,[2] the master mind controlling the institution might well be termed a "souphead." So, also, it may be accepted as a matter of judicial observation that, during the lightning-like rapidity with which some judges

---

[2]{Ed. Note: "Bread and circuses," a phrase from the Roman poet Juvenal, *Satires* X, 81.}

255

and lawyers alike, with equal rapidity betake themselves to the nearest boniface, and there discard everything edible for this attractive and toothsome decoction, as though to evince that in some esoteric manner the rapid administration of the work typified by the blindfolded goddess is dependent upon the momentary acquisition and rapid ingestion of that ever ready and most inviting dietetic staple. If, therefore, we apply the legal maxim *noscitur a sociis* {one is known by the company one keeps} to the situation, the "souphead" maintains respectable and satisfactory relationships in all the dignified walks of life, and proverbially one is known by the company he keeps.

In the light of these circumstances it will be quite universally conceded that the head which invented this popular gastronomic edible, like the genius who discovered the attraction of gravitation or the rotundity of the earth, is entitled to the applause and gratitude, rather than the condemnation, of mankind. Obviously, therefore, the term cannot be deemed either undignified or offensive, and the defendant, whether conscious of his complimentary ebullition or not, cannot be adjudged guilty of disorderly conduct.

The conviction, however, must be sustained upon the ground first stated.

The following case is a "classic" gemstar of judicial humor, and the undisputed grandaddy of *all* "trade defamation" lawsuits.

DICKES v. FENNE
King's Bench, Michaelmas Term, 15 Charles II
82 E.R. 411; March, N.R. 60 (1640)

PER CURIAM (*including* ROLLS *and* BARCKLEY, J.J.)

In an action upon the case for words, the words were these: The defendant having communication with some of the customers of the plaintiff, who was a brewer, said, that he would give a peck of malt to his mare, and she should piss as good beer as Dickes doth brew. And that he laid {suffered as a result} *ad grave damnum* {to his extreme damage}, &c. Porter for the defendant; that the words are not actionable of themselves, and because the plaintiff hath alleged no special damage, as loss of his customers, &c. the action will not lie. Rolls; that the words are actionable; and he said, that it had been adjudged here, that if one say of a brewer, that he brews naughty beer, without more saying, these words are actionable, without any special damage alledged. But the whole Court was against him (Crooke only absent) that the words of themselves, were not actionable, without alledging special damage; as the loss of his customers, &c. which is not here. And therefore not actionable. And Barckley said, that the words are only comparative, and altogether impossible also. And he said, that it had been adjudged, that where one says of a lawyer, that he had as much law as a monkey, that the words were not actionable; because he hath as much law, and more also. But if he had said, that he hath no more law than a monkey, those words were actionable. And it was adjourned.

One who is the victim of an assault and battery may sue the attacker and recover money damages to compensate for the injuries suffered. This legal principle is graphically illustrated in the following case, a vile, odious and lamentable depiction of early twentieth-century urban violence in America.

TRICOLI v. CENTALANZA
Supreme Court of New Jersey
100 N.J.L. 231; 126 A. 214 (1924)

JAMES F. MINTURN, J.

"Run away, Maestro Juan, I am going to kill you." Such was the ferocious threat that disturbed the atmosphere, not of prehistoric Mexico, where upon desolate plains the savage coyote still bays at the moon, nor yet of classic Verona, where dramatic memories of the houses of Montague and Capulet still linger to entrance the romantic wayfarer, but from the undiluted atmosphere of Bloomfield Avenue, where it winds its attractive course through the prim rococo shades of modern Montclair, which upon the day of succeeding Christmas in 1923 sat like Roman immortals upon its seven hills, and from its throne of beauty contemplated with serene satisfaction the peace and tranquility of the modern world.

The Maestro, however, with true chivalric disdain, refused to retreat, but determined at all hazards, like Horatius, to hold the

257

bridge, or rather the stoop, upon which he stood. Like a true Roman, inoculated with the maximum percentage of American patriotism, he turned defiantly to the oncoming house of Centalanza, and proclaimed in the bellicose language of the day, "You too son of a gun."

In the days of Montague and Capulet, aristocratic rapiers and swords defended the honor of their respective houses; but in this day of popular progress the Maestro and the Centalanza sought only the plebian defense of fists and a shovel. As a result of a triangular contest, the physician testified that the Maestro was battered "from head to buttocks"—a distribution of punishment, it may be observed, which, while it may not be entirely aesthetic in its selection of a locum tenens, was to say the least equitably administered and distributed. Indeed, so much was the Maestro battered that his daily toil lost him for 12 days, and the trial court estimated that this loss, together with his pain and suffering, and the aggravation of the trespass, entitled him to receive from the house of Centalanza $210.

The latter, however, has appealed, and alleges that the Maestro proved no substantial cause of action against them. But the learned trial court, upon this contested state of facts, concluded, and we think properly, that there was an issue of fact thus presented, since the suit was for assault and battery in the nature of trespass *vi et armis* {with force and arms}. But the defendants Centalanza insist that two distinct encounters took place, one by both defendants, and the other by one only, and they ask: How can such a physical contretemps be admeasured, so as to impose upon each member of the house of Centalanza his fair share of compensation for his physical contribution to the melee? The inquiry possesses its latent difficulties, but, since it is an admitted rule of law that the court will not distribute the damages between tortfeasors, upon any theory of equitable admeasurement, the house of Centalanza obviously must bear the entire loss, without seeking a partition thereof. *Ex turpi causa oritur non actio* {An action does not arise from a base (illegal or immoral) consideration; citation omitted}.

Indeed, it would prove to be a rare feat of judicial acumen, were the court to attempt to give due credit to Donato Centalanza for the prowess he displayed in his fistic endeavors, and to assess to Raffale Centalanza his meed of financial contribution for the dexterity with which he wielded his handy implement of excavation. It is doubtful, even in these days of the mystic prize ring, whether such a metaphysical

258

test may be included among the accredited mental accomplishments of a quasi-militant judiciary, which, while it occasionally indulges in a caustic punch, still strenuously endeavors to maintain the proverbial respectability and regal poise of its ancestral prototype. In such a sit- uation we are not inclined to impose this extraordinary and novel field of jurisdiction upon our inferior courts. The occurrence of trespass *vi et armis* confers upon the trial court the right to assess exemplary dam- ages as smart money, and this the trial court properly did under the circumstances of the case {citation omitted}.

It is contended, however, that the actual damage sustained by the Maestro was inconsequential, and that the rule, *De minimis non curat lex* {the law is not concerned with trifles}, applies. It must be obvious, however, that damage which to the attending physician seemed to penetrate the Maestro "from head to buttocks" may seem trivial to us as noncombatants, but to the Maestro it manifestly seemed otherwise, and doubtless punctured his corpus, as well as his sensibilities. Indeed, he well might declare in the language of the gal- lant Mercutio of Verona, concerning the extent of his wound: "It is not as wide as a church door, or as deep as a well, but 'twill serve."

The judgment will be affirmed.

Those with the courage and vision to blaze new trails on the cutting edge of fashion or technology have often served as objects of ridicule by their less-inspired contemporaries. In this case, a hairdresser sued a newspaper over an article which poked fun at her novel hairdressing techniques.

MORGANROTH v. WHITALL
Court of Appeals of Michigan
161 Mich. App. 785; 411 N.W.2d 859 (1987)

DAVID SAWYER, JUDGE

> *Truth is a torch that gleams through the fog without dispelling it.*
> —*Claude Helvetius,* **De l'Esprit**

In this heated dispute, the trial court granted summary disposi- tion in favor of defendants on plaintiff's claims of libel and invasion of privacy by false light. Plaintiff now appeals and we affirm.

Plaintiff alleges that she was libeled and cast in a false light by an article written by defendant Whitall which appeared in the Sunday supplement of the *Detroit News* on November 11, 1984. The article was entitled "Hot Locks: Let Shila burn you a new 'do." The article was accompanied by two photographs, one depicting plaintiff performing her craft on a customer identified as "Barbara X" and the second showing Barbara X and her dog, identified as "Harry X," following completion of the hairdressing. Central to the article was the fact that plaintiff used a blowtorch in her hairdressing endeavors. According to the article, plaintiff's blowtorch technique was dubbed "Shi-lit" and was copyrighted.[1]

The article also described two dogs, Harry and Snowball, the latter belonging to plaintiff, noting that the canines have had their respective coats colored at least in part. The article also indicated that the blowtorch technique had been applied to both dogs. Additionally, the article described plaintiff's somewhat unusual style of dress, including a silver holster for her blowtorch and a barrette in her hair fashioned out of a $100 bill. Much of the article devoted itself to plaintiff's comments concerning her hairdressing and the trend of what, at least in the past, had been deemed unusual in the area of hairstyles.

Plaintiff's rather brief complaint alleges that the article, when read as a whole, is false, misleading and constitutes libel. More specifically, the complaint alleges that the article used the terms "blowtorch lady," "blowtorch technique" and the statement that plaintiff "is dressed for blowtorching duty in a slashed-to-there white jumpsuit" without any factual basis and as the result of defendants' intentional conduct to distort and sensationalize the facts obtained in the interview. The complaint further alleges that the article falsely portrayed plaintiff as an animal hairdresser, again as part of a deliberate action by defendants to distort and sensationalize the facts. In her brief on appeal, plaintiff also takes exception to her being cast as an animal hairdresser and claims as inaccurate the portrayal in the article that she does "mutt

---

[1]Sic. While this is not an intellectual property case, we note in passing that it would seem more reasonable that the blowtorch technique would be subject to patent law and the term "Shi-lit" would constitute a trademark, rather than coming under the terms of copyright law. However, we leave it to a more appropriate forum to decide this burning issue if it should ever become relevant.

Mohawks for dogs" and the reference to "two canines who have been blowtorched." . . .

The elements of defamation were stated by this Court in Sawabini v. Desenberg {citation omitted}:

> The elements of a cause of action for defamation are: "(a) a false and defamatory statement concerning plaintiff; (b) an unprivileged publication to a third party; (c) fault amounting at least to negligence on the part of the publisher; and (d) either actionability of the statement irrespective of special harm (defamation *per se*) or the existence of special harm caused by the publication (defamation *per quod*)." . . .

The *Sawabini* court further commented on the appropriateness of dismissing a defamation claim by summary disposition:

> The court may determine, as a matter of law, whether the words in question, alleged by plaintiff to be defamatory, are capable of defamatory meaning. . . .

In determining whether an article is libelous, it is necessary to read the article as a whole and fairly and reasonably construe it in determining whether a portion of the article is libelous in character. . . .

Reading the article as a whole, we believe that it is substantially true; therefore plaintiff's complaint lacks an essential element of her defamation claim, namely falsity. In looking at plaintiff's specific allegations of falsity, for the most part we find no falsehood. Considering as a group the various references to plaintiff's using a "blowtorch" in hairstyling, we note that *The Random House College Dictionary*, Revised Edition (1984), defines "blowtorch" as follows:

> [A] small portable apparatus that gives an extremely hot gasoline flame intensified by air under pressure, used esp. in metalworking.

In looking at the photographic exhibits filed by defendants, we believe that the instrument used by plaintiff in her profession can accurately be described as a blowtorch.[2] Accordingly, while the use of the term "blowtorch" as an adjective in connection with references to

---

[2]We acknowledge that *The Random House Dictionary's* definition did not list hairdressing as an example. However, we are not persuaded that the dictionary's editors intended their examples to be exclusive. See also *blowtorch, Webster's New World Dictionary*, 2nd College Edition (1976).

plaintiff or her hairdressing technique may have been colorful, it was not necessarily inaccurate and certainly not libelous. As for the reference that plaintiff was "dressed for blowtorching duty in a slashed-to-there white jumpsuit," we have examined the photographic exhibits submitted by defendant at the motion hearing and we conclude that reasonable minds could not differ in reaching the conclusion that plaintiff did, in fact, wear a jumpsuit "slashed to there."

Finally, while having disposed of the allegedly libelous claims contained in the complaint, we briefly turn to the additional allegations of false statement listed in plaintiff's brief on appeal. In her brief, plaintiff claims that defendants inaccurately described her as being a hairdresser for dogs, giving dogs a Mohawk cut, and using a blowtorch on the dogs. While it appears that plaintiff did do hairdressing on dogs, it is not necessarily certain at this point that she did, in fact, use the blowtorch on the dogs. . . .

Moreover, inasmuch as it appears undisputed that plaintiff at least dyed the fur of the dogs, which would constitute hairdressing of dogs, we are not persuaded that the article, when read as a whole, becomes libelous because of an inaccurate reference to using the blowtorch on the dogs. This is particularly true since, by plaintiff's conduct, she asserts that blowtorching is a safe practice when performed on humans. Therefore, it would appear that, from plaintiff's perspective, blowtorching would also be safe on dogs, even if she did not engage in such a practice. Furthermore, her claim that she was libeled by labeling her as both a dog hairdresser and a human hairdresser is unsupported in light of the tinting of the dogs' hair. Since the undisputed factual showing indicates that plaintiff did blowtorch her human clientele and style her pooch's fur, we will not split hairs at this point to conclude that the statement that she used her blowtorch on dogs, even if inaccurate, is libelous.

For the above-stated reasons, we conclude that, when reviewing the article and accompanying photographs as a whole, the article was not libelous.

On appeal, plaintiff also argues that the article invaded her privacy by casting her in a false light. . . . False light invasion of privacy is described in Ledl v. Quik Pik Stores {citation omitted} as:

[p]ublicity which places plaintiff in a false light in the public eye. . . .

In discussing what is necessary to state a cause of action for invasion of privacy, this court stated in Reed v. Ponton {citation omitted}:

> When there has been no misappropriated use of, or physical intrusion into, the private life, employment, property, name, likeness, or other personal place or interest, so that the privacy action is premised solely upon a disclosure of secret or confidential matter or upon being put publicly in a "false light," then if (without deciding) mere words of mouth can never be actionable (except by a slander action) the oral communication must be broadcast to the public in general or publicized to a large number of people. . . .

As indicated in the above discussion under the theory of defamation, with the exception of certain references to hairdressing dogs, none of the conduct attributed to plaintiff in the article was false. Therefore, it could not place plaintiff in a false light. With reference to the assertions concerning her hairdressing of dogs, we do not believe that a rational trier of fact could conclude that, even if inaccurate, those references are unreasonable or put plaintiff in a position of receiving highly objectionable publicity.

The article did not indicate that plaintiff harmed, injured or inflicted pain upon the dogs. Rather, at most, the article inaccurately stated that plaintiff used techniques on the dogs, such as blow-torching, which she also used on humans. While the article may have overstated the techniques that she uses on dogs, inasmuch as she advocates those techniques for use on humans, we cannot conclude that plaintiff would believe it highly objectionable that those techniques also be performed on dogs.

Similarly, she cannot have been placed in false light as being both the hairdresser of dogs and humans inasmuch as the tinting of the canines' fur would constitute hairdressing. Thus, it would not be placing plaintiff in a false light to indicate that she served both dog and man. Accordingly, we believe that summary disposition was also properly granted on the false light claim.

In summary, although the manner in which the present article was written may have singed plaintiff's desire for obtaining favorable coverage of her unique hairdressing methods, we cannot subscribe to the view that it was libelous. We believe that the trial court aptly summarized this case when it stated that "this Court is of the Opinion that the Plaintiff sought publicity and got it." Indeed, it would appear that the root of plaintiff's dissatisfaction with defendants' article is that the publicity plaintiff received was not exactly the publicity she had in mind. While the publicity may have been inflammatory from plaintiff's vantage point, we do not believe it was libelous. At most, defendants treated the article more lightheartedly than plaintiff either anticipated or hoped. While this may give plaintiff cause to cancel her subscription to the *Detroit News,* it does not give her cause to complain in court.

Affirmed. Costs to defendants.

For centuries, humankind's propensity to employ insults, put-downs, expletives, epithets, name-calling and similar exchanges of "pleasantries" has provided fertile ground for lawsuits. The following 670-year-old dispute arose from the not-so-polite discourse between a man and a woman. The judge apparently weighed the seriousness of the insults hurled in order to determine which party would prevail.

BOLAY v. BINDEBERE
Court of the Bishop of Ely at Littleport
reprinted in 4 Selden Society 133 (1321)

ANONYMOUS, JUDGE

Littleport. Court there on Wednesday next after the feast of S. Luke in the fifteenth year of King Edward the Second.

It is found by inquest that Rohese Bindebere called Ralph Bolay thief and he called her whore. Therefore both in mercy.[1] And for that trespass done to the said Ralph exceeds the trespass done to the said Rohese, as has been found, therefore it is considered that the said Ralph do recover from the said Rohese 12d. {12 shillings} for his taxed damages.

---

[1]{Ed. Note: "Both in mercy": both parties acted wrongly, and therefore were subject to the jurisdiction of the court.}

Neither the IRS nor income tax is usually considered a topic of great humor or levity. Consistent with its ground-breaking, avant-garde tradition, however, the popular and long-running television show "Saturday Night Live" presented a skit that parodied a supposedly fictional tax consultant named "Fast Frank." Predictably (if not inevitably), a living, breathing tax consultant (i.e., Maurice Frank) surfaced and filed a lawsuit, contending that he had been defamed by the skit.

FRANK v. NATIONAL BROADCASTING CO., INC.

New York Supreme Court, Appellate Division
119 A.D.2d 252; 506 N.Y.S.2d 869 (1986)

SYBIL HART KOOPER, JUSTICE

We have occasion today to address the issue of when humor or jest at the expense of an identifiable private person becomes defamation. It is an issue that since the turn of the century has arisen but rarely in New York's Appellate Courts, and never at all with respect to the medium of television. . . .

The facts, which are not disputed, are fairly simple. The plaintiff, Maurice Frank, a resident of Westchester County, is described in his amended complaint as being "engaged in business as an accountant, tax consultant and financial planner." The defendants Richard Ebersol and Lorne Michaels are the producers of the late night television comedy program "Saturday Night Live." "Saturday Night Live" (hereinafter SNL) is broadcast weekly throughout New York and the United States by the defendant National Broadcasting Company, Inc. (hereinafter NBC).

The plaintiff's complaint concerns an SNL broadcast initially aired nationwide on April 14, 1984, the day before the general deadline for the filing of 1983 income tax returns. The program that evening included a segment known as the "Saturday Night News," the name of which implies a parody of standard, televised news broadcasts. It is a skit contained within the "Saturday Night News" which is the subject of the instant defamation suit.

The plaintiff refers to the objectionable skit as the "Fast Frank Feature." In the skit a performer was introduced to the audience as a

265

tax consultant with the same name as the plaintiff, Maurice Frank. The performer allegedly bore a "noticeable physical resemblance" to the plaintiff. This character then gave purported tax advice which the plaintiff described in his complaint as "ludicrously inappropriate." Specifically, the complaint recites the following monologue as defamatory:

> Thank you. Hello. Look at your calendar. It's April 14th. Your taxes are due tomorrow. You could wind up with your assets in a sling. So listen closely. Here are some write-offs you probably aren't familiar with—courtesy of "Fast Frank" Got a houseplant? A Ficus, a Coleus, a Boston Fern—doesn't matter. If you love it and take care of it—claim it as a dependent.
>
> Got a horrible acne? ... use a lotta Clearasil ... that's an Oil-Depletion Allowance. You say your wife won't sleep with you? You got withholding tax coming back. If she walks out on you—you *lose* a dependent. *But* ... it's a home improvement—write it off.
>
> Should you happen, while filling out your tax form, to get a paper cut—thank your lucky stars—that's a medical expense and a disability. Got a rotten tomato in your fridge? Frost ruined your crops—that's a farm loss. Your tree gets Dutch Elm Disease. ... Sick leave—take a deduction. Did you take a trip to the bathroom tonight? If you *took* a trip ... and you did *business*—you can write if off. Wait, there's more. Did you cry at *Terms of Endearment*? That's a *moving* expense. A urologist who's married to another urologist can file a joint return.
>
> Got a piece of popcorn stuck between your teeth?. ... Or a sister who drools on her shoes? ... You got money comin' back—and I can get it for you *fast,* because I'm Fast Frank. Call me. I have hundreds of trained relatives waiting to take your call. At Fast Frank's, we guarantee your *refund* will be greater than what you *earned.* ...

In June 1984, the plaintiff's attorney wrote to the defendant Ebersol requesting both a public apology and compensation. It appears, however, that only a private, written apology was offered. Thereafter, in August 1984, the April 14, 1984, SNL program, including the "Fast Frank Feature," was rebroadcast nationwide.

The plaintiff commenced the instant action in November 1984 and served an amended complaint in March 1985. The first two causes of action in his amended complaint sought damages for defamation as a result of the two broadcasts of the "Fast Frank Feature." As

266

the alleged defamation was broadcast by television, it is therefore classified as a libel. . . .

In reviewing defamation cases, it is the principal duty of the courts to reconcile the individual's interest in guarding his good name with cherished First Amendment considerations. This balancing of interests is evident in the requirement that "actual malice" must be demonstrated before a public official can recover damages in defamation, a stringent standard necessitated by the "profound national commitment" to "uninhibited, robust and wide-open" debate upon public issues. . . . In some instances, the protection of the First Amendment approaches the absolute: for example, the expression of one's opinion, no matter how pernicious, distasteful or unpopular it may be, is not actionable on the theory that defamation requires falsity, and in this country "there is no such thing as a false idea." . . .

The terms *humor* and *comedy* are not and cannot be synonymous with the term *opinion*. As forms of expression, humor and comedy have never been held to be entitled to absolute or categorical First Amendment protection. . . . Indeed, the danger implicit in affording blanket protection to humor or comedy should be obvious, for surely one's reputation can be as effectively and thoroughly destroyed with ridicule as by any false statement of fact. "The principle is clear that a person shall not be allowed to murder another's reputation in jest." . . .

But it is equally clear that not every humorous article, comedic routine or antic performance will subject its author or performer to liability for defamation. As Judge Learned Hand once observed, "[i]t is indeed not true that all ridicule * * * or all disagreeable comment * * * is actionable; a man must be not too thin-skinned or a self-important prig." . . . Frequently too, courts, including those of this State, have requested claims of damages for defamation where the allegedly defamatory statements were patently humorous, devoid of serious meaning or intent and impossible of being reasonably understood otherwise.

The principal factors distinguishing humorous remarks that are defamatory from those that are not appear to be whether the statements were intended to injure as well as amuse and whether they give rise to an impression that they are true. This is the standard that was established in New York in Triggs v. Sun Printing & Publishing Assn.

267

{citation omitted}. There, the defendant published a series of newspaper articles concerning the plaintiff, a professor at the University of Chicago. In each of the articles, the plaintiff was portrayed as egotistical in the extreme, a man who believed, among other things, that his own brand of colloquial language and slang would be a vast improvement upon Shakespeare.

The articles also cast aspersion on Triggs's patriotism; told how he had taken "a year of solemn consultation" before naming his new son; and referred to Triggs as "the god" who was "born great, discovered himself early and has a just appreciation of the value of this discovery." With thinly veiled contempt, the articles closed, stating that it had been one of the pleasures of life to introduce people to the "shrine" of the plaintiff, a "true museum piece." . . . {The Court in *Triggs* held, *inter alia,* as follows}:

> We are of the opinion that one assaulting the reputation or business of another in a public newspaper cannot justify it upon the ground that it was a mere jest, unless it is perfectly manifest from the language employed that it could in no respect be regarded as an attack upon the reputation or business of the persons to whom it related.

How laughter-provoking statements are viewed will depend in large part upon the context in which they are delivered. A recent case in California involved the well-known television personality and comedian Robin Williams. A stand-up comedic routine performed by Mr. Williams at a San Francisco night club was recorded, and the video and audio tapes were thereafter distributed. A videotape of the performance was also carried over the Home Box Office cable television channel. Part of Williams's routine concerned wines, and, in one version, ran as follows:

> There are White wines, there are Red wines, but why are there no Black wines like: Rege a Motherfucker? It goes with fish, meat, any damn thing it wants to [comment from a member of the audience] * * * Thank you, Lumpy * * * Isn't it nice, though, having someone like Mean Joe Green advertising it—You better buy this or I'll nail your ass to a tree [Polygram Records v. Superior Court {citation omitted}].

A suit seeking damages for personal defamation, among other things, was thereafter brought by a Mr. David H. Rege, the distributor of "Rege" wines from his San Francisco store, Rege Cellars. The

California court examined the statements using a standard similar to our own, to wit, if the offensive words were "not fairly susceptible of a defamatory meaning," the action should be dismissed. . . .

In that case, there was an additional question, not present here, of whether Mr. Williams had intended to refer to Mr. Rege's product. In dismissing the action, the court relied upon the fact that the statements were unquestionably uttered as part of a comedy routine, and could not be interpreted in any other way. Williams's descriptions of "Rege wine" were "obvious figments of a comic imagination impossible for any sensible person to take seriously." . . . The court noted that the audience "knew [Williams] as a comedian, not a wine connoisseur." . . .

In the instant case, it can also be asserted without hesitation that no person of any sense could take the so-called tax advice of "Fast Frank" seriously. If anything, the statements here are even more plainly the obvious figments of a comic imagination. A wine might possibly be made dark enough to look black. It might also taste bad, and unquestionably persons who might be regarded as ruffians can and do advertise many products. Income taxes, on the other hand, and persons connected with their collection and even preparation, have been a fertile source of the comic imagination since their adoption.

No person who has ever had the dubious pleasure of filling out a 1040 federal tax form would, in his most extravagant fantasies, believe that he could claim his favorite Boston Fern as a dependent. No person exists who is so gullible as to believe that his acne medication entitles him to an oil-depletion allowance or that the departure of a spouse from the marital premises—however welcome—may be listed as a deductible "home improvement." Moreover, just as it is inconceivable that anyone hearing Robin Williams's monologue would thereafter avoid Mr. Rege's wines in the belief that they were possessed of an unnatural wine color, or had other peculiar qualities, no one who saw the "Fast Frank Feature" could believe that the plaintiff was inclined to prepare income tax returns claiming paper cuts as medical expenses.

The contested statements here were so extremely nonsensical and silly that there is no possibility that any person hearing them could take them seriously. Neither were the statements themselves so malicious or vituperative that they would cause a person hearing them to

hold the plaintiff in "public contempt, ridicule, aversion or disgrace."
... We believe that the lunacy of the statements themselves, presented as they were as a small comic part of a larger and obviously comic entertainment program, coupled with the fact that they were neither a malicious nor vicious personal attack, requires a finding that they were not defamatory as a matter of law. Rather, this case involves just that sort of humor which is "of a personal kind that begets laughter and leaves no sting," and it thus cannot form the basis of a lawsuit. . . .

Certainly, this is an area in which cases will stand or fall on their own peculiar facts. We hold today that in certain situations and under some circumstances the authors of humorous language will be insulated from liability in defamation cases even where the comic attempt pokes fun at an identifiable individual. The line will be crossed, however, when humor is used in an attempt to disguise an intent to injure; at that point a jest no longer merits protection, because it ceases to be a jest. As was the case in Triggs *(supra)*, the defense of humor will not immunize the authors of a malicious or abusive attack upon a plaintiff's character or reputation. In this case, no such malice or abuse can be found in a comic dialogue that offers a Coleus as a tax-deductible dependent. . . .

Order affirmed.

In the following case, the Pennsylvania Supreme Court had to decide whether a railway company should be held liable for the conduct of its driver who operated a street car in a rough, jerking manner, resulting in an injury to one of the passengers. The court ruled "No," and Justice Musmanno, as usual, filed an eloquent and spirited dissenting opinion.

SMITH v. PITTSBURGH RAILWAYS COMPANY
Supreme Court of Pennsylvania
405 Pa. 340; 175 A.2d 844 (1961)

BENJAMIN R. JONES, JUSTICE

On January 28, 1957, appellant Roselyn K. Smith, and her sixteen-year-old daughter, Carol Smith, were passengers on an uncrowded street car owned and operated by the Pittsburgh Railways

Company, appellee. Appellant and her daughter were seated on a long seat located lengthwise in the extreme right front portion of the street car. According to appellant, the street car ride was "rough" and the car "was jerking just as though he [the motorman] was playing with the pedal" and, as the street car approached the so-called Bloomfield stop, passengers expecting to alight at that stop came forward and "he [the motorman] jerked that street car again" and a man, standing near where appellant was seated, was thrown off balance by the jolt and "the heel of his foot just stomped right down on the great toe of [appellant's] left foot" causing severe injuries. Furthermore, according to appellant, the street car was about to stop when the jolt occurred.[1]

As the car approached the Bloomfield stop, Carol Smith left her seat to ask the motorman for a street car schedule and she "had [her] hand on the railing when the motorman started the car real fast" and she fell to the floor.[2] Except for the statement that other passengers were "thrust back" there is no evidence that the alleged "jolt" or "jerk" affected any other passengers in the street car.

{*At trial, after appellant had presented her evidence, the Court entered a "non-suit" against her, thus terminating the litigation in favor of the appellee.*}

An examination of the testimony produced by appellant failed to show that the movement of this street car was so unusual and extraordinary as to be beyond the reasonable anticipation of the passengers therein, and it is clear that the evidence falls far short of the standard of proof required to fasten liability upon the appellee. . . .

Judgment affirmed.

MICHAEL A. MUSMANNO, JUSTICE (*dissenting*)

On January 28, 1957, the motorman of the Pittsburgh Railways Company street car involved in this litigation, who was apparently angry with himself and the world in general, picked up passengers on the northside of Pittsburgh and then furiously headed across the Allegheny River into downtown Pittsburgh and out to Bloomfield. His

---

[1]According to the complaint, the "jerk" or "jolt" occurred when the street car was "started up without warning" by the motorman.

[2]Carol Smith stated:"I wasn't holding on to it [the railing] but I had my hand on it" and "I put my hand on the pole just to brace myself while I was going forward * * * "

speed was such that from time to time the trolley pole jumped the overhead high voltage wire, whereupon he would jerk the car to a stop, leap off to reengage the trolley, swearing all the while and intermixing with his profanity a variety of indelicate and indecent phrases. As he bounded over the rails he applied the power in fits and starts as if playing the pedals of a pipe organ, thereby shaking up the passengers to such a degree that one of them exclaimed: "This is the roughest ride we have ever had." Other passengers described the rough trip as a "terrible ride."

As the car approached the Bloomfield stop, the motorman slowed down and the alighting passengers prepared to disembark. Suddenly the motorman, possibly realizing that he was moving into the stop too uneventfully, threw on a sudden burst of power and jolted the car forward as if he had decided not to stop after all. In consequence, *all* the passengers were thrown backward and one of them, a sixteen-year-old girl, measured her length on the floor. Her mother testified that the girl was "terribly embarrassed because her dress went up when she fell."

Still another passenger, a large, heavy, six-foot gentleman, went into an involuntary jig to maintain equilibrium and balance. He executed a few steps backwards and then eventually braked his anticipatory fall by anchoring one foot firmly to what he thought was the floor. It turned out to be the foot of another passenger. The weight of his body and the violence with which he bore down fractured the big toe of the left foot of the startled passenger, who is the plaintiff in this lawsuit which terminated with a jolt in the Court below in a Court-imposed non-suit.

This court has affirmed that non-suit in an Opinion which would suggest that the Court assumes that the ride of the momentous street car was as smooth and tranquil as that of a gondola moving over the Grand Canal of Venice. The Majority Opinion states:

> An examination of the testimony produced by appellant fails to show that the movement of this street car was so unusual and extraordinary as to be beyond the reasonable anticipation of the passengers therein and it is clear that the evidence falls far short of the standard of proof required to fasten liability upon appellee [the street car company].

Are passengers to anticipate that a street car will be operated in such headlong fashion that the trolley pole does a St. Vitus dance on the roof? Are they to foresee that an angry and mysteriously infuriated motorman will do a dance on the power pedal? Is a trip on a street car to be considered a usual one when one passenger is hurled to the floor, another does an impromptu ballet, and all of them are thrown back?

How unusual must a street car ride be when a passenger suffers a fractured toe from the pirouetting of a six-foot passenger before there may be a recovery for the injury? Even the attorney for the street car company admitted the jolt, of which the plaintiff complains, was a "*violent* jolt." Is violence now so much a part of daily existence that it no longer arouses surprise and cannot stir the law into enforcing redress for injuries suffered as a result of the violence?

The personal characteristics of the motorman in this case would have no bearing, generally speaking, on the manner in which he operated his car. However, since the whole street car was under his absolute domination and control, his conduct may help the legal observer to determine whether he did operate the car in a manner to cause the result suffered by the plaintiff. In describing the motorman, the plaintiff employed a phraseology of her own which would not be without meaning to the jury. She said that the motorman was "snotty." The dictionary defines this colloquial and slangly word as meaning contemptible, dirty, offensive, nasty, snooty, offish and supercilious. A motorman who could be nasty and snooty would be just the kind of motorman who would slam on his brakes and precipitately throw on his power regardless of what happened to his passengers.

The plaintiff added that the motorman was also "snippy." This is not as pungent a description as "snotty," but, added to everything else said about the motorman, reveals an operator given to impetuosity. The dictionary defines "snippy" as being short-tempered, tart and snappish. It would not be too much to assume that a motorman who is nasty, snooty, snappish, short-tempered and supercilious would be just the kind of motorman who would operate his car with such angry abandon and unconcern over the safety of his passengers that he would lose his trolley three or four times in a short run and then slam on his brakes with such instantaneous violence as to produce the toe-smashing event heretofore narrated.

The plaintiff's counsel in his brief cites all three cases, all of which support his position that this case should have been submitted to the

273

jury. In Sanson v. Philadelphia Rapid Transit Company {citation omitted}, the plaintiff-passenger signaled the motorman he intended to get off at the next stop. The motorman acknowledged the signal and began to slow down. As the plaintiff, however, rose from his seat and took hold of the handle of the door the motorman suddenly increased the speed of the car, causing the plaintiff to be thrown to the platform. Verdict for the plaintiff was sustained.

In Tilton v. Philadelphia Rapid Transit Company {citation omitted}, the plaintiff was non-suited after testifying that the car suddenly stopped and he was thrown forward striking the seat ahead of him. This Court removed the non-suit. . . .

In Angelo v. Pittsburgh Railways Company {citation omitted}, the plaintiff was injured when the bus in which she was riding suddenly swerved to one side and made a violent and unusual stop throwing her against a pole in the car to her injury. She recovered a verdict and the defendant appealed. The Superior Court affirmed the verdict. . . .

In the case at bar, the defendant company should have been required to show that the motorman could not have avoided the extraordinary circumstances in the car when, because of his operation, the car jolted, jerked and otherwise so carried on that a large passenger was thrown off balance and came down heavily on the foot of the plaintiff who was innocently sitting in the car minding her own business and now has a disabled foot, which will impede her walking, even if she determined she would never ride street cars again.

The Majority does not attempt to analyze these three cases or show how they differ in principle from the principle controlling the facts in the case at bar. It merely says that these cases "are clearly *inapposite.*" [Emphasis supplied {by Musmanno}.] Even the brief treatment I have given them demonstrates that they are quite *apposite*, and certainly far more apposite than the cases which, like a long train of cars, have been cited by the Majority.

And thus, because of all this inappositeness, Mrs. Smith is out of court. She boarded a street car, she paid her money and accordingly had the right to be taken to her destination with the care that a common carrier is required to exercise in accordance with the law of the land. A motorman who, from the evidence adduced at the trial, revealed to himself to be masterfully incompetent and superbly insolent, and with personal traits inapposite to the skill required properly

274

to run a street car, so operated the car as to fracture her foot. She hob-
bled into court for a redress of her grievance and she was compelled
to hobble out with her grievance unredressed.

And she will now hobble through life still unredressed, not
because a jury passed on her rights, but because a long series of inapposite cases passed over her.

EPILOGUE

. . . And for a farewell to our jurisprudent, I wish unto him the gladsome light of jurisprudence, the lovelinesse of temperance, the stabilitie of fortitude, and the soliditie of justice.

—Edward Coke[1]

The man of firm and noble soul
No factious clamours can control:
No threatening tyrant's darkling brow
Can swerve him from his just intent;
Gales the warring waves which plough,
By Auster on the billows spent,
To curb the Adriatic main
Would awe his fixed determined mind in vain.

Aye, and the red right arm of Jove,
Hurtling his lightning from above,
With all his terrors there unfurled,
He would unmoved, unawed behold.
The flames of an expiring world.
Again in crushing chaos rolled,
In vast promiscuous ruin hurled,
Might light his glorious funeral pile,
Still dauntless 'mid the wreck of earth he'd smile.

—Horace[2]

---

[1]From Epilogue: Edward Coke, *The First Part of the Institutes of the Laws of England or a Commentary upon Littleton*, 17th ed., vol. II, p. 395a (1817).

[2]Horace, *Ode* III.3, Byron translation, as reprinted in *Oxford Book of Latin Verse*, p. 482–483 (1912).

277

GLOSSARY*

AFFIRMED The appellate court ratifies and confirms the decision of the lower court or trial court. It decrees, orders and declares that the former judgment or ruling is valid and correct and must stand as rendered. When the appellate court "affirms" a decision, it formally concurs or agrees that the court below was correct and the decision stands as originally entered.

ANSWER A formal written statement made by a defendant setting forth the grounds for a defense to a lawsuit filed by the plaintiff. An answer is a pleading by which the defendant tries to oppose the plaintiff's claims, either by denying them entirely or by alleging new or separate matters, which defendant contends should prevent recovery by plaintiff in the case.

CERTIORARI In Latin, *certiorari* means "to be informed of." It is issued by a superior court to a lower one, requiring it to produce a certified record of the case in question. The writ of certiorari mandates an inspection of the proceedings occurring in the lower court to determine whether there have been any irregularities. The U.S. Supreme Court sees this type of writ most commonly, and utilizes it as a discretionary device to select the cases it wishes to hear.

CHANCERY COURT A court that administers "equity" and conducts its proceedings according to the forms and principles of equitable jurisprudence. The term *equity* means ideal or impartial justice, evenhandedness and fairness. In theory, it involves common notions of "justice" as opposed to strict conformity to statutes or laws; justice ascertained by natural reason and right; unwritten law of remedial justice. Most of the chancery courts have been abolished in the United States in favor of courts of law, although many of the "equitable" principles are still valid.

COMPLAINT The initial document or pleading filed with the court, by which an action is commenced. It must set forth a short and plain statement of the grounds upon which the court's jurisdiction depends, a short and plain statement of the claim showing that the plaintiff is entitled to relief, and a demand for judgment or relief. The complaint must be served with a "summons" (which gives the court jurisdiction over the defendant and also provides formal notification that an action has been commenced against the defendant, and that an answer or other response to the action is required to be filed at the time and place named in the summons).

DEFENDANT The person against whom relief or recovery for damages is sought in a civil lawsuit. A defendant is the party denying or defending against the claims and allegations set forth in the lawsuit filed by the plaintiff. Once a defendant has been served with a summons and complaint, he or she will generally file an answer or other response with the court. A defendant is also the person accused of wrongdoing in a criminal case.

DEMURRER A formal method by which a defendant may dispute the legal sufficiency of the plaintiff's allegations. A demurrer is a pleading by defendant, which .

---

*Acknowledgment and thanks to *Black's Law Dictionary*, fifth ed., West Publishing Co. (1979), and *Legal Thesaurus* by William C. Burton, Macmillan Publishing Co. (1980).

admits that the facts alleged in the plaintiff's complaint are true, but sets forth reasons why those facts do not give the plaintiff any legal right to recover against him or her. For example, the action may be barred by the statute of limitations. A demurrer may also contend that the complaint is defective in some other manner, or that conclusions of law in the complaint are incorrect or that other reasons exist why defendant should not be required to answer. A demurrer effectively stalls the lawsuit, since the plaintiff cannot proceed or force defendant to answer until the issues raised by the demurrer are resolved by the court.

GUARDIAN AD LITEM   A person appointed by a court to prosecute, defend or otherwise represent the interests of a minor (or incompetent) person in legal matters.

IN RE   In the matter of; concerning; regarding. This is how a case is titled when there are no true adversarial parties, or when one party makes an application to the court on his or her own behalf. Usually, however, it is used in conjunction with legal proceedings involving a specific property or a thing such as a bankruptcy estate, a probate estate, a coroner's inquest, a proposed public highway, or the like.

NON-SUIT   A term broadly applied to a variety of means by which courts may terminate a lawsuit without determining the actual merits of the case. Examples include an adverse judgment against a plaintiff who refuses or neglects to proceed to trial (thereby leaving the legal issues undetermined) or is in default under local court rules or fails to comply with court orders.

PLAINTIFF   A person who files a lawsuit; the party who complains or sues in a civil (non-criminal) action. A person who seeks relief for an injury to body and/or a violation of rights. If it is a criminal case, the party who complains or sues is the prosecutor, acting on behalf of the appropriate governmental entity.

PLEADING or PLEA   An allegation or averment of a matter or fact stated affirmatively by a person in a formal written document submitted to the court.

PRO PER (IN PROPRIA PERSONA)   In one's own proper person. The party is representing his or her own interests in a legal action. A similar term is *pro se*, which means "for himself; in his own behalf; in person." These two terms are generally used to designate a party who does not retain an attorney and appears for himself or herself in court.

REMANDED   The action whereby an appellate court sends the case back to the lower or trial court with instructions to correct certain specified irregularities.

REVERSED   To overthrow, vacate, set aside, make void, annul, repeal or revoke. To reverse a judgment means to overthrow it by contrary decision or ruling, undo or annul it on account of error.

STATUTE OF LIMITATIONS   A law that provides a specific time limitation for commencing a lawsuit for the enforcement of certain rights of action; that is, declaring that no lawsuit shall be maintained unless brought within a specified period of time after the right that the plaintiff seeks to vindicate has accrued. For example, in California, the statute of limitations for a personal injury lawsuit is one year from its accrual. On the other hand, in most jurisdictions, murder has no statute of limitations, and the prosecution may file criminal charges at any time during the life of the suspect.

SUMMARY JUDGMENT   The process whereby a party to an action requests the court to enter an immediate judgment on a claim in favor of the requesting party on the grounds that there is no genuine issue of material fact to be decided and that the requesting party is entitled to prevail as a matter of law.

TROVER   Originally, an action against a person who found another's goods and wrongfully converted them to his own use. Now it refers to the recovery of the "value" of personal property wrongfully taken or converted by another for his own use. It is a possessory action, which the plaintiff can maintain only when he or she has a general or special interest in the property and had the right to possession of the property at the time that it was taken.

VACATE   To annul; to set aside; to cancel or rescind. To declare that an entry of judgment is void.

WRIT   An order issued from a court requiring the performance of a specified act, or giving authority to have it done.

INDEX

Appeals, Fifth Circuit, 602 F.2d 743 (1979); John R. Brown, 64

GUTHRIE v. POWELL: Supreme Court of Kansas, 178 Kan. 587; 290 P.2d 834 (1955); William W. Harvey, 232

H

HALL v. HALL: High Court of Chancery, 21 E.R. 447; Dick. 710 (1788); Edward Thurlow, 164

HALL v. MOORING: Court of Appeals of Georgia, 12 Ga. App. 74; 76 S.E. 759 (1912); James Robert Pottle, 98

HAMPTON v. NORTH CAROLINA PULP CO.: U.S. District Court, E.D. North Carolina, 49 F. Supp. 625 (1943); Isaac M. Meekins, 36

HARPER v. LOVELL: Supreme Court of Tennessee, 105 Tenn. 614; 59 S.W. 337 (1900); John S. Wilkes, 214

HAWKEYE DISTILLING COMPANY v. NEW YORK STATE LIQUOR AUTHORITY: New York Supreme Court, Special Term, 118 Misc.2d 505; 460 N.Y.S.2d 696 (1983); Richard W. Wallach, 77

HILL, IN RE JAMES: Justice Court of California, Tuolumne County, Coroner's Report No. 18 (1850); R. C. Barry, 190

J

JACKSON COCA-COLA BOTTLING CO. v. CHAPMAN: Supreme Court of Mississippi, 106 Miss. 864; 64 So. 791 (1914); Richard F. Reed, 14

JOD, IN RE SIRUS: Justice Court of California, Tuolumne County, Case No. 515 (1851); R. C. Barry, 2

JORDACHE ENTERPRISES, INC. v. HOGG WYLD, LTD.: U.S. Court of Appeals, Tenth Circuit, 828 F.2d 1482 (1987); Deanell Reece Tacha, 43

K

KENT © NORMAN v. REAGAN: U.S. District Court, D. Oregon, 95 F.R.D. 476 (1982); James A. Redden, 162

KERNESLAWE, IN RE JOHN OF: Assize Court of Northumberland County, Northumberland Assize Roll, 7 Edward I (1279), 202

KEYES v. KEYES: Superior Court of New York City, Equity Term, 6 Misc. 355; 26 N.Y.S. 910 (1893); David McAdam, 137

KIRK, IN RE: Supreme Court of New Jersey, 101 N.J.L. 450; 130 A. 569 (1925); James F. Minturn, 252

KMICZ v. KMICZ: County Court of Luzerne County, Pennsylvania, 50 Pa. C.C. 588 (1920); Henry A. Fuller, 126

KOPLIN v. QUADE: Supreme Court of Wisconsin, 145 Wis. 454; 130 N.W. 511 (1911); John Barnes, 12

KROBRE v. HEED: Justice Court of California, Tuolumne County, Case No. 606 (1851); R. C. Barry, 71

L

LODI v. LODI: Court of Appeals of California, Third Appellate District, 173 Cal. App.3d 628; 219 Cal. Rptr. 117 (1985); Richard M. Sims III, 165

LOVE, IN RE ROBIN E.: U.S. Bankruptcy Court, S.D. Florida, 61 B.R. 558 (1968); A. Jay Cristol, 58

LUSSAN v. GRAIN DEALERS MUTUAL INSURANCE COMPANY: U.S. Court of Appeals, Fifth Circuit, 280 F.2d 491 (1960); John R. Brown, 10

283

M

MAIN v. MAIN: Supreme Court of Iowa, 168 Iowa 353; 150 N.W. 590 (1915); Silas M. Weaver, 139

McDONALD v. JOHN P. SCRIPPS NEWSPAPER: California Court of Appeals, Second Appellate District, 210 Cal. App.3d 100; 257 Cal. Rptr. 473 (1989); Arthur Gilbert, 156

METRO. GOV'T OF NASHVILLE v. MARTIN: Supreme Court of Tennessee, 584 S.W.2d 643 (1979); Joseph W. Henry, 88

MILES v. CITY COUNCIL OF AUGUSTA, GEORGIA: U.S. District Court, S.D. Georgia, 551 F. Supp. 349 (1982); Dudley H. Bowen, 31

MONTALDA, IN RE JUAN: Justice Court of California, Tuolumne County, Coroner's Report No. 21 (1850); R. C. Barry, 191

MONTGOMERY v. MARYLAND CASUALTY COMPANY: Supreme Court of Georgia, 169 Ga. 746; 151 S.E. 363 (1929); Stirling Price Gilbert, 19

MORGANROTH v. WHITALL: Court of Appeals of Michigan, 161 Mich. App. 785; 411 N.W.2d 859 (1987); David Sawyer, 259

MURPHY v. STEEPLECHASE AMUSEMENT CO., INC.: Court of Appeals of New York, 250 N.Y. 479; 166 N.E. 173 (1929); Benjamin N. Cardozo, 236

MYLWARD v. WELDON: Chancery Court of England, Reg. Lib-A 1596, fol. 672 (1596); reprinted in *Monroe's Acta Cancellariae 1545–1625*, vol. 1, p. 692; Anonymous, 55

N

NEWLY, IN RE T.: Justice Court of California, Tuolumne County, Coroner's Report No. 5 (1850); R. C. Barry, 189

NIDDESDALE, IN RE GILBERT OF: Assize Court of Northumberland County, Northumberland Assize Roll, 40 Henry III (1256); Anonymous, 192

P

PACETTI v. THE STATE OF GEORGIA: Supreme Court of Georgia, 82 Ga. 297; 7 S.E. 867 (1888); Logan E. Bleckley, 76

PARADINE v. JANE: Court of King's Bench, Michaelmas Term [1558–1774] All E.R. Rep. 172; 82 E.R. 897, Aleyn 26, Sty. 47 (1647); Lord Bacon and Henry Rollen, 117

PAVLICIC v. VOGTSBERGER: Supreme Court of Pennsylvania, 390 Pa. 502; 136 A.2d 127 (1957); Michael A. Musmanno, 130

PEOPLE OF CALIFORNIA v. GLEGHORN: California Court of Appeals, Second Appellate District, 193 Cal. App.3d 196; 238 Cal. Rptr. 82 (1987); Steven J. Stone, 171

POTTS v. HOUSE: Supreme Court of Georgia, 6 Ga. 324 (1849); Joseph H. Lumpkin, 202

R

RAMIREZ, IN RE JESUS: Justice Court of California, Tuolumne County, Case No. 516 (1851); R. C. Barry, 54

REGINA v. COLLINS: Court of Appeal of England, Criminal Division, [1972] 3 W.L.R. 243, [1972] 2 All E.R. 1105, 56 Cr. App. R. 554 [1972]; Edmund Davies, 144

ROBINSON v. PIOCHE, BAYERQUE & CO.: Supreme Court of California, 5 Cal. 460 (1855); Solomon Heydenfeldt, 227

ROOS v. LOESER: California Court of Appeals, First Appellate District, 41 Cal. App. 782 (1919); Frank H. Kerrigan, 15

S

SAY, IN RE DR. JAMES: Justice Court of California, Tuolumne County, Coroner's Report No. 4 (1850); R. C. Barry, 189

SCHWARTZ v. WARWICK-PHILADEL-PHIA CORPORATION: Supreme Court of Pennsylvania, 424 Pa. 185; 226 A.2d 484 (1967); Michael A. Musmanno, 227

SEARIGHT v. STATE OF NEW JERSEY: U.S. District Court, D. New Jersey, 412 F. Supp. 413 (1976); Vincent P. Biunno, 154

SMITH, T., & FELIPE VEGA, IN RE: Justice Court of California, Tuolumne County, Case No. 60 (1850); R. C. Barry, 91

SMITH v. PITTSBURGH RAILWAYS COMPANY: Supreme Court of Pennsylvania, 405 Pa. 340; 175 A.2d 844 (1961); Benjamin R. Jones, 270

STAMBOVKSY v. ACKLEY: Supreme Court of New York, Appellate Division, 572 N.Y.S.2d 672 (1991); Israel Rubin, 207

STATE OF MISSOURI v. KNOWLES: Court of Appeals of Missouri, 739 S.W.2d 753 (1987); Anthony P. Nugent, Jr., 182

STEVENS v. THE STATE OF GEORGIA: Supreme Court of Georgia, 77 Ga. 310 (1886); Logan E. Bleckley, 29

SWINDLE v. MUNFORD: Supreme Court of Georgia, 59 Ga. 337 (1877); Logan E. Bleckley, 116

T

TEAGLE v. CITY OF PHILADELPHIA: Supreme Court of Pennsylvania, 430 Pa. 395; 243 A.2d 342 (1968); Michael A. Musmanno, 234

TOM, IN RE HUNGRY: Justice Court of California, Tuolumne County, Coroner's Report No. 20 (1850); R. C. Barry, 191

TOVER, IN RE JAMES: Justice Court of California, Tuolumne County, Case No. 500 (1851); R. C. Barry, 97

TRICOLI v. CENTALANZA: Supreme Court of New Jersey, 100 N.J.L. 231; 126 A. 214 (1924); James F. Minturn, 257

TRUSTEES OF COLUMBIA UNIVERSITY v. JACOBSEN: Superior Court of New Jersey, Appellate Division, 53 N.J. Super. 574; 148 A.2d 63 (1959); Sidney Goldmann, 175

TWO POTS, IN RE: Assize Court of Northumberland County, Northumberland Assize Roll, 7 Edward I (1279); Anonymous, 192

U

UNITED STATES ex rel. MAYO v. SATAN AND HIS STAFF: U.S. District Court, W.D. Pennsylvania, 54 F.R.D. 282 (1971); Gerald J. Weber, 152

UNITED STATES v. SENTOVICH: U.S. Court of Appeals, Eleventh Circuit, 677 F.2d 834 (1982); Frank M. Johnson, Jr., 72

UNITED STATES v. SPROED: U.S. District Court, D. Oregon, 628 F. Supp. 1234 (1986); James M. Burns, 25

V

VANN v. IONTA: Municipal Court of City of New York, Borough of Queens, 157 Misc. 461; 284 N.Y.S. 278 (1935); Nicholas M. Pette, 107

W

WADDELL v. THE STATE OF GEORGIA: Supreme Court of Georgia, 27 Ga. 262 (1859); Joseph H. Lumpkin, 70

WEBSTER v. BLUE SHIP TEA ROOM, INC.: Supreme Judicial Court of Massachusetts, 347 Mass. 421; 198 N.E.2d 309 (1964); Paul Cashman Reardon, 102

WESTERN RAILROAD, THE, v. THORNTON & ACEE: Supreme Court of Georgia, 60 Ga. 300 (1878); Logan E. Bleckley, 123

WILEY v. SLATER: New York Supreme Court, Appellate Division, 22 Barb. 506 (1856); William F. Allen, 7

WILLIAMS v. JOHNS: Chancery Court of England, 21 E.R. 355; Dick. 477 (1773); Sir Henry Bathurst, 61

WILLIAMS, IN RE GEORGE: Justice Court of California, Tuolumne County, Coroner's Report No. 3 (1850); R. C. Barry, 188

Z

ZIM v. WESTERN PUBLISHING COMPANY: U.S. District Court of Appeals, Fifth Circuit, 573 F.2d 1318 (1978); Irving L. Goldberg, 217

ABOUT THE EDITORS

JOHN B. McCLAY
Attorney-at-Law

John B. McClay has practiced law in Orange County, California, since 1980 and is cofounder and co–lead counsel of McClay & Alani, a Professional Law Corporation. McClay is a graduate of the University of California at Berkeley (B.S., Business Administration, 1976) and Pepperdine University School of Law (J.D., 1979), where he was named to the Dean's Honor List and served on the *Pepperdine Law Review.*

WENDY L. MATTHEWS
Attorney-at-Law

Wendy L. Matthews has practiced law in Orange County, California, since 1989 and established the Law Offices of Wendy L. Matthews in 1991. Her civil litigation practice emphasizes personal injury, business and probate law. Matthews studied geology at Monterey Peninsula College before transferring to the Gemological Institute of America (G.G., 1978). As a gemologist, she has served as a consultant and expert witness in connection with litigation involving gem fraud. She has completed postgraduate studies at the University of Cambridge and is a graduate of Western State University College of Law (B.S.L., 1986; J.D., 1988).

McCLAY & ALANI
A Professional Law Corporation

McCLAY & ALANI, a Professional Law Corporation, established in 1988, emphasizes real property litigation and commercial asset management law, representing developers, commercial landlords and asset management companies throughout Southern California. Please direct all communication, comments, criticism, suggestions and (especially) references to additional clever cases and/or materials to:

McCLAY & ALANI
A Professional Law Corporation

1630 East Palm Avenue, Santa Ana, California 92701

Telephone: (714) 558-1535/Telecopier: (714) 558-8024

INVITATION TO CONTRIBUTE AND REFER ADDITIONAL CASES AND MATERIALS

A follow-up volume, *Corpus Juris Humorous II*, is currently being compiled and edited. All readers are invited and encouraged to contribute and refer any information concerning additional humorous, extraordinary, outrageous, unusual, colorful, infamous, clever and/or witty reported judicial opinions and related materials from any source whatsoever. Please direct all such contributions, referrals and other communications to:

MAC-MAT

c/o

McCLAY & ALANI

A Professional Law Corporation

1630 East Palm Avenue

Santa Ana, California 92701

Telephone: (714) 558-1535

Telecopier: (714) 558-8024